DIMENSIONS OF FAMILY THERAPY

DIMENSIONS OF FAMILY THERAPY

Edited by
MAURIZIO ANDOLFI
Family Therapy Institute and Italian Society for Family Therapy
Rome, Italy

and

ISRAEL ZWERLING
Hahnemann Medical College and Hospital
Philadelphia, Pennsylvania

Foreword by
SALVADOR MINUCHIN

THE GUILFORD PRESS
New York

© 1980 The Guilford Press, New York
A Division of Guilford Publications, Inc.
200 Park Avenue South, New York, N.Y. 10003

All rights reserved

No part of this book may be reproduced, stored in a retrieval system, or transmitted, in any form or by any means, electronic, mechanical, photocopying, microfilming, recording, or otherwise, without written persmission from the Publisher

Printed in the United States of America

Library of Congress Cataloging in Publication Data

Main entry under title:

Dimensions of family therapy.

    "Several of the chapters were initially presented at the Second International Conference on Family Therapy... Florence, Italy, on June 21–24, 1978."
    Includes Bibliographies.   1. Family psychotherapy—Congresses. I. Andolfi, Maurizio.   II. Zwerling, Israel, 1917–   III. International Conference on Family Therapy, 2d, Florence, 1978.
RC488.5.D54   616.89'156   79-25485
ISBN 0-89862-601-3

CONTRIBUTORS

PÅL ABRAHAMSEN, M.D. Lovisenberg Hospital, Oslo, Norway

MAURIZIO ANDOLFI, M.D. Family Therapy Institute and Italian Society for Family Therapy, Rome, Italy

DONALD A. BLOCH, M.D. Ackerman Institute for Family Therapy, New York, New York

CHARLOTTE BUHL, PH.D. Gaustad Hospital, Oslo, Norway

PHILIPPE CAILLÉ, M.D. Sagene Family Guidance Center, Oslo, Norway

MONY ELKAÏM, M.D. La Gerbe Mental Health Center; Institute of Family and Human Systems Studies; and National Science Research Fund; Brussels, Belgium

ILDA FICHER, PH.D. Department of Mental Health Sciences, Hahnemann Medical College and Hospital, Philadelphia, Pennsylvania

JAMES L. FRAMO, PH.D. Department of Psychology, Temple University, Philadelphia, Pennsylvania

ROBERT GARFIELD, M.D. Master's of Family Therapy Degree Program, Department of Mental Health Sciences, Hahnemann Medical College and Hospital, Philadelphia, Pennsylvania

ALAN S. GURMAN, PH.D. Outpatient Clinic, Department of Psychiatry, University of Wisconsin Medical School, Center for Health Sciences, Madison, Wisconsin

DAVID V. KEITH, M.D. Department of Psychiatry, University of Wisconsin Medical School, Center for Health Sciences, Madison, Wisconsin

DAVID P. KNISKERN, PSY.D. Department of Psychiatry, University of Cincinnati College of Medicine, Cincinnati, Ohio

PAOLO MENGHI, M.D. Family Therapy Institute, Rome, Italy

Contributors

ANNA M. NICOLÒ, M.D. Family Therapy Institute, Rome, Italy

PEGGY PAPP, A.C.S.W. Brief Therapy Project, Ackerman Institute for Family Therapy, New York, New York, and Philadelphia Child Guidance Clinic, Philadelphia, Pennsylvania

CARMINE SACCU, M.D. Family Therapy Institute, Rome, Italy

ALBERT E. SCHEFLEN, M.D. Ackerman Institute for Family Therapy, New York, New York

MARA SELVINI PALAZZOLI, M.D. Center for the Study of the Family, Milan, Italy

BENTE SØRBYE, M.S.W. Family Guidance Center of Buskerud County, Drammen, Norway

M. DUNCAN STANTON, PH.D. Addicts and Families Program, Philadelphia Child Guidance Clinic; University of Pennsylvania School of Medicine; and Family Therapy Program, Drug Dependence Treatment Center, Philadelphia Veterans Administration Hospital; Philadelphia, Pennsylvania

CARL A. WHITAKER, M.D. Department of Psychiatry, University of Wisconsin Medical School, Center for Health Sciences, Madison, Wisconsin

ISRAEL ZWERLING, M.D., PH.D. Department of Mental Health Sciences, Hahnemann Medical College and Hospital, Philadelphia, Pennsylvania

FOREWORD

In June 1978, the International Conference on Family Therapy met in Florence, Italy. Under the ghost of Dante, we mused on our condition. Family therapy has become established; we no longer need to fight for recognition and validation. But it seems we have promoted ourselves, not to heaven, but to a purgatory of complex divisions. The first generation of family therapists had a sense of purpose and unity in their attack on mechanistic paradigms. Now that we are no longer on the defensive, our differences are appearing. And now that we have established a point of view, our differences become interesting.

It is not a bad place to be, this "in between," far from a unified theory of family, family development, or family change—but without an external enemy. The need to establish schools and maintain their purity is slowly waning with the spread and acceptance of a systems paradigm. A decade ago, a myriad of techniques clustered, ascended to the level of generalization, and became schools. We built individual towers like the medieval manors of San Gimignano, from which we could watch the horizon while preparing our defenses. Now second- and third-generation family therapists like Andolfi can draw upon the models of several "schools." The pragmatic utilization of many different techniques has become possible, and we are all enriched by the integration.

Our tasks are just beginning. We describe the family as an open system, delving into the mysteries of microscopic and macroscopic structures, and paraphrase Ashby, Bertalanffly, and Maruyama. But we do not have good descriptions of the diversity of tasks, function, and structure in the spectrum of normal families, useful studies of family development, or even usable descriptions of the family as a whole—a living organism. Our descriptions, controlled by the structure of language, emphasize sequences when what we need to describe is Gestalt. We do not yet have a way of integrating into family therapy the knowledge gained by our colleagues who study individual or societal structures. While we have increased our armamentarium of therapeutic techniques (and the chapters by Andolfi, Papp, Selvini Palazzoli, Caillé, Keith and Whitaker, and others show a marvelous creative diversity and ingenious artistry in expanding our capacity to transform families), we do not have a shared view of the process of transformation. While we agree, in our different ways, on the importance of the therapist as a change agent, our training is a quilt of educational strategies about what the training should be: return home for change, role-play your family, be in family therapy, be in individual therapy, be yourself, learn in live supervision....

Discipline seems to have the effect of narrowing our view of society as a context. All family therapists talk about the family "in context." Yet when a social psychiatrist like Elkaïm or Zwerling writes, we can see how glibly we tend to put our boundaries around the nuclear or extended family, stigmatizing the family for what may be an adaptation to a dysfunctional social context. In contemplating the future of family therapy, Bloch describes three consequences of the emergence of new paradigms: the end of blame, the end of objectivity, and the end of absolutes. The loss of such clear anchors leaves us a field mined with question marks.

This book, then, in many ways represents "where we're at." In Florence we had an international case (though the American points of view were still the most represented), some shared premises, and a host of uncertainties. This book presents our questions very well. The fact that we do not yet have the answers does not in the least detract from the importance of developing the questions.

SALVADOR MINUCHIN
Philadelphia Child Guidance Clinic

PREFACE

There are not many phenomena in the history of the healing arts which rival the dramatic, almost explosive, burgeoning of the field of family therapy over the past two decades. The hesitantly planted seed of the idea of effecting change in individuals by changing the structure and function of their families through techniques applied to entire family units, in a framework of traditional lineal thinking about treatment techniques such as "repeopling," or challenging family rules and myths, or exposing covert alliances and scapegoating, has flowered into an entirely new conceptual model for describing and changing human behavior. And the excitement that tends to be generated by a new discovery has indeed been a feature of the growth of family theory and family therapy, as is eloquently demonstrated by the diversity of approaches to theory, practice, and training included in this book. Several of the chapters were initially presented at the Second International Conference on Family Therapy, sponsored by the Società Italiana di Terapia Familiare in Florence, Italy, on June 21–24, 1978, and it is unfortunate that there is no way to capture in print the lively discussions engendered by these presentations.

At the heart of the matter is the recognition of the family as a system, with emergent properties beyond those of its individual members. It has proved a very difficult step to shift our focus from the forces and counterforces in the intrapsychic apparatus of an individual patient to the systemic properties of a family; it is proving a much less difficult step to generalize from the family system to larger social units. Once family therapy opened the door to a systemic approach to studying social determinants of behavior, it was immediately apparent that one could only study a family in its community and, in turn, could only study a community in the context of the society and the culture in which it is embedded. Several chapters in this book are directed at the exploration of approaches to the study of the family in the community, and it may well be that family therapy will prove to have been the opening wedge into a still broader, more comprehensive field of contextual therapy.

Preface

Partly as a consequence of the pioneering roles played by Americans in the earliest development of family therapy, and partly as a reflection of American ethnocentrism, family therapists in the United States have tended to think of the field as uniquely theirs. Our hope is that this volume will help dispel this illusion. We would expecially call attention to the sophisticated clinical contributions of Dr. Caillé from Norway and Drs. Andolfi and Selvini Palazzoli from Italy, the challenge of Dr. Elkaïm from Belgium that we beware lest family therapy become still another bit of technology used to blame now families rather than individuals for social ills, and the remarkable technique for training family therapists described by Drs. Andolfi and Menghi.

Those of us who were privileged to participate in the Second International Conference on Family Therapy will not soon forget the experience. This volume encompasses much of the wisdom, and we hope it communicates as well some of the excitement, for those interested in learning about families and family therapy who could not attend.

MAURIZIO ANDOLFI
ISRAEL ZWERLING

CONTENTS

Foreword
vii

Preface
ix

1. Family Therapy and Community Psychiatry
Israel Zwerling
1

SOCIETY AND THE FAMILY

2. Social Policy and Family Policy
Israel Zwerling
11

3. Family System and Social System: Some Examples of Interventions in an Impoverished District of Brussels
Mony Elkaïm
19

4. Drug Abuse and the Family
M. Duncan Stanton
29

COUPLE THERAPY

5. Marriage and Marital Therapy: Issues and Initial Interview Techniques
James L. Framo
49

6. The Use of Fantasy in a Couples' Group
Peggy Papp
73

Contents

7. Divorcing: Clinical Notes
   Donald A. Bloch
   91

8. Treatment of Sexual Disorders in a Community Program
   Ilda Ficher
   109

SCHIZOPHRENIA

9. Family Communication and Social Connectedness in the Development of Schizophrenia
   Albert E. Scheflen
   125

10. Add Craziness and Stir: Psychotherapy with a Psychoticogenic Family
    David V. Keith and Carl A. Whitaker
    139

11. Why a Long Interval between Sessions? The Therapeutic Control of the Family–Therapist Suprasystem
    Mara Selvini Palazzoli
    161

12. Interaction in Rigid Systems: A Model of Intervention in Families with a Schizophrenic Member
    Maurizio Andolfi, Paolo Menghi, Anna M. Nicolò, and Carmine Saccu
    171

13. Communicational Aspects of Therapeutic Systemic Transaction with the Psychotic Family
    Philippe Caillé, Pål Abrahamsen, Charlotte Buhl, and Bente Sørbye
    205

TRAINING

14. Research on Training in Marriage and Family Therapy: Status, Issues, and Directions
    David P. Kniskern and Alan S. Gurman
    221

Contents

15. A Model for Training in Family Therapy
    Maurizio Andolfi and Paolo Menghi
    239

16. Family Therapy Training at Hahnemann Medical College and Hospital
    Robert Garfield
    261

17. The Future of Family Therapy
    Donald A. Bloch
    273

DIMENSIONS OF FAMILY THERAPY

I

Family Therapy and Community Psychiatry

ISRAEL ZWERLING

There are compelling reasons for combining family therapy and community psychiatry in the title of a single presentation. To start with, in the United States, there has been an extraordinary concurrence in their development—the "family therapy movement" and the "community psychiatry movement" both emerged following World War II, both consolidated their positions in the mental health arena in the decade following 1950, and both experienced a measure of formal recognition in the early 1960s: family therapy in the form of the establishment of its first journal, *Family Process*, in 1962, and community psychiatry in the form of the passage of the Community Mental Health Act in 1963. There are, of course, powerful integrating forces that make these two concurrent developments much more than coincidences, and I would like to sketch briefly both some of the conceptual and some of the functional ties that ineluctably bind family therapy and community psychiatry together.

    I distinguish *community psychiatry* from traditional psychiatry by three fundamental criteria: first, the target of services is the entire population of a defined community rather than individual persons who are identified as patients; second, it places the promotion and maintenance of mental wellness on an equal priority level with the treatment of mental illness; and third, it seeks both the sources and the avenues of correction of mental illness in sociocultural determinants of human behavior, as well as in biological and psychological determinants. These may appear to be rather innocent shifts in the focus of psychiatric effort, but their implications are indeed profound. As a consequence of the orientation of community psychiatry to all residents of a defined catchment area, there has been a perceptible blurring of the sharp line that separated the psychodynamically oriented care available to those who could afford the services of a private psychiatrist from the custodial, organically oriented care available to the indigent. The traditional use of the "waiting list" becomes anachronistic when the mission of community psychiatry is to identify and treat mental illness in the community: I can with much more grace ask you to wait until my clinic or ward has an opening if you have come to me asking for my help than if I have myself, in the first place, identified you as in need of my help. Similarly, I cannot gracefully continue my traditional practice of referring to others people I do not really know how to treat successfully—drug addicts, or old people, or children, or delinquent adolescents—when these people are identified by their communities as most in need of mental health services. How I define the condition to which I address my efforts and just what these efforts entail in a traditional psychiatric practice are entirely a matter between me and my patient, with the occasional exception of insurance companies asking about the "illness" for which they are reimbursing my patient; it is another matter when a community tells me to stop blaming the victims of unbearable life circumstances with a label of mental illness. These are some of the consequences flowing from the "catchment area" concept.

Coequal concern with the maintenance of mental health in place of the exclusive concern with treating mental illness has in its turn had a profound impact on traditional psychiatry. So long as my focus was on "illness," the appropriateness of the traditional medical model to the practice of psychiatry could hardly be questioned. There were two of us—my patient and myself—and only I knew the cause of the patient's dis-ease (etiology); only I could name it (diagnosis); and only I could cure it (treatment). To be sure, I had a corps of helpers—*ancillary therapists*, I called them (psychologists, social workers, rehabilitation and industrial counselors and other such lesser professionals)—but there was no question at all as to who was the captain of the medical ship. But once the goal of enhancing mental health is added to the goal of treating mental illness, boundaries begin to be blurred, and the definition of mental health inevitably merges into the broadest concern with the quality of life. What is the role of a psychiatrist in a program to improve reading levels in community schools, or to reduce adolescent gang wars, to cite just two programs for enhancing community mental health currently under way in my own mental health center? I have so frequently been asked what a nice psychoanalyst like myself is doing in an urban ghetto storefront clinic that I have developed a routine answer: I cite a verse from Rabbi Hillel's prayer, "If not I then who; if not now, then when?" I will come back to this point later.

It is, needless to say, the third identifying parameter of community psychiatry—the addition of sociocultural to biological and intrapsychic determinants of human behavior in the search for causes and for modes of intervention—that provides the most immediately evident ties that bind family therapy and community psychiatry. Not long after I became aware of the family as a superordinate social entity—as a *system*, with properties and characteristics beyond the mere sum of those of its constituent members—I found myself in frequent dialogues with analytic colleagues who insisted that they saw nothing new in family therapy; that indeed they were themselves, as analysts, family therapists; that concepts such as *sibling rivalry, oedipal conflict, schizophrenogenic mothers,* and *passive fathers* were all family concepts. I would argue that these were unidirectional concepts having to do only with how others in the family may have affected their patient; that they were concepts about family fragments and not about family systems; that their concern was about the impact of the family upon *a* patient and mine was upon the family as *the* patient. This was some 20 or more years ago, but the same issues have applied over the years, in much the same way, with regard to the application of social role theory and cultural value orientation theory to the understanding of and the intervention with disturbed behavior. Initial insistence that these were only facets of individual psychology has given way to a recognition of the properties of social systems as relevant parameters to be studied, side by side with—and *not* in place of—intrapsychic and neurobiological parameters.

I have found a lucid explication of the central issue that unites family therapy and community psychiatry in Richard Rabkin's very readable little book *Inner and Outer Space*.[5] His basic approach is to define the difference between social and traditional psychiatry on the basis of *where* each establishes the locus of illness. Once processes inside the individual person—biological and/or psychological—are acknowledged to be adaptations to events occurring outside that person, an entirely new perspective, of the sort I am proposing, emerges with regard to the three systems levels (the neurobiological, the psychological, and the sociocultural) that must be explored if one is to achieve the deepest understanding of an instance of disturbed behavior. Dr. Rabkin's extrapolations of the three systems levels to the several parameters of psychopathology and therapy are illustrated in Table 1.

I would like to summarize briefly a few of the specific programs that have been reported that illustrate a family–community approach to a mental health problem.

Two recent contributions, one by Bernice Tucker and Ernest Dyson[6] and the other by Harry Aponte,[1] describe essentially similar programs for therapeutic intervention in cases of school referrals by conjoint family–school interviews. The traditional psychiatric approach to the behavioral problem of a child in a schoolroom was to refer the child to a child guidance clinic for treatment, often with a concurrent transfer of the child out of the class or the school. The advent of systems-oriented consultation services in community programs brought about the recognition that the problem that precipitated the referral developed in a classroom that was part of a school, and that the more appropriate locus

TABLE 1. THREE SCHOOLS OF THOUGHT AND THE METAPSYCHOLOGICAL MODELS

Model	Organic	Psychoanalytic	Social psychiatric
Genetic	Chromosomes	Oral, anal, phallic, genital	Epigenetics
Structural	Brain	Id, Ego, Superego	Networks, interfaces
Dynamic	Neurophysiology	Conflict	Cycles, spirals
Economic	Energy as in physics, chemistry	Libido	"The great chain of life"
Topographical	States of consciousness	Conscious, preconscious, unconscious	Contrite fallibilism
Pathogenesis and diagnosis	APA diagnosis medical model		Social breakdown syndrome
Treatment	Chemical, surgical	Psychoanalysis	"Family" therapy

for treating the problem child was the system within which the problem had developed, the system whose disequilibrium was made manifest by the problem, that is, the classroom or the school. A further step has now been proposed by Tucker and Dyson and by Aponte, namely, that the "problem child" is a product of two systems, of two sets of values, the family and the classroom–school, and that the disturbances within and between these systems, manifested by the "problem behavior," are best understood and resolved by a meeting of the family and the school staff. Aponte has made the point succinctly: "A child with a problem cannot be seen as the sole repository of his problems, nor necessarily should his family. A mental health professional must look at the context of the child with all its ecosystems." The particular approaches advocated by the contributors I have cited raise quite different questions from those to which I here address myself. My point is simply to illustrate the inevitable ways in which community psychiatry and family therapy intertwine, once one begins to think in terms of systems.

Another quite different area, in the sequence I have noted—from traditional approaches to an individual symptomatic person, to work with the community agency dealing with that person, and finally to a joint family-and-agency approach—may be seen in the widely occurring practice among crisis intervention services of introducing family techniques to emergency police units. Everstine, Boden, and Everstine[2] recently described one such project, in which a family-oriented team works with a number of California police departments responding to such emergencies as violent family fights, suicide attempts, and in this particular instance, crises of any sort involving adolescents. The authors pointed out that "The police are used, particularly by the poor, in the way that family physicians and the clergy are used by the middle class." At the same time, the police are traditionally an agency whose "training, temperament, and motivation fall short of equipping them to cope with emotionally charged and highly ambiguous psychological emergencies." They then describe a remarkable collaborative model between a family therapy crisis team and the police departments of 10 California jurisdictions, with case illustrations that compellingly make the value of this model evident. I vividly recall, early in my own development as a community psychiatrist, a futile effort to teach family process to the police squad of the youth division of the precinct in my catchment area: I failed to see the completely disparate values between an effective police system and an effective family therapy system.

A third illustration of a community mental health program in which there is increasing use of the family systems model is in consultation services to day-care centers. Minard[4] has described a sophisticated systems approach to the family and to the day-care center in an illustrative case report of a 4-year-old boy with a behavioral problem, pointing out the applicability of Murray Bowen's conceptualization of systems dynamics to both the family and the center. It should be clear that essentially, any community mental health program not addressed to an individual client lends itself to this approach.

One of the early spin-offs from the community mental health movement was the emergence of the "paraprofessional," which has opened an area filled with contending forces that are still far from resolution. The initial rationale was quite simple: there were many times more patients identified as needing our help than available mental health professionals could hope to serve, and there were many time-consuming chores in the helping process that did not require the extensive training of the professional. Why not, then, provide the minimal training—perhaps "instructions" would better fit our view of what we were doing at the time—necessary to perform these chores, preferably to people from the community whose residents were our patients? It very quickly became apparent that our sights in training "indigenous mental health workers" had been set much too low. In my own experience, the very first thing I was aware of was that much of what I perceived as the "symptomatology" of our patients, when interpreted by our mental health workers turned out to be culturally prescribed behaviors different from my own—not pathological, just different from my own—and many behaviors I looked for, and to the absence of which I ascribed some pathological implications, turned out to be behaviors proscribed by or unfamiliar to the culture of my patients. Where there had been language barriers that had turned off prospective patients, there were now compadres who made them feel welcome. I had allies to cover my awesome ignorance of the "street" culture—allies who, for example, saw through the manipulative behaviors of drug addicts long before I did, and who taught me aspects of family lifestyles that were totally alien to me.

The emergence of extremely competent, even gifted, therapists from the initial pool of paraprofessionals, in retrospect, should have been largely predictable. We were selecting small numbers of persons from the large population of minority ghetto residents who had been blocked from access to the sources of professional training available to the white

English-speaking population. Some of the paraprofessional workers were of only modest ability; many, however, were truly superb. The result of this early experience has been largely a division of employment patterns into two extremes: elitist programs that suffer from too limited a use of paraprofessionals, and antiprofessional, anti-intellectual programs that insist that there is nothing a paraprofessional cannot do as well as a psychiatrist, a psychologist, or a psychiatric social worker. And in the middle of the spectrum, the paraprofessional who escapes these extremes is assailed by the problems of role blurring inherent in his/her other role—most centrally, a division of loyalty to the community and to the professional staff, each seeing him or her as *their* representative.

In virtually every community mental health program I know, the paraprofessional staff function as family therapists, usually as cotherapists with mental health professionals but often enough alone or with other paraprofessionals or with trainees as therapists. It seems to me premature at this time to attempt to formulate a policy with regard to the appropriate use of paraprofessionals, but it is gratifying to see the emergence of reports describing in some detail the actual training programs, work assignments, and family therapy approaches utilized by responsible training centers; I would especially urge your attention to reports by Umbarger[7] and by Meyerstein.[3] Both offer descriptions of the conceptual framework within which they view the problems, as well as some indications of how they choose their paraprofessional trainees and of what and how they teach. More, and more detailed, studies such as these are needed, as well as even more crucial outcome studies. It seems almost self-evident to me that in the long run, the questions about what paraprofessionals can be expected to do as family therapists and how they can best be trained for their roles will be answered by the empirical assessment of their clinical capabilities and not by assessments of the merits of the arguments of the elitistism–anti-intellectualism debate.

The uncertain role of paraprofessionals leads to another observation I wish to make with regard to the "fit" between family therapy and community psychiatry, a point to which I referred early in this report. Within the first few months of my having organized the Division of Social and Community Psychiatry at the Albert Einstein College of Medicine in 1956, I called attention to an unanticipated phenomenon that was proving to be a formidable administrative problem, namely, the blurring of interprofessional boundaries. When we had, the previous year, organized our wards and clinics, there had been no question about who was to be assigned which role, who was responsible to whom, or who was in charge. We no sooner moved out of the college and hospital and into the community than we began to ask "Who *can* do this or that?" as problems never previously encountered by us arose, and the answers followed none of the traditional hierarchical lines. Within the first year, a nurse had clearly emerged as our most talented organizer of community groups, a psychologist was the most sought after supervisor of individual therapy, and a licensed practical nurse was in charge of inpatient-community liaison. In much the same way, it was clear from the very beginning of the family therapy movement that it "belonged" to no single profession, and it remains the case—as family therapy begins now to emerge as a new and separate discipline in its own right—that no single dimension of prerequisite training or experience can claim universal acceptance by family therapy trainers. Family therapy and community psychiatry both represent challenges to the boundaries that compartmentalize mental health professionals into the several traditional disciplines.

I have barely skimmed the surface of the interrelationship between family therapy and community psychiatry. They jointly offer a challenge to all facets of the helping professions, from traditional service delivery systems to the traditional educational structure in which separate graduate schools separately teach separate bodies of students and separately license them to perform largely the same functions, with distinctions in their professional titles but without real differences in their professional roles. This challenge has revolutionary implications for our field. It is a challenge that has not yet been met.

REFERENCES

1. Aponte, H. J. The family–school interview: An eco-structural approach. *Family Process*, 1976, *15*, 303–311.
2. Everstine, D. S., Bodin, A., & Everstine, L. Emergency psychology: A mobile service for police crisis calls. *Family Process*, 1977, *16*, 281–292.
3. Meyerstein, I. Family therapy training for paraprofessionals in a community mental health center. *Family Process*, 1977, *16*, 477–493.
4. Minard, S. Family systems model in organizational consultation. *Family Process*, 1976, *15*, 313–320.
5. Rabkin, R. *Inner and outer space.* New York: W. W. Norton & Co., 1970.
6. Tucker, B. Z., & Dyson, E. The family and the school: Utilizing human resources to promote learning. *Family Process*, 1976, *15*, 125–141.
7. Umbarger, C. The paraprofessional and family therapy. *Family Process*, 1972, *11*, 147–162.

SOCIETY
AND THE FAMILY

2

Social Policy and Family Policy

ISRAEL ZWERLING

INTRODUCTION

The front page of *The New York Times* of June 19, 1978, carried an article headlined "U.S. Family Conference Delayed Amid Dispute and Resignation." It reported the controversy stirred up by the appointment by the Secretary of Health, Education, and Welfare of Mrs. Patsy Fleming as director of a White House Conference that was to have convened experts from the social, behavioral, and political sciences next spring to assess the state of the contemporary family and to recommend a national family policy. Mrs. Fleming is a divorced black woman. The newspaper article stated that her appointment by Mr. Califano had evoked criticism from religious and other groups, and she had therefore been asked to share the directorship with a white Catholic male from an intact family. Mrs. Fleming promptly resigned, and rather than face the criticism certain to develop if *her* resignation was accepted, the entire conference plan was "postponed." I see in microcosm, in this episode, all three of the points I wish to make: first, that there is no national family policy in the United States; second, that there is virtually no issue of national policy that does not have an impact—direct or indirect, mediate or immediate—on the contemporary family; and third, that any attempt to establish a national family policy, or even to resolve any individual broad family problem, necessarily and ineluctably evokes oppositional forces and that these, in turn, evoke counterforces, which preclude the establishment of a consistent family policy or even the resolution of an individual broad family issue.

Philippe Ariès[1] has recently developed the argument that the family has served historically as the social institution of last resort, that is, that "in an attempt to fill the gap created by the decline of the city and the urban forms of social intercourse it had once provided, the omnipotent, omnipresent family took upon itself the task of trying to satisfy all the emotional and social needs of its members." The relationship that Ariès describes is more frequently presented in obverse form by contemporary students of the family, who generally focus on the gradual attrition of instrumental family functions as more and more of the activities that characterized traditional family life have been surrendered to social and professional agencies and institutions. For many of us, it was the thinness of the glue of the purely emotional bonds tying family members together that was the source of its vulnerability; without the multiple functional ties between husband and wife and between parents and children, the stresses on family unity become overwhelming. Ariès now adds another dimension, regarding the emotional ties themselves. He points out that the separation of the place of work—essentially a site that demands restraint and control—from the family residence, and the role of the automobile and television, in further isolating families from the streets and from public places, have sealed the family off from any consistent external or community source of emotional gratification. "Henceforth, the only function of the streets and cafes was to enable the physical movement between home and work or restaurant. These are no longer places of meeting, conversation, recreation. From now on, the home, the couple, the family claim to fulfill all those functions"—and further—"the family has had a monopoly on emotions, on raising children, and on filling leisure time. This tendency to monopolize its members is the family's way of coping with the decline of the public sector." Not only, then, have family members increasingly become tied together exclusively by emotional bonds, but the family has become the exclusive institution in which emotional bonds can be reliably developed. It is for me useful, however much it is also alarming, to view the many evidences of the instability and fragility of the contemporary family in the light of these twin processes. It is alarming because as the family increasingly becomes a social unit whose members are held together exclusively by love and increasingly becomes the *sole* social unit in which love is expressed, it inevitably and necessarily must simultaneously become increasingly sensitive to any social change that alters the status of any of its members. Another, simpler way of saying this is, of course, that increasingly every issue of national policy can be expected to have an impact on the family.

It takes only a moment of reflection to recognize the immediacy of this impact with regard to abortion, unemployment, transportation, wel-

Social Policy and Family Policy

fare, the Equal Rights Amendment, housing, school desegregation, inflation, affirmative action, national health insurance, social security, day care, energy—there is patently no domestic issue, and ultimately no foreign policy issue, that is without identifiable consequences to family life. I would like to discuss briefly three issues that have recently prompted contributions to the family literature—the increasing entry of women into the work force, housing, and welfare—to spell out this argument in some detail.

The Working Mother

The data concerning the increasing representation of women in the work force are widely quoted and are very likely already familiar to an audience concerned with the family. Most impressive has been the increase of mothers of preschool children in the labor force; their representation has risen by 300%, from 13% in 1948 to over 50% in 1979.

Clearly many implications for family life flow from these data. The day-care industry has burgeoned as one consequence of the working mother, and all the assumptions about the crucial role of object constancy in early personality development are being tested currently in a social experiment of massive proportions. The essentially complementary relationship between husband and wife tends more and more to become a symmetrical relationship, and all the assumptions about the crucial role of a clear, sharp differentiation of sexual roles between the parents in the formation of a clear and consistent gender identity in the child are similarly being tested. The inevitable pressure of a working wife on the marital relationship is toward a more egalitarian, more democratic union, and the fundamental tenets of Parsonian family sociology regarding the instrumental role of the husband and the expressive role of the wife as essential prerequisites for a harmonious marital relationship are now also under suspension. I was particularly unnerved by an economic analysis of the implications of the working mother presented by Dr. Isabel Sawhill,[6] which I would like to summarize very briefly.

Dr. Sawhill's starting assumption, hardly assailable, is that child rearing is a labor-intensive occupation: feeding, dressing and undressing, watching over, and singing or talking or reading to or playing with infants and children demand many hours of each day. As the price of this time increases—that is, as the potential income represented by the time required for childbearing and child rearing increases—the motivation for having and rearing children can be expected to decrease. We are clearly at a point now where capital-intensive devices (e.g., television, records, and comic books) have increased to the point where we are alarmed about the "dehumanization" of the child-rearing process. Dr. Sawhill concluded that

> the likely prospect is an increase in the labor-market participation of women as the higher value of their time makes home-based activities, including the rearing of children, more expensive. There will not only be fewer children but also fewer marriages as the wage differential between the sexes narrows. Does this mean that the nuclear family will wither away? I suspect that in a quantitative sense it will diminish in importance, but that the quality of life for children and the relationships between husbands and wives can only improve. In the past, marriage was too often an economic necessity for women, and childbearing either the unintended outcome of sex or an insurance policy against the insecurities of old age. In the future, economics and technology are likely to ensure that the act of having a child and the decision to share life with another adult are freely and consciously chosen for the personal satisfactions they entail rather than as a means to some other end. Personal values and psychological needs met by marriage, children, and family life will be the final arbiters of choice.

This may be an optimistic perspective; Dr. John Calhoun[2] has estimated that within 100–150 years two-thirds of the families in our population will be childless, and he reported that the UN Commission on Population Control on which he serves is already considering the special problems of child rearing in situations in which there are no peer groups of children and in which adults compete for access to child-rearing activities.

Housing

In the period following World War II, the United States witnessed a dramatic, massive expansion of housing resources, which, from the viewpoint of American family life, can only be described as mindlessly irresponsible. In the period from 1930 to 1945, one-and-one-half times as many families had occupied homes that were already in existence as occupied newly built homes; in the decade of the 1950s, when 16 million new homes were built, almost one-and-one-half times as many families occupied newly built homes as occupied existing homes.[7] This process continued until 1973, at an even more accelerated rate, except for a building lull at the height of our involvement in the Vietnam war in the mid-1960s, a lull that ended abruptly after the urban riots in 1968. It is instructive to examine where these new housing units were built, and what kinds of units they were, and how the decisions about building them were made. It is painfully clear that no family impact study was first done.

Under normal circumstances, when a housing shortage evolves slowly, the expectable adaptations of a society are to delay marriage, to postpone childbearing, to subdivide existing housing into smaller units, and to accommodate residential support services—transportation, schools, recreational areas, shopping facilities, etc.—to the gradual increase in population density. The confluence of forces that created the housing shortage following World War II did not produce this sequence; the enormous number of young adults returning from military service to sweethearts and wives, the large number of families migrating north from rural southern areas and from Puerto Rico in response to the wartime job opportunities in the industrial cities, all coming after the prolonged period of reduced construction during the prewar depression and the war years—these simply overwhelmed the normal adaptations. The high standards of size and quality established by local building codes in response to federal regulations, and the resultant high cost of new construction, dictated the process by which new houses were built in the suburbs, on vacant land surrounding existing housing (we increased suburban housing units from 11 million in 1950 to 27 million in 1973) and occupied by the more affluent, while inner-city housing gradually deteriorated. Anthony Downs[3] has described what he calls the "trickle-down process," in which the more affluent keep moving into newer and newer housing units in more peripheral areas as their existing units age; these units are then occupied by less affluent families, who in turn are replaced in their center-city units by still less affluent families, until eventually families too poor to maintain the oldest housing units (whose maintenance costs, of course, meanwhile keep rising) move into these units, and these areas become slums. Downs estimated that this "trickle-down" cycle takes from 40 to 60 years.

The impact of this solution to the postwar housing crisis on family life has been complex, and in my view largely negative. Affluent families were provided attractive suburban housing, but with the attendant isolation that Ariès has stressed and to which I referred above. Center-city families were relieved of the intense overcrowding but found themselves in segregated, ghettoized slums; in rat-infested apartments; and in areas where community services (sanitation, transportation, schools, etc.) were severely reduced. The federally funded mortage terms (highly favorable for suburban homes; prohibitive in center-city slums), the tax benefits of home ownership, the highway systems (also federally financed) linking the suburbs to the commercial, recreational, and cultural areas of the city, all ensured this "solution" to the housing crisis. It is noteworthy that it was not until muggings, rapes, and robberies reached the city areas frequented by the affluent that "crime in the streets" became a salient political issue. Crime in the ghetto had been a feature of life on slum streets for years, but apparently of no special interest to the polity.

Welfare

No national issue matches income support policy in the extent to which it commands the attention of students of the family, and of the population as a whole as well. Keniston et al.[5] devoted almost half of their immensely popular book *All Our Children* to this issue. The antifamily features of our welfare structure would require more time simply to list and describe than is available for an entire conference. Aid to Families with Dependent Children (AFDC), the major cash-benefit welfare program in our country, is not available to a woman and her children if there is an able-bodied man in the household, a fact that is responsible directly for desertion and divorce, or for the pretense of abandonment, by countless unemployed husbands. The promptness with which welfare payments are reduced as income from a job begins has served as a strong deterrent to work as a way to reunite families torn apart by the need to survive through AFDC eligibility. Social insurance programs are very specifically tied to the legal status of relationships; eligibility is established by marriage, and this criterion continues regardless of the later outcome: divorce or desertion does not eliminate eligibility and automatically eliminates any preexisting benefits based on a previous relationship; it is for this reason that so many elderly widows and widowers live together but stay unmarried, to protect the two social security incomes. Recent studies of the family (Gutman,[4] perhaps most notably) have

Social Policy and Family Policy

documented the extent to which oppressed black families, in slavery and in freedom, have relied on kinship networks for security and for child rearing. Patently, adding the kinship network of the father to that of the mother doubles the number of people who are potential resources for the care of the child. AFDC rules about eligibility for child support, in the presence of unemployment rates of up to 40% for young adult black men, generally can be counted on to achieve two predictable results: they rob the father of an opportunity to fulfill his obligation to his child, and they rob the child of access to the father's kinship system.

There has been no dearth of alternatives to the present welfare system; Keniston *et al.* devoted a major portion of their book to a detailed description of one such alternative. In a way, it seems to me that we can begin to perceive an answer to the question "Why has such an antifamily program persisted for so long?" when we read the epilogue to *All Our Children,* a brief section titled "A Vision of the Possible." Keniston wrote:

> The society we imagine would be one that put children first, not last, that saw the development of a vital, resourceful, caring, moral generation of Americans as the nation's highest priority. The devotion that individual parents now feel to their own children would be broadened to include everyone's children. The next generation's strength and well-being would become everyone's responsibility. "How will it affect all our children" would be the first question we ask of every new technology, each innovation, all policies.

A bit further in his vision of the possible, he added, "It would be a society where parents had available to them the kinds of help they needed and where they had a powerful voice in every institution affecting them and their children. It would be a society where present excessive inequalities of income, power, and dignity were much reduced." In effect, Keniston and the Carnegie Council on Children were suggesting that nothing short of a radical revision of our social structure can make it possible for their recommendations to be implemented.

This is the crux of the matter, as I see it. We have no consistent national family policy in the United States because such a policy is not possible within the existing social structure. We continue to apply a simplistic linear approach to individual issues that we carefully isolate, each from all the others: if we have a drug problem, we organize a drug program; for a housing problem, we establish a housing program, or several housing programs. We do this, I believe, not because we do not know about general systems and feedback circuits but because a systems approach, with the welfare of people as the target of the social system, would require the kind of complete reconstruction of our society that we quite clearly are not now prepared to undertake. Keniston and Ariès and many others are calling for a restoration of sense of community: "The next generation's strength and well-being would become everyone's responsibility," Keniston wrote. But the public school system in Chicago (and in a dozen other cities) may not have funds to complete the school year 1979–1980, and California's Proposition 13 promises to sweep the nation, and a national health insurance program keeps receding at the same time that the benefits in the leading proposals keep diminishing. Nor do we have unlimited time in which to work all this out. The inability of our society to support our families as a matter of national policy occurs in a demographic context in which some 70% of the population supports the 30% who are too young or too old to work. We have now about 22 million persons over 65 years of age; by the year 2000, it is estimated there will be 32 million, and the 70% who support the nation will have shrunk to 60% or less. If 70% of us are already so reluctant to support the other 30%, how will 60% of us feel about supporting the other 40%? We might begin to prepare for what lies ahead by reading John Donne's "Devotions" together and by reminding ourselves that the bell tolls for us all.

REFERENCES

1. Ariès, P. The family and the city. *Daedalus*, 1977, 106, 227.
2. Calhoun, J. Report to "Symposium on the Human Family," Washington, D.C., September 9, 1978.
3. Downs, A. Housing policies and family life. *Daedalus*, 1977, 106, 163.
4. Gutman, H. G. *Black family in slavery and freedom.* New York: Pantheon Books, Inc., 1976.
5. Keniston, K. and the Carnegie Council on Children. *All our children.* New York: Harcourt Brace Jovanovich, 1977.
6. Sawhill, I. V. Economic perspectives on the family. *Daedalus*, 1977, 106, 115.
7. U.S. Bureau of Census. *Historical statistics of the U.S., Part 2,* 1975.

3

Family System and Social System
Some Examples of Interventions in an Impoverished District of Brussels

MONY ELKAÏM

In an article I wrote in conjunction with Albert Scheflen[4] in 1973, we criticized the role of the expert in the area of mental health:

- In a given situation, one event from among all possible events is described as the principal event and is given pride of place in the explanation of the phenomenon or symptom.
- Having isolated this explanatory element and overlooking the tentative nature of the explanation, the expert gives it a causal status.
- This cause is then elevated to a higher level of abstraction and codified, which causes the initial information to shrivel still further.
- At that stage, all the expert can do is reduce the diverse elements of a situation to those that he or she deems relevant.

This criticism, in my view, seems also to apply in the area of family therapies. When we are confronted with the families we have to work with, irrespective of the role of economic, sociocultural, or political factors, the tools at our disposal enable us to understand and to take action on the sole basis of intrapsychical or relational patterns.

We then intimate to the families that their problems are exclusively bound up with their past or their current relationships. To cap that, although our action is not without some efficacy, we unwittingly but in fact become so many more social control agents who play their part in obscuring a number of political considerations. As a result, we contribute to the reproduction of the following cycle:

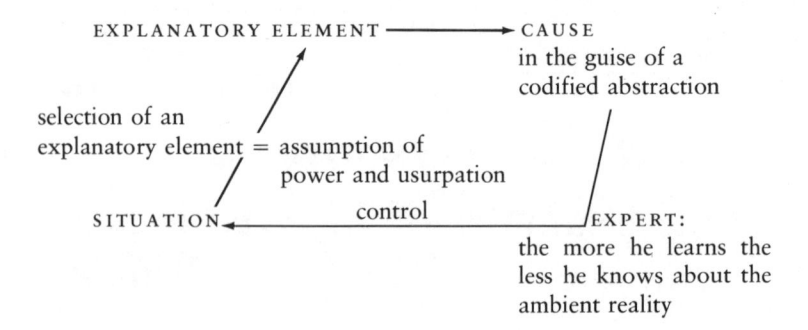

```
              EXPLANATORY ELEMENT ──────► CAUSE
                         ↗                in the guise of a
                        /                 codified abstraction
     selection of an   /
     explanatory element = assumption of
                      /   power and usurpation
                     /    control
        SITUATION ◄─────────────────────► EXPERT:
                                          the more he learns the
                                          less he knows about the
                                          ambient reality
```

Are we thus condemned to being reducing agents and to some degree responsible for a certain mystification whenever we find ourselves faced with a request labeled *psychiatric?*

Together with a group of mental health workers belonging to the La Gerbe sociocultural development team in Brussels, we have attempted research in the direction of what we call *defamilization*. We mean by this term that we refuse to reduce the "causes" of a symptom to the purely family context and that we try to bring about situations in which we can relate our action to an economic, social, cultural, or political dimension. The use of this approach has led us to develop a number of modes of action along four mutually complementary tracks:

- Network therapies based on the problem of an individual or a family.
- Creation of solidarity networks for the benefit of isolated persons.
- Therapeutic action with the family with concomitant action in the living or working environment.
- Multiple-family therapy or family therapies with different families with common problems.

In this article, I propose to dwell more particularly on the two latter modes of action as illustrated by very recent experience. The first two modes of action will be dealt with in subsequent articles. Suffice it to say that our approach is rather different from that of Ross Speck.[7] As a precondition for the creation of a solidarity network, we try to give network members an insight into the way in which the problem of an individual is that of a group caught up in the same contradictions.

Family System and Social System

Therapeutic Action with the Family and Concomitant Action in the Living or Working Environment

In the Living Environment

The case of the following family* may bring out the way we work with a family in the "conventional" manner while giving rise to contexts allowing of the integration of other than purely family elements.

> The family comprises three persons: the grandmother, Jacqueline, aged 70; the mother, Monique, aged 30; and the daughter, Marguerite, aged 9.
>
> Two years ago, the mother, who was employed at a cash desk, was the victim of an automobile accident. Since, a series of symptoms have occurred: depression, anxiety, difficulties with her balance, increase in weight. The mother then stopped working. Having signed a document stating that her disability was not due to her accident, she has not received any compensation. She and her daughter live at the grandmother's in a very simple two-room apartment. Their only income is provided by the grandmother's widow pension.
>
> Marguerite has difficulties at school, suffers from anxiety and phobias in certain specific situations (physical education and swimming).
>
> At the first family therapy session, it immediately emerged that the grandmother was doing the decision making for her granddaughter, the mother having no maternal role at all. For example, the little girl asks her grandmother not to wake her up in the morning.
>
> THERAPIST (*to the mother*). Mrs. X, do you never wake up Marguerite?
> MOTHER. No—it happened once when Mother was away.
> THERAPIST. Well. Why shouldn't you be the one to wake your daughter up in the morning?
> MARGUERITE (*to her mother*). May I say why?
> MOTHER. Yes.

---

*Coordination of this action was very largely ensured by Françoise Moyersoen of La Gerbe.

MARGUERITE. Because she never sleeps at night, so that in the morning around seven o'clock, when I have to get up, she goes to sleep... so it's never possible.
MOTHER. But the fact is that I am awake.
MARGUERITE. What I mean to say is that she just can't get up because she's about to fall asleep.
MOTHER. It isn't quite like that. Err—it's a bit like that, just a bit. But, let's say since I'm at Mother's place, you see, err—I'm not sure she'd really allow it... I did when Mother was away—she'd gone into hospital, I dressed her, it was lovely, we used to wake up...

Steps were then taken to redraw generational lines, the therapist siding with the grandmother in order to allow the mother to come more into the picture. Concomitantly, further work had been carried out in the community. A team from La Gerbe had written to the mother:

On Sunday afternoon we are organizing a meeting of a number of young mothers living in the district who are often very much alone and who would like to get to know others and to discuss the problems they have encountered with their children and many other things. We thought you would like to come along, alone or with your child, as you prefer.

The mother came to the meeting with her daughter. A group was set up that decided to meet every other Sunday afternoon. Monique and Marguerite came to play an active part.

An attorney working in conjunction with the team tried to help Monique to approach the insurance company with a view to obtaining compensation. After a period during which she had to stop attending for health reasons, Monique came back. When the meetings finished, she started sending her daughter home quite frequently in order to spend some time with one or another of the group members.

At these meetings, Marguerite led the games of the youngest.

As for the grandmother, we have learned that she has started to visit her old friends again when Monique and Marguerite are away.

The bustle of activity that is now a feature of the family apartment, where many visitors from the district come and go, does not appeal to the neighbors, who have complained to the police and accused Monique of running a bordello! Monique is coping with the situation. Shortly afterwards, together with another mother from the district she set up a "clothes mart" where they sold used clothing to people living in the neighborhood. She then became one of the leaders of a neighborhood group set up near her home.

In the meantime, despite Monique's persistent financial and physical problems, there was a gradual wane in the complaints expressed by the family at the first session.

In the Working Environment

The contradictions in which a "mentally ill" person gets caught up are not exclusively those of a member of a family; they are those of someone who is also a tenant, a worker, or a member of a community, and so on. We think it is important not to encounter "patients" solely in a context where the only facets we explore are the psychological or family facets. Hence this other experience, which was conducted by La Gerbe in liaison with other mental health workers* close to the Belgian socialist trade union FGTB. The SETCA (Union of Belgian Employees, Technicians, and Cadres, the FGTB trade branch) contacted two firms through their shop floor representatives in order to arrange for each of them to take on five persons whom the official psychiatrists had diagnosed as being mentally ill. Only the management of one of these firms (engaged in distribution) agreed to try the experiment. A general meeting was then held of the shop stewards in that firm, the great majority of whom expressed their support.

The five persons taken on were assigned to handling stores and replenishing shelves. Their ages ranged from 16 to 30 (one woman and four men). Four of them had psychiatric records. One was described as "prepsychotic, disharmonic mentally retarded," another as "psychotic and depressive," the third as "anxiety-fraught psychotic," and the fourth as "mentally retarded illiterate having presented an interpretative delirium." The fifth had no psychiatric record but had been dismissed from all previous jobs on account of "relational difficulties."

---

*Jacques Ternest and Anne-Marie Appelmans. La Gerbe's most active members in this project were Maggy Tilman and Sylvette Norre.

The agreement with the five persons taken on by the firm stipulated that a family therapy would be conducted and that we could also intervene at the place of work whenever tensions emerged that might lead to these patients' being fired. The union representatives and the management agreed that we could operate within the firm.

This research—which, in addition to inserting or reinserting patients into working life, attempts to "depsychiatrize" the contradictions they have to contend with—is still in its early stages. Although some have experienced a problem-free insertion, others have preserved in their working environment their power of subversion, which calls in question the meaning of work as well as the way in which workers look upon their solidarity.

Multiple-Family Therapy

In an article published in 1977,[1,2] we described an example of this type of therapy that had had a successful outcome. It dealt with a meeting of immigrant Moroccan families in Belgium whose adolescent children had been having problems at school and with delinquency.

Unlike Peter Laqueur,[6] in multiple-family therapy we try to bring together families from the same socioeconomic and cultural background and experiencing the same type of problems. During the meetings, we try to create a context that reduces our team's psychological interventions to a minimum. As the dialogue proceeds, the participants come to realize that the problems of the "designated patients" are the problems of a group caught up in the same contradictions. It is no longer a matter merely of the behavior of one or the other individual but of the shared lot of the members of the network. Mutual assistance then takes on another meaning; it grows out of the awareness of belonging to the same community of the oppressed.

Here I should like to summarize some aspects of a session we had with a group of Turkish and Moroccan families whose children were having problems with delinquency:

> During this session, it was very difficult to move from the stage of blame to the stage of solidarity. Neither did it prove possible to create an effective support network. On the basis of that finding, we undertook a more systemic appraisal of the function that de-

Family System and Social System

linquency could assume in this community of immigrant workers and altered our approach.*

From the outset of the session, the parents clearly see the community of problems but in a manner that reproduces the dominant ideology. They are good parents who are sacrificing themselves for their children, who cause them nothing but worry. The parents complain in common about their children's behavior, recalling that they have come to find work in Europe so that their children can study; they compare the little they spend on their own clothing with the excessive amounts spent on the children's clothing; the children do not look after their clothes.

Throughout all this, the children say nothing to contradict their parents.

Then the parents start to talk about Belgian institutions, with which they side against their children.

Here is an example, translated from the Arabic, of what was said by an invalid non-French-speaking father:

I want first of all to thank you for the good you are doing, we shall not forget what you are doing for us, how you are helping us so that our children can study and don't hang about in the streets.

I said to my son, "On Saturday, go to the swimming pool, and on Sunday, go to the movies, but apart from that do your schoolwork and don't misbehave." It's a disgrace—the police come along and tell me, "This is what your son has been up to." What can I answer? Once two policeman brought him home. He had been stealing; they said, "Is this your son?" I answered, "Yes." I wanted to hit him. The policeman said to me, "No. Don't hit him." This is what happened to me—they came to my home. I said to them, "Come in, my other son speaks French." My other son said, "My father doesn't smoke, doesn't go to the movies, doesn't go to bars..." The policeman answered, "All children are like that, tell your father we are sorry." The policeman said, "Tell your father we are sorry. We are sorry we came." It was as if he were ashamed; he said, "We're sorry." I answered, "I'm sorry as well." I added, "Take him away; if he stays here I'll kill him." They took him to Brasschaet [institution for young delinquents], where he stayed for four months. When his mother went to see him, he begged her, "Let me out of here, it's the last time, I won't do it again." We went to the judge—he agreed. When he came out he went to a school. She [pointing to Maggy Tilman, one of the workers responsible for arranging the meeting], gentille, bien [in French], found a school. It's a good school where you can learn a trade. He didn't go regularly. One day he would go, another day he wouldn't.

---

*Béatrice de Crayencour and Maggy Tilman of La Gerbe coordinate this work and are mainly responsible for carrying it out.

Then the headmaster told me, "He doesn't want to study, he doesn't want to go to school." To him, he said, "Your father is a very respectable man. Why aren't you like your father? I can see that you are always clean, you are well dressed and are never short of money."

We could not help being struck by the way in which this father identified with the Belgian institutions, attaining through his son's deviance the status of a man who is looked up to and treated with deference.

A little later in the course of the session the adult brother of one of the adolescents asked, "Why does this never happen to Belgians—why should it only happen to us?"

A MEMBER OF LA GERBE. Why wasn't there the same type of problem in Morocco?
AN ADOLESCENT. Because in Morocco the police are very severe. If you try to steal in Morocco, in Turkey, in Albania, you know where you end up? In the cemetery.
A MEMBER OF LA GERBE. What does that mean?
AN ADOLESCENT. In Morocco or in Turkey, if you touch anything, they chop your hands off. Here, they don't do anything. If you rob a bank, they put you in jail for a year; then when you come out, you start again; they let you...

As soon as we started talking about possible solutions, the young people left the room on various pretexts.

A little later, one of the women members of the team from La Gerbe tried to get one of the teenagers to talk about what he found wrong with school. He refused to do so in front of his parents, whereas he had previously had a lot to say to her on the subject.

Confronted with this situation, I wondered to what extent we might apply the systemic model I had used in the approach to the families of cases of anorexia nervosa[3] to the system made up of a fraction of the community of immigrant workers from Morocco and Turkey. Everything gave the impression that the delinquency was a pseudochange created by a system subjected to major pressures for transformation (because of conditions obtaining in the host country) but whose rigid rules (bound up, inter alia, with the conditions prevailing in the country of origin) prevent any modification of the homeostasis.

Family System and Social System

The vulnerability of this system is particularly observable in connection with the educational prospects of immigrant children. The fact is that when they arrive in Belgium, they are too old to be assigned to classes with children of the same level of educational development. They are also too backward to keep up with schoolchildren of their own age. In addition, the schools in the neighborhood are overcrowded. Similarly the parents expect from their children's success at school educational and economic status without realizing that most of their children soon find themselves in schools leading only to badly paid manual jobs. Thus many children are excluded from the neighborhood schools and are gradually propelled into delinquency by an environment that fosters consumption (fairgrounds, cafés, etc.).

These young people's delinquency can thus be understood as a symptom the function of which is to protect both the system of their parents' community and the values of the Belgian social system.

Ironically one of the fathers of the group—an unemployed, marginalized, non-French-speaking invalid—is so obsessed by his son's deviance that he feels himself allied to the institutions that contribute to excluding himself as well as his son.

Immigrant families confronted with all sorts of external difficulties and values that threaten their traditional rules avoid facing up to these problems by devoting their attention to the delinquent child. At the same time, this delinquency also "protects" the mystifying values of the broader social system by offering an identified scapegoat to a society that prefers to blame the victim rather than to call into question its own structures.

In taking the example of families with cases of anorexia nervosa, where, I believe, the patient who "protects" the family treats its members as objects of care as opposed to subjects, we wondered whether the behavior of these teenaged delinquents wasn't to some extent comparable. They also behave as if they believed their parents to be incapable of coping with external pressures or the institutions that concern them.

Starting from that hypothesis, we decided systematically to involve parents in the solutions to the problems raised by their children and to help these parents, in conjunction with other groups from the neighborhood, to set up pressure groups capable of lobbying the institutions on which they and their children depend. This phase of the experiment is now beginning.

All these examples call on the environment external to the family in an attempt to integrate sociocultural, economic, and political elements into our action. The political element is not the exclusive preserve of the superstructures. A couple or a family experience power relations that Félix Guattari would describe as "micropolitical"[5] and that are inseparable from the external political context.

We are not convinced that working with a couple or a family *ipso facto* means familization. A further need is to create an approach whereby we can analyze this day-to-day political component without falling into normalizing patterns. This is also one of our current research topics.

REFERENCES

1. Castel, R., Elkaïm, M., Guattari, F., & Jervis, G. L'alternative politique face aux techniques. In M. Elkaïm (Ed.), *Réseau-alternative à la psychiatrie*. Paris: Union Générale d'Éditions, 1977.
2. Duhamel, J. M., D., H., et les autres: Le groupe des adolescents. In M. Elkaïm (Ed.), *Réseau-alternative à la psychiatrie*. Paris: Union Générale d'Éditions, 1977.
3. Elkaïm, M. Une approche systémique de quelques cas d'anorexie mentale. Paper presented to the second international conference on the theme: Family Therapy in the Community, Florence, June 1978. In *Cahiers critiques de thérapie familiale et de pratiques de réseaux*. Paris: Éditions Gamma, 1979.
4. Elkaïm, M., & Scheflen, A. Antipsychiatrie et revision épistémologique. *Mosaïque*, No. 18, Brussels, 1973.
5. Guattari, F. *La révolution moléculaire*. Paris: Éditions Recherches, 1977.
6. Laqueur, P. Multiple family therapy: Questions and answers. In D. Bloch (Ed.), *Techniques of family psychotherapy: A primer*. New York: Grune and Stratton, Inc., 1973.
7. Speck, R. V., & Attneave, C. N. *Family networks*. New York: Vintage Books, 1974.

4

Drug Abuse and the Family*

M. Duncan Stanton

In recent years the importance of the family in the genesis, maintenance, and alleviation of drug problems has received increasing recognition. A number of literature reviews[26,35,49,53,58,60,61] and over 370 related papers[54] have appeared. People in the drug abuse field, except for those who take an extreme genetic or sociological view of addiction, have come to realize that drug problems develop within a family context and that most abusers are not isolates who have no primary ties. In other words, problems that arise in abusers' lives can usually be linked to the interpersonal forces and relationships that surround them. While it is not disputed that many other factors (e.g., environmental, physiological, economic, conditioning, and genetic) can also be critical, family variables have come to assume a position of salience in the arena of addictive symptomatology.

Concepts of the Family, Symptoms, and Treatment

Before proceeding to the specifics of drug abuse, it is important to provide some conceptual clarification vis-à-vis the family and the role of symptoms within it. A major problem that has existed both in the drug abuse area and in the larger field of mental health has been the simplistic view of the family that has predominated. Except for consideration of the early developmental years, the family has been viewed as a more-or-less

---

*A similar version of this chapter appeared under the title "Some Overlooked Aspects of the Family and Drug Abuse." In B. Ellis (Ed.), *Drug abuse from the family perspective: Coping is a family affair* (publication of the Office of Program Development, National Institute on Drug Abuse). Washington, D.C.: U.S. Government Printing Office, 1980.

inert influence that, at worst, can bring additional "stress" on the symptomatic member. However, its importance in symptom *maintenance* has generally gone unrecognized. In instances where the family *is* mentioned, discussion has usually been couched in, for example, mother–addict or father–addict dyads or in terms of the characteristics of these people as individuals; the concept of the family as a *system* of people composed of the members *and* their interactions has rarely been applied. Such individually and dyadically oriented concepts are not really in tune with what we have learned about families over the past 20–25 years.

Related to the above is the role of the symptom per se within the family system. A symptom can be seen as a particular kind of behavior that functions as a homeostatic mechanism regulating family transactions[32]; that is, it maintains the dynamic equilibrium among the members. It is a communicative act that serves as a sort of contract between two or more members and often occurs when a person is "in an impossible situation and is trying to break out of it" (p. 44).[25] The person is locked in a sequence or pattern with the rest of his family or significant others and cannot see a way to alter it through nonsymptomatic means.[59] More specifically, the symptom may help, for instance, in the labeling of a member as helpless and incompetent and, therefore, unable to leave home. It might serve as a problem that unifies the family and keeps it intact, much as a catastrophe unites people who experience it together. Similarly it might have diversionary qualities, drawing the attention of other members to the symptom bearer and away from their own difficulties.

Lennard and Allen[37] have emphasized that in order for drug abuse treatment to "take hold," the social context of the abuser must be changed. Applying this principle to the family, one could assert, as have Bowen,[9] Haley,[24] and others, that in order for the symptom to change, the *family system* must change. Conversely, treatment that changes an individual must also have effects on his or her interpersonal system. However, if broader system change (rather than change primarily in the individual) does not occur, the chances for prolonged cure are reduced, for there can be considerable pressure on the "improved" symptomatic member to revert back to the old ways. This idea has important implications for the way in which drug abuse treatment is approached.

We are dealing here with events and behaviors that often lie outside the purview and experience of most treaters and researchers; the actions of family members other than the symptom bearer are rarely or only occasionally observed within the context of most conventional programs. When the larger system is actually encompassed, we must make a conceptual leap into new ways of thinking about symptoms such as substance abuse. Such a view is radically different from and discontinuous with individually or intrapsychically oriented cause-and-effect explanations. It is a new orientation to human problems. Einstein stated that the theory to which we subscribe determines what we see, and it is hoped that through application of this different perspective, the reader will be better able to understand the material to follow.

Addict Family Patterns and Structures

It is beyond the scope of this paper to cover the extensive body of demographic, psychosocial, and interactional literature that has accumulated on the families of drug abusers. Such coverage appears in the aforementioned reviews. Instead a brief overview will be given of the predominant patterns and structures that have emerged from the body of existent research. Their relevance to treatment will also be noted. Emphasis here and throughout this report is on findings about families in which a member shows heavy, compulsive drug use rather than occasional or experimental use.

Family of Origin

Drug misuse appears initially to be an adolescent phenomenon. It is tied to the normal, albeit troublesome, process of growing up, experimenting with new behaviors, becoming self-assertive, developing close (usually heterosexual) relationships with people outside the family, and leaving home. Kandel, Treiman, Faust, and Single[34] propose, from their data, that there are three stages in adolescent drug use and that each has different concomitants. The first is the use of legal drugs, such as alcohol, and is mainly a social phenomenon. The second involves the use of marijuana and is also primarily peer-influenced. The third stage, frequent use of other illegal drugs, appears contingent more on the quality of the parent–adolescent relationship than on other factors. Thus it is concluded that more serious drug misuse is predominantly a family phenomenon.

The importance of adolescence in the misuse of drugs becomes more apparent when family structure is considered. The prototypic drug abuser's family—as described in most of the literature—is one in which one parent is intensely involved with the abuser, while the other is more punitive, distant, and/or absent. Usually the overinvolved, indulgent, overprotective parent is of the opposite sex of the abuser. Sometimes this overinvolvement even reaches the point of incest.[16,19,70] Further, the abusing offspring may serve a function for the parents, either as a channel for their communication or as a disrupter whose distracting behavior keeps their own fights from crystallizing. Conversely, the abuser may seek a "sick" state in order to position himself or herself, childlike, as the focus of the parents' attention. Consequently the onset of adolescence, with its threat of losing the adolescent to outsiders, heralds parental panic. The family then becomes stuck at this developmental stage, and a chronic, repetitive process sets in, centered on the individuation, growing up, and leaving home of the "identified patient."

It is probably most helpful to view the above process as at least a triadic interaction, minimally involving two adults (usually parents) and the abuser. If the drug-using youth is male, the mother may lavish her affections on him because she isn't getting enough from her husband, while the husband retreats because his wife undercuts him—for example, when he tries to discipline the son appropriately. This kind of thinking is much more attuned to the family system, and only a few studies and papers have subscribed to it. Schwartzman[51] noted how all members help to keep the drug addict in a dependent, incompetent role, while Alexander and Dibb,[2,3] Huberty,[30] Noone and Reddig,[44] Reilly,[46] and Stanton, Todd, and associates[64] have presented data on how the family serves to undermine the drug abuser's self-esteem and how drug-taking helps to maintain family stability and homeostasis. Stanton, Todd, Heard, Kirschner, Kleiman, Mowatt, Riley, Scott, and VanDeusen[63] conceptualized drug taking as serving the dual function of simultaneously letting the addict be distant, independent, and individuated, while at the same time making him or her dependent, in need of money and sustenance, and loyal to the family. They have called this conception "pseudo-individuation." Even as an adult, the drug user may be kept closely tied into the family, serving much the same function as during adolescence, when the problem (probably) had its onset. This model of compulsive drug use fits much of the data and helps to explain the repetitiveness of serious misuse and the continuity both (1) across generations and (2) throughout much of a compulsive user's own lifetime. While there is evidence for more frequent substance abuse among parents of drug abusers, relative to parents of nonabusers,[58] the view presented here accentuates the importance of the "identified patient" in the family versus his/her siblings. The limitations of a simple "modeling" theory of drug abuse are underscored, since a particular offspring is usually selected for this role; all children in a family are not treated similarly. Even if they all have equal opportunity to observe the drug-taking patterns of their parents, they generally do not all take drugs with equal frequency. Modeling parents' behavior is only a partial explanation of drug taking by their children.

It is not necessarily obvious that addicts in their late 20s and early 30s are still involved with their families of origin. Their age, submersion in the drug subculture, frequent changes in residence, possible military service, etc., all seem to imply that they are cut off, or at least distanced, from one or both parents. However, there is increasing evidence that despite their protestations of independence, the majority of addicts maintain close family ties. Even if they do not reside with their parents, they may live nearby, and the frequency of contact is high. Twenty years ago, Mason[40] noted the overinvolvement between male addicts and their mothers. This phenomenon was also hinted at by Chein, Gerard, Lee, and Rosenfeld[12] and was documented in an early study by Vaillant,[69] in which he found that 72% of the addicts in his sample still lived with their mothers at age 22. When those whose mothers had died prior to the addict's 16th birthday were deducted, the percentage rose to 90%. As late as age 30, 47% were living with a female blood relative (59% when corrected for those with living mothers). Ellinwood, Smith, and Vaillant[19] also noted a tendency for male addicts to be living alone with their mothers, while Thompson[67] reported that an increasing and substantial minority of the addicts in Vancouver, B.C., remained with their parents. Noone and Reddig[44] found that 72.5% of their 323 clients (average age 24.4) either currently lived with their families of origin or had done so within the previous year. Andreoli[4] has stated that at least 80% of the heroin addicts in Italy live with their parents, and a similar percentage has been noted by Choopanya for addicts in Thailand.* In tracking addicts for long-term follow-up, Bale, Cabrera, and Brown[5] noted that addicts usually have a long-standing contact such as a parent or relative, and Goldstein, Abbott, Paige, Sobel, and Soto[22] reported that addicts "tend to utilize a given household (usually their parents) as a constant reference point in their lives" (p. 25). These authors give examples of how even the "street" addict periodically gets in touch with his or her

---

*K. Choopanya, Health Department, Bangkok, Thailand, personal communication, April 1978.

permanent address, renews relationships with his or her family, etc. Along these lines, Coleman* noted in an examination of the charts of 30 male heroin addicts that the person they requested to be contacted in case of emergency was invariably the mother and was almost never the person with whom they lived (i.e., wife or girlfriend) for clients who did not live with their mothers. A 1972 survey of our own (presented in Stanton[56] and Stanton et al.[63]), taken among 85 addicts at the Philadelphia VA Hospital Drug Dependence Treatment Center and using anonymous questionnaires, showed that of those with living parents, 66% either resided with their parents or saw their mothers daily; 82% saw at least one parent weekly. These figures become more striking when one realizes that the average age of these men was 28 and that all of them had previously been separated from home and in the military for at least several months. The least frequent contact rate was among those over age 35. The only dissenting study on this point was performed in Vancouver by Alexander and Dibb,[2] who felt that most addicts were not closely tied to their parents. However, they did not obtain family contact data; they only inspected existing records to see where, at intake, former patients had reported they were living. It is our experience, and that of Noone and Reddig,[44] that this method is highly unreliable in that much depends on the focus of the intake interviewer. Also, if an addict does not want his or her parents contacted or has reservations about the program, he or she may provide an incorrect or alternative address, such as that of a girlfriend. Further, Ross[48] found that addicts tend to operate out of two addresses, one of which was "drug-related" and the other "family-related," and it is quite possible that many of Alexander and Dibb's subjects reported the former when providing intake information. In sum, this is a facet of the addict family pattern that has not generally been recognized, partly because many addicts deny this closeness or tend to protect their parents. However, anonymous questionnaires or observations of actual behavior have, for the most part, yielded data consistent with a close addict–family tie hypothesis.

Family of Procreation

Concerning marriage and the family of procreation, it has generally been concluded that the heterosexual dyadic relationships that addicts become

---

*S. B. Coleman, personal communication, March 1979.

involved in are a repetition of the nuclear family of origin, with roles and interaction patterns similar to those seen with the opposite-sex parent.[26,53,66,73] In a certain number of these marriages, both spouses are addicted, although it is more common for one or neither of them to be drug-dependent at the beginning of the relationship.[20,70] If the marital union is formed during addiction, it is more likely to dissolve after methadone treatment than if initiated at some other time.[1] Also, nonaddicted wives tend to find their husbands' methadone program to be more satisfactory than do addicted wives.[13] Equally important, the rate of marriage for male addicts is half what would be expected, while the rate for multiple marriages is above average for both sexes.[45] Chein et al.,[12] Scher,[50] and Stanton et al.[63] have noted that parental permission is often quite tentative for the addict to have a viable marital relationship: although he or she attempts flight into marriage, there is often a certain pull or encouragement for him or her to go back. Consequently he or she usually returns home, defeated, to the parents.

Comparison with Other Symptoms or Disorders

Since a number of disorders, in addition to drug abuse, show a pattern of overinvolvement with one parent and distance or absence of the other, the question arises as to how drug abusers' families differ from other dysfunctional families. In a recent paper, Stanton et al.[63] have tried to clarify this issue, drawing both from the literature and from their own studies.* In brief, the cluster of distinguishing factors of addicts' families appears to include the following:

1. There is a higher frequency of multigenerational chemical dependency—particularly alcohol among males—plus a propensity toward other addictionlike behaviors such as gambling and television watching (such practices provide modeling for children and also can develop into family "traditions").
2. There is more primitive and direct expression of conflict, with quite explicit (as opposed to covert) alliances, for example, between the addict and the overinvolved parent.
3. The parents' behavior is characterized as "conspicuously unschizophrenic" in quality.

*The reader is referred to the original paper for the references that document these conclusions.

4. The addict may have a peer group or subculture to which he or she (briefly) retreats following family conflict—the illusion of independence is greater.
5. Mothers of addicts display "symbiotic" child-rearing practices further into the life of the child and show greater symbiotic needs than mothers of schizophrenics and normals.
6. There is a preponderance of death themes and premature, unexpected, or untimely deaths within the family.
7. The symptom of addiction provides a form of "pseudo-individuation" at several levels, extending from the individual–pharmacological level to that of the drug subculture.

Finally, there are data to indicate that offspring of people who immigrated either from another country or from a different section of the United States have high addiction rates, so acculturation variables and parent–child cultural disparity may play a major role in the development of drug addiction.[2,57,68,69]

Treatment and the Drug Abuser's Family

Family Factors That Neutralize Treatment for Drug Abuse

From the early papers (e.g., Berliner,[6] Hirsch,[29] Mason,[40] Wolk & Diskind[73]) to the present, many writers have attested to the importance of the family in the maintenance of addiction. Not only is the drug taking of one member often overlooked by relatives, it is frequently either openly or covertly encouraged.[26,35,53,60,67,71] Further, in addition to supporting the drug-taking pattern, the family may actually work to sabotage those treatment efforts that begin to succeed in reducing or eliminating it. Examples have been commonly reported in the literature, such as the wife of the recovering alcoholic who buys him a bottle of liquor for his birthday, or the parent of the heroin addict who gives him money to purchase drugs. Thus the family is crucial in determining whether or not someone *remains* addicted.

Addicts who are married or are living with a spouse-type partner are involved in at least two intimate interpersonal systems: that of the "marriage" and that of the family of origin. Since more time is spent in the marital context, this system would appear to be more influential in maintaining the drug pattern. A number of writers (e.g., Gasta & Schut,[21] Wellisch[70]) have emphasized the importance of drugs in many such relationships, and Hejinian and Pittel[27] give data indicating that while addicts' spouse-type partners generally voice strong support for the abuser's abstinence, there is also evidence of an unconscious collusion to remain addicted. However, our own studies[62,63,64] have underscored the interdependence between the marital couple and one or both of their respective families of origin. In line with the observations of Chein *et al.*[12] and Scher,[50] we have observed that a "rebound" effect often occurs from marital quarrels, resulting in the addict's returning to his or her parents. We have found that couples' therapy often produces stress on the marriage and triggers another rebound, so that treatment has to begin by including both systems; the key is to start with the parent–addict triad and move more toward the family of procreation in accordance with parents' readiness to "release" the addict.[62,63]

Several investigators have looked at family effects on posttreatment adjustment. For example, Vaillant[69] found that a high percentage of heroin addicts returning to New York City from the federal drug program at Lexington, Kentucky, went to live with either their mothers or a female blood relative; the rate of readdiction in this group was also very high. Thompson[67] noted a similar pattern. Zahn and Ball's[75] data with Puerto Rican addicts indicated that cure was associated with living with one's spouse, while noncure tied in with living with one's parents or relatives. Stanton *et al.*[63,64] observed that prognosis was better in addict families in which the parents were most easily able to release the addict to the spouse or outsiders during the course of treatment.

Positive Family Influence

While the above discussion deals with ways in which the family can neutralize the treatment effort, family involvement can also prove beneficial.[17] The inherent leverage of significant others can be used to help the drug-abusing member to *overcome* his or her problem, rather than serving as a force that *maintains* it. For example, Eldred and Washington[18] found in interviews with 158 male and female heroin addicts that the people the patients thought would be most helpful to them in their attempts to give up drugs were the members of their families of origin or their in-laws; second and third choices were an opposite-sex partner and the patient himself or herself. In interviews with 462 heroin addicts, MACRO Systems[39] researchers found that the family was second only to treatment (70.9% and 79.6%) as the influence the addicts perceived as most important in changing their lives. Finally, Levy[38] indicated in a five-year follow-up of narcotic addicts that patients who successfully overcame drug abuse most often had family support.

Family Treatment

Concerning non-drug-related disorders, the field of family therapy appears to have come of age. Dozens of books, hundreds of articles, and five journals exist in the area. In a review of the literature, Gurman and Kniskern[23] located over 200 studies of family or marital treatment that presented outcome data. Of those studies in which family therapy was directly compared with other modes of treatment, it emerged with superior results in two-thirds of the studies and equal results in the remainder. Gurman and Kniskern also noted that among the various "schools" of family therapy, the most impressive results have been obtained with a "structural" approach,[43] corresponding, in general, with results that have emerged from family therapy in the drug abuse field.[60]

Family treatment is a relative newcomer to the field of drug abuse. However, it has found rapid acceptance. Data from a recent survey of 2,012 drug treatment facilities by Coleman and Davis[14] indicate that the majority of our nation's drug abuse treatment programs provide some kind of family services—in many cases, family or marital therapy—as part of their therapeutic armamentarium. In at least 40 of these programs, involvement of the family is mandatory.[15]

Recently Stanton[60] has reviewed the literature on family treatment for drug problems, locating 74 papers pertaining to 68 different studies or programs. A number of approaches were used, such as multiple-family therapy, and couples' groups, but the largest proportion employed conjoint family therapy, that is, treatment of individual families. Most of the papers held that such approaches are beneficial and effective. Of the 68 studies, 8 mentioned the efficacy of their techniques without providing data, 20 presented case studies with outcomes, and 14 quantified their outcomes; 6 of the 14 involved comparisons with other forms of treatment or control groups; 4 of the 6[28,52,56,64,74] showed family treatment to be superior to other modes, while the remaining 2[72,76,77] obtained equivalent, or equivocal, results. The author concluded that family treatment shows considerable promise for effectively dealing with problems of drug abuse.

FAMILIES WITH LITTLE OR NO DRUG ABUSE

Clues as to the reduction and prevention of drug misuse can be obtained from studies of families who rarely or never use drugs. A number of reports present data on control or "normal" families. In comparison to drug-using families, the non- or low-use families show the following characteristics: offspring perceive more love from both parents, particularly the father[42,65]; there is less discrepancy between how the parents would ideally like their children to be and how they actually perceive them, and the children are seen as more assertive[3]; the parents and their offspring's friends are compatible, the parents have more influence than the peers, and less approval of drug use is voiced by parents and peers[33]; more spontaneous agreement is observed in problem solving, but if it does not occur, the members are slower but more efficient in reaching solutions[41]; the families function more democratically or quasi-democratically, with shared authority and better communication.[11,31] In her study of white middle-class, non-drug-using families, Cannon[11] also found them (1) better able to prepare their children for adult life than families of drug-using adolescents; (2) more likely to make the best of existing circumstances and to underplay frustrations; and (3) generally more cohesive. In addition, she noted that they showed more rigidity than the norm, and she attributed this finding to the fact that a majority of them were referred for participation in the study by religious groups.

Finally, the work by Blum and associates[8] led to a number of conclusions about families that were at low, medium, or high "risk" for drug misuse. The low-risk families manifested a "benevolent dictatorship" structure with diversity of self-expression and adherence to traditional sexual roles. They also showed the following: religious involvement, along with love of God and country; more emphasis on child rearing, discipline, and self-control and less allowance of freedom for children; emphasis on family togetherness and cohesion; greater ability to plan and have fun together; and a tendency for the offspring to be more enamored of control and obedience and also reliable, honest, and sensible. An important variable was their sense of family tradition, that is, that the family had existed over generations—an ethos that seemed to engender loyalty to family standards. It was noted that some of them tended to "have adamant beliefs that status quo is right, that racial segregation is desirable, and that those who want social change are menaces," while some offspring were found lacking in flexibility and were "smug, dogmatic, subservient, uninspired and uninspiring" (p. 105). The authors posited that some of the moderate-risk families showed better adaptation because, even if their offspring had engaged in minor drug experimentation, they appeared to be rather self-reliant, flexible, zealous, and curious, and not overly dogmatic, neurotic, or sociopathic. These families tended to "give in" somewhat in child rearing but maintained a basic firmness.

Prevention

Family Treatment

Of the various approaches to psychotherapy—whether for drug abuse or other problems—family treatment has perhaps the clearest implications for prevention because (1) more people are involved when one sees a family; (2) it engages people (e.g., parents) who may not otherwise have entered treatment themselves but who engender problems in others (e.g., offspring); and (3) if effective, a system is changed that, prior to treatment, had the potential to produce problems in other offspring. For instance, if parents are helped to improve the ways in which they handle a son or a daughter with a problem, they are becoming more competent parents. It is hoped that their experience will provide them with ways of dealing with younger children as these grow older; that is, the lessons learned with one offspring can be transferred to others. In fact, the work of Klein, Alexander, and Parsons[36] with delinquents indicates that family therapy can result in clear-cut prevention of future problems among siblings. Further, if the family situation is changed so that a drug abuser is set free of a need for the parents and therefore, in part, the need for drugs, she or he is on the road to becoming a more competent person and, in the long run, a more competent spouse and parent herself or himself. This, then, is primary prevention.

Education

Several years ago, Blum[7] opined that drug education has rarely helped young people's decision-making about use. A subsequent review also concluded that this approach is generally ineffective or equivocal in reducing overall drug use, although some programs may attenuate more extreme use by certain individuals.[10] However, a recent report by Resnik[47] indicates that drug information, in small doses, can be effective, especially if it is presented *in a family setting*. Similarly Stanton[58] has stated that education for prevention needs to be aimed more directly at parents and families, as opposed to, for example, school systems. It should be based on a sophisticated knowledge of family patterns, structures, and child-rearing practices. Information on such topics as how to deal with grandparents, how to allow an adolescent autonomy, and when to be firm might be appropriate. Familial triads and larger units should be discussed, rather than perpetuating such limited individual and dyadic concepts as the "personality" of the drug user or the mother–son relationship. The adaptive role that drug use can serve in the family could be dealt with, in addition to warnings, for instance, of how antagonisms between one parent and a child may arise if the parents are divided. Emphasis needs to be placed on strengthening the *boundaries between the generations*. Parents should be helped to recognize how their child, in an effort both to get his or her own way and to survive, can play them off against each other if they are not of a similar mind on disciplinary procedures. Finally, stress should be given to the positive ways that families can deal with drug-related problems, and a sense of hope should be conveyed. For, indeed, there does appear to be hope.

REFERENCES

1. Africano, A., Fortunato, M., & Padow, E. The impact of program treatment on marital unions in a methadone maintained patient population. *Proceedings of the 5th National Conference on Methadone Treatment*, 1973, *1*, 538–544.
2. Alexander, B. K., & Dibb, G. S. Opiate addicts and their parents. *Family Process*, 1975, *14*, 499–514.
3. Alexander, B. K., & Dibb, G. S. Interpersonal perception in addict families, *Family Process*, 1977, *16*, 17–28.

4. Andreoli, V. *Current drug abuse treatment approaches in Italy.* Paper presented at the National Drug Abuse Conference, Seattle, Wash., Apr. 1978.
5. Bale, R., Cabrera, S., & Brown, J. Follow-up evaluation of drug abuse treatment. *American Journal of Drug and Alcohol Abuse,* 1977, 4, 233–249.
6. Berliner, A. K. Narcotic addiction, the institution and the community. *International Journal of the Addictions,* 1966-1967, 1-2, 74–85.
7. Blum, R. *A new perspective on drug education.* Paper presented at the meeting of the National Coordinating Council on Drug Education, Washington, D.C., June 1972.
8. Blum, R., & associates. *Horatio Alger's children.* San Francisco: Jossey-Bass, Inc., 1972.
9. Bowen, M. The use of family therapy in clinical practice. *Comprehensive Psychiatry,* 1966, 7, 345–374.
10. Bry, B. H. Research design in drug abuse prevention: Review and recommendations. *International Journal of the Addictions,* 1978, 13, 1157–1168.
11. Cannon, S. R. *Social functioning patterns in families of offspring receiving treatment for drug abuse.* Roslyn Heights, N.Y.: Libra Publications, 1976.
12. Chein, I., Gerard, D., Lee, R., & Rosenfeld, E. *The road to H.* New York: Basic Books, Inc., 1964.
13. Clark, J. S., Capel, W. C., Goldsmith, B. M., & Stewart, G. T. Marriage and methadone: Spouse behavior patterns in heroin addicts maintained on methadone. *Journal of Marriage and the Family,* 1972, 34, 496–501.
14. Coleman, S. B., & Davis, D. I. Family therapy and drug abuse: A national survey. *Family Process,* 1978, 17, 21–29.
15. Coleman, S. B., & Stanton, M. D. An index for measuring agency involvement in family therapy. *Family Process,* 1978, 17, 479–483.
16. Cuskey, W. *An assessment of the clinical efficacy of the Mabon Parents Demonstration Project* (Report prepared for the Services Research Branch, National Institute on Drug Abuse). Philadelphia: Cuskey, Ipsen & McCall Consultants, Inc., Nov. 1977.
17. Dell Orto, A. E. The role and resources of the family during the drug rehabilitation process. *Journal of Psychedelic Drugs,* 1974, 6, 435–445.
18. Eldred, C. A., & Washington, M. N. Interpersonal relationships in heroin use by men and women and their role in treatment outcome. *International Journal of the Addictions,* 1976, 11, 117–130.
19. Ellinwood, E. H., Smith, W. G., & Vaillant, G. E. Narcotic addiction in males and females: A comparison. *International Journal of the Addictions,* 1966, 1, 33–45.
20. Fram, D. H., & Hoffman, H. A. Family therapy in the treatment of the heroin addict. *Proceedings of the 5th National Conference on Methadone Treatment,* Vol 1. National Association for the Prevention of Addictions to Narcotics, 1973, pp. 610–615.
21. Gasta, C., & Schut, J. *Planned detoxification of addict marital pairs: Diagnosis and treatment strategies.* Paper presented at the meeting of the National Drug Abuse Conference, San Francisco, May 1977.

22. Goldstein, P. J., Abbott, W., Paige, W., Sobel, I., & Soto, F. Tracking procedures in follow-up studies of drug abusers. *American Journal of Drug and Alcohol Abuse,* 1977, *4,* 21-30.
23. Gurman, A. S., & Kniskern, D. P. Research on marital and family therapy: Progress, perspective and prospect. In S. L. Garfield & A. E. Bergin (Eds.), *Handbook of psychotherapy and behavior change: An empirical analysis* (2nd ed.). New York: John Wiley & Sons, Inc., 1978.
24. Haley, J. Whither family therapy. *Family Process.* 1962, *1,* 69-100.
25. Haley, J. *Uncommon therapy.* New York: W. W. Norton & Company, Inc., 1973.
26. Harbin, H. T., & Maziar, H. M. The families of drug abusers: A literature review. *Family Process,* 1975, *14,* 411-431.
27. Hejinian, C. L., & Pittel, S. M. *Can marriage survive addiction and treatment?* Paper presented at the National Drug Abuse Conference, Seattle, Wash., Apr. 1978.
28. Hendricks, W. J. Use of multifamily counseling groups in treatment of male narcotic addicts. *International Journal of Group Psychotherapy,* 1971, *21,* 84-90.
29. Hirsch, R. Group therapy with parents of adolescent drug addicts. *Psychiatric Quarterly,* 1961, *34,* 702-710.
30. Huberty, D. J. Treating the adolescent drug abuser: A family affair. *Contemporary Drug Problems,* 1975, *4,* 179-194.
31. Hunt, D. G. Parental permissiveness as perceived by the offspring and the degree of marijuana usage among offspring. *Human Relations,* 1974, *27,* 267-285.
32. Jackson, D. D. The study of the family. *Family Process,* 1965, *4,* 1-20.
33. Jessor, R. Predicting time of onset of marijuana use: A developmental study of high school youth. In D. Lettieri (Ed.), *Predicting adolescent drug abuse: A review of issues, methods and correlates* (DHEW Publication No. [ADM] 76-299, National Institute on Drug Abuse). Washington, D.C.: U.S. Government Printing Office, 1975.
34. Kandel, D. B., Treiman, D., Faust, R., & Single, E. Adolescent involvement in legal and illegal drug use: A multiple classification analysis. *Social Forces,* 1976, *54,* 438-458.
35. Klagsbrun, M., & Davis, D. I. Substance abuse and family interaction. *Family Process,* 1977, *16,* 149-173.
36. Klein, N. C., Alexander, J. F., & Parsons, B. V. Impact of family systems intervention on recidivism and sibling delinquency: A model of primary prevention and program evaluation. *Journal of Consulting and Clinical Psychology,* 1977, *45,* 469-474.
37. Lennard, H. L., & Allen, S. D. The treatment of drug addiction: Toward new models. *International Journal of the Addictions,* 1973, *8,* 521-535.
38. Levy, B. Five years after: A follow-up of 50 narcotic addicts. *American Journal of Psychiatry,* 1972, *7,* 102-106.
39. MACRO Systems, Inc. *Three-year follow-up study of clients enrolled in*

treatment programs in New York City: Phase III—Final Report. Submitted to NIDA by MACRO Systems, Inc., June 1975.
40. Mason, P. The mother of the addict. *Psychiatric Quarterly Supplement,* 1958, *32* (part 2), 189–199.
41. Mead, D. E., & Campbell, S. S. Decision-making and interaction by families with and without a drug-abusing child. *Family Process,* 1972, *11,* 487–498.
42. Mellinger, G. D., Somers, R. H., & Manheimer, D. I. Drug use research items pertaining to personality and interpersonal relations: A working paper for research investigators. In D. J. Lettieri (Ed.), *Predicting adolescent drug abuse: A review of issues, methods and correlates* (DHEW Publication No. [ADM] 76–299, National Institute on Drug Abuse). Washington, D.C.: U.S. Government Printing Office, 1975.
43. Minuchin, S. *Families and family therapy.* Cambridge, Mass.: Harvard University Press, 1974.
44. Noone, R. J., & Reddig, R. L. Case studies in the family treatment of drug abuse. *Family Process,* 1976, *15,* 325–332.
45. O'Donnell, J. A. *Narcotic addicts in Kentucky.* Washington, D.C.: U.S. Government Printing Office, 1969.
46. Reilly, D. M. Family factors in the etiology and treatment of youthful drug abuse. *Family Therapy,* 1975, *2,* 149–171.
47. Resnik, H. S. (Ed.). *It starts with people: Experiences in drug abuse prevention* (DHEW Publication No. [ADM] 78–590, National Institute on Drug Abuse). Washington, D.C.: Porter, Novelli and Associates, 1978.
48. Ross, S. A study of living and residence patterns of former heroin addicts as a result of their participation in a methadone treatment program. In *Proceedings of the Fifth National Conference on Methadone Treatment,* Washington, D.C., 1973 (Vol. 1). New :York: NAPAN, 1973, pp. 554–561.
49. Salmon, R., & Salmon, S. The causes of heroin addiction—A review of the literature, Part 2. *International Journal of the Addictions,* 1977, *12,* 937–951.
50. Scher, J. Patterns and profiles of addiction and drug abuse. *Archives of General Psychiatry,* 1966, *15,* 539–551.
51. Schwartzman, J. The addict, abstinence and the family. *American Journal of Psychiatry,* 1975, *132,* 154–157.
52. Scopetta, M. A., King, O. E., Szapocznik, J., & Tillman, W. *Ecological structural family therapy with Cuban immigrant families.* Paper submitted for publication, 1980.
53. Seldin, N. E. The family of the addict: A review of the literature. *International Journal of the Addictions,* 1972, *7,* 97–107.
54. Stanton, M. D. The family and drug misuse: A bibliography. *American Journal of Drug and Alcohol Abuse,* 1978, *5*(2), 151–170.
55. Stanton, M. D. Forum: Family therapy for the drug user: Conceptual and practical considerations. *Drug Forum,* 1978, *6,* 203–205.
56. Stanton, M. D. Some outcome results and aspects of structural family therapy with drug addicts. In D. Smith, S. Anderson, M. Buxton, T. Chung,

N. Gottlieb, & W. Harvey (Eds.), *A multicultural view of drug abuse: The selected proceedings of the National Drug Abuse Conference—1977.* Cambridge, Mass.: Schenkman Publishing Co., Inc., 1978.
57. Stanton, M. D. The client as family member: Aspects of continuing treatment. In B. S. Brown (Ed.), *Addicts and after-care: Community integration of the former drug user.* Beverly Hills, Calif.: Sage Publications, 1979.
58. Stanton, M. D. Drugs and the family. *Marriage and Family Review,* 1979, *2(1),* 1–10.
59. Stanton, M. D. Family therapy: Systems approaches. In G. P. Sholevar, R. M. Benson, & B. J. Blinder (Eds.), *Handbook of emotional disorders in children and adolescents* (tentative title). New York: Spectrum, 1980.
60. Stanton, M. D. Family treatment approaches to drug abuse problems: A review. *Family Process,* 1979, *18,* 251–280.
61. Stanton, M. D. Family treatment of drug problems: A review. In R. L. Dupont, A. Goldstein, & J. O'Donnell (Eds.), *Handbook on drug abuse* (National Institute on Drug Abuse publication). Washington, D.C.: U.S. Government Printing Office, 1979.
62. Stanton, M. D., & Todd, T. C. Structural family therapy with drug addicts. In E. Kaufman & P. Kaufmann (Eds.), *The family therapy of drug and alcohol abuse.* New York: Gardner, 1979.
63. Stanton, M. D., Todd, T. C., Heard, D. B., Kirschner, S., Kleiman, J. I., Mowatt, D. T., Riley, P., Scott, S. M., & VanDeusen, J. M. Heroin addiction as a family phenomenon: A new conceptual model. *American Journal of Drug and Alcohol Abuse,* 1978, *5(2),* 125–150.
64. Stanton, M. D., Todd, T. C., & associates. *The family therapy of drug addiction.* New York: Guilford Press, 1981, in press.
65. Streit, F., Halsted, D. L., & Pascale, P. J. Differences among youthful users and nonusers of drugs based on their perceptions of parental behavior. *International Journal of the Addictions,* 1974, *9,* 749–755.
66. Taylor, S. D., Wilbur, M., & Osnos, R. The wives of drug addicts. *American Journal of Psychiatry,* 1966, *123,* 585–591.
67. Thompson, P. Family of the addict explored. *The Journal* (Addiction Research Foundation, Toronto), 1973, *2,* 8.
68. Vaillant, G. E. Parent–child cultural disparity and drug addition. *Journal of Nervous and Mental Disease,* 1966, *142,* 534–539.
69. Vaillant, G. E. A 12-year follow-up of New York narcotic addicts: III. Some social and psychiatric characteristics. *Archives of General Psychiatry,* 1966. *15,* 599–609.
70. Wellisch, D. D., Gay, G. R., & McEntee, R. The easy rider syndrome: A pattern of hetero- and homosexual relationships in a heroin addict population. *Family Process,* 1970, *9,* 425–430.
71. Wellisch, D., & Kaufman, E. Family therapy. In E. Senay, V. Shorty, & H. Alksne (Eds.), *Developments in the field of drug abuse.* Cambridge, Mass.: Schenkman Publishing Co., Inc., 1975.
72. Winer, L. R., Lorio, J. P., & Scrafford, I. *Effects of treatment on drug abuser*

and family. Report prepared for the Special Action Office for Drug Abuse Prevention, Executive Office of the President, Washington, D.C. (Grant No. DA 4 RG 003), 1974.
73. Wolk, R. L., & Diskind, M. H. Personality dynamics of mothers and wives of drug addicts. *Crime and Delinquency,* 1961, 7, 148–152.
74. Wunderlich, R. A., Lozes, J., & Lewis, J. Recidivism rates of group therapy participants and other adolescents processed by a juvenile court. *Psychotherapy: Theory, Research and Practice,* 1974, 11, 243–245.
75. Zahn, M., & Ball, J. Factors related to the cure of opiate addition among Puerto Rican addicts. *International Journal of the Addictions,* 1972, 7, 237–245.
76. Ziegler-Driscoll, G. Family research study at Eagleville Hospital and Rehabilitation Center. *Family Process,* 1977, 16, 175–189.
77. Ziegler-Driscoll, G. Family treatment with parent addict families. In D. Smith, S. Anderson, M. Buxton, T. Chung, N. Gottlieb, & W. Harvey (Eds.), *A multicultural view of drug abuse: The selected proceedings of the National Drug Abuse Conference—1977.* Cambridge, Mass.: Schenkman Publishing Co., Inc., 1978.

COUPLE THERAPY

5

Marriage and Marital Therapy
Issues and Initial Interview Techniques

JAMES L. FRAMO

In this paper, I first briefly outline some theoretical views about marriage. Then I present a rough classification of the kinds of problems that bring couples to therapy. I then discuss in brief the issue of individual versus conjoint treatment for marital problems. These observations are followed by a discussion of my general goals of therapy, and I conclude with specific details on how I conduct initial interviews with couples. These observations are not being presented as a comprehensive or encyclopedic account of marital therapy, not even of my own approach. They are an approximation of my way of organizing the material presented by couples who come for help; they represent the translation of theory into practice. In this paper, I attempt to describe some of the things I have learned about marriage and marital therapy, based on over 20 years of working with couples and families. The focus is largely on the earliest, engagement phase of treatment, when, by the kinds of questions I ask, I prepare the couple for what lies ahead. The real work of marital therapy comes later. I do not presume that I could begin to describe in words the later *process* of therapy and change; I don't think anyone's written accounts have ever accomplished *that*.

SOME THEORETICAL PROPOSITIONS ABOUT MARRIAGE

The following theoretical notions about marriage are not presented in any systematic order; they represent, in random fashion, some of the varied conceptual ideas, including my own, put forth by professionals about marriage. Since no observations can be addressed to all the multiple levels of intimate relationships, they may appear contradictory, and some of them may even seem downright absurd. One of the things that makes the subject of marriage so fascinating is that whatever you want to say about marriage is true and not true. Everyone knows everything about marriage, and no one really knows very much. Marriage experts are as subject to distortion about marriage as anyone else.

1. It has been postulated that people select mates on the basis of need complementarity, that, for example, the logical man will choose an emotional wife.[34] On the other hand, it has been proposed that those who marry tend to have similar needs.[22] Both statements are probably true, depending on the depth and level of inference.

2. Social learning theory, translated into clinical practice by the behavior therapists, views marriage in terms of sequences of rewarding and negative behaviors between partners. Therapy from this point of view consists of establishing *quid pro quo* negotiations that can increase mutual positive reinforcements.[26] (Husband to wife: "I will listen to you more if you will not spend so much time on the telephone.")

3. Conventional psychoanalytic views on marriage stress that the discrepancy between conscious and unconscious demands creates marital problems, expressed first in the choice of a mate and then in the subsequent evolution of the relationship. Kubie[20] described how conflicts stemming from the family of origin and based on the need to "wipe out old pains or pay off an old score" can create profound marital conflict and estrangement, particularly when the partners are misled by romantic feelings.

4. Dicks[5] extended traditional psychoanalytic theory, using object relations theory to deal with the interlocking collusion and bilateral reciprocity that go on between married partners (or in any intimate relationship). He stressed the unconscious complementariness of marriage—a kind of division of function by which each partner supplies part of a set of qualities. The partners' joint personality enables each half to rediscover lost aspects of the primary object relations that they had split off and that in their involvement with the spouse they reexperience by projective identification.

5. The definition of what is appropriate and normal is based on the way one's original family viewed and did things. When people marry, there occurs a mixture of two "normal" family systems, each of which was "right," giving rise to profound bewilderment and misunderstanding. Yet the very differences between spouses are what attracted them to

each other in the first place, since a way was opened, through the spouse, for conflicts from that old family to be worked out and lived through. I have postulated that mate selections are made with profound accuracy and, collusively, in two-way fashion. The partners carry psychic functions for each other, and they make unconscious deals: "I will be your conscience if you will act out my impulses." The relationship between the intrapsychic and the transactional constitutes the core of my own approach.[7]

6. People tend to marry those who are at the same basic level of personality differentiation, however different their social functioning may appear to be; the spouses, moreover, have opposite patterns of defensive organization.[3]

7. The secret agendas of marriage partners defy reality. People make impossible demands on marriage, based on the idea that one's spouse should make one happy. No one can make this work. It is not possible to go through life, with or without a partner, without experiencing some pain and loneliness. Yet people act as if their spouse *owes* them happiness as an inalienable right. You can't make anyone love you, and no one can make you happy. People do not marry people, not real ones anyway: they marry what they *think* the person is; they marry illusions and images. Many end their marriages because the spouse does not match the internal image. Jourard[19] said that a real marriage can begin at just the point where the marriage appears to be finished. The exciting adventure of marriage is finding out who the partner really is.

8. Marriage is more than the sum of its parts; it is a system within other systems, kept in balance by such universals as how dependency flows back and forth, the power struggles, who is one down and who is one up, who pursues and who distances, who fights and who withdraws, who approaches whom sexually, who does what jobs around the house, how the kids are handled, who deals with the in-laws, who is the day person and who is the night person, who is going to take care of whom, and who determines the values about what the good life should be. Spouses, over time, often switch positions along these dimensions.

9. All lasting marriages go through stages, or what Warkentin and Whitaker[30] have called "serial impasses" (starting with the honeymoon, through the first pregnancy and subsequent children, through the "ten-year syndrome," etc.). These authors stated that the bilateral transference on which the marriage was originally based has become exhausted by the ten-year impasse, and the couple have "fallen out-of-

love." They already know how to hurt each other; in marital therapy, they may learn how to love each other. It is only after they have fallen "out of love" that they learn to behave lovingly. People are quite different at various stages of their marriage; Jourard[19] has stated that he has had many marriages over time, all with the same person. Uneven growth spurts can make spouses feel like strangers to each other.

Warkentin and Whitaker[31] also believe that the usual rules of social behavior do not apply to intimate relationships, that fairness is not appropriate, consistency is impossible, and factual honesty is not relevant: "All is fair in love and war, and marriage is both."

10. Societal and cultural factors, of course, all affect marriage. No one can deny that governmental policies, a developing ethos of individualism, the women's movement, the high divorce rate, changing population trends, world events, and inflation have an impact on family and marital life. It is also true that differences in race, age, religion, or social class are influences on marital outcomes. But there is a sector of the marriage relationship that is impervious to external conditions and events, a kind of private world that is unique to the couple alone. This is the part of the marriage that is usually not open even to the view of the marital therapist, for it is underground, sometimes not known to the partners themselves. But the force of this private experience (his marriage, her marriage, and their marriage) can have powerful effects on feelings and behavior. Marriage can be the greatest or the most humiliating experience of one's life. Whitaker[32] said that marriage is "an experience which threatens one's being and wrenches one down to the roots. Like hypnosis, marriage is an altered state of consciousness. . . . The deeper one goes the more possible it is for things to happen" (p. 70). Marriage can be like a sterile field, where you can't catch anything but nothing will grow in it. Marriage can be like a beech tree, beautiful to admire from afar but cold and dark underneath. Or marriage can make you feel like a million bucks.

11. One intriguing hypothesis about marriage developed by Napier,[24] one that tends to scare almost everyone, is that people tend to marry their worst nightmare. More precisely, this author suggests that partners who feared rejection or abandonment in their families of origin are likely to marry those who felt engulfed by their parents. The former partner is seeking greater closeness in the relationship, whereas the latter partner pushes for more separateness. The partners, who selected each other on the basis of their deepest fears, also selected the one person who

offers the opportunity for mastery of those fears. When you marry, you don't just marry a person; you marry a family. Sometimes people try to improve on their original family when they marry.[23] One client said, "I married her because her family seemed so warm and accepting—something I never had in my own family."

12. Family problems tend to repeat themselves from one generation to the next. The greatest gift that parents can give their children is a viable marriage relationship and a sense of self. Strengthening marriages, in my judgment, is the best way for the children to be free to live their own lives. After all, the primary function of family life, when all is said, is preparation of the young for the next generation.

A Preliminary Classification of Marital Problems

The following categories of kinds of problems and couples that come for help are based on my own private practice experience and are frankly impressionistic. The couples I have seen are largely upper middle class, educationally and economically, and they tend to be more motivated and sophisticated about therapy than most people seen in public clinics. I must mention, however, that even in private practice, the dropout rate for conjoint marital therapy is high; about one-fifth of the couples I see do not return for a second session. There are various reasons that couples have not stayed in treatment: some couples could not afford the fee and were too embarrassed to tell me; one partner wanted the therapy and the other did not (perceiving the marital therapy as a commitment to the marriage); some couples did not "connect" with me or sensed that I was reluctant to work with them; some couples with a very tenuous relationship were afraid that if the therapy continued, they would end up divorced; some people had no concept of how therapy worked and were disappointed that their problems were not solved in the first session; and there were various other reasons for dropping out that I could not figure out.

Not all the couples I see are married; the partners "living together," however, are deeply involved in a relationship that they either want to make better or need help to terminate. In this paper, I discuss all these relationship problems as "marital problems."

The following classification of marital problems is presented in order of the treatment outcomes I am able to effect operationally. That is to say, I personally find those categories in the early part of the list less difficult to treat than those toward the latter part. This scale of difficulty is very crude, and, to be sure, there have been couples in the last few categories who have had good treatment outcomes, as well as those who initially looked very promising but got nowhere in therapy. The more experience I have, the more respectful I am of the enormous complexity of marriage relationships and the difficulty of changing them.

I do not believe that this classification scheme is precise enough to be called *marital diagnosis*. Diagnosis would imply that specific treatment strategies have been devised for each category, which is certainly not the case.

1. There are couples, recently married or married a long time, whose marriages are basically sound and whose problems are relatively superficial. Although most couples who come to marital therapy state as their chief complaint, "We do not communicate," these couples' problems really can be handled as communication ones. By clarifying misunderstandings and utilizing the sessions to really listen to the other, this kind of couple essentially rehabilitate their own marriage and leave therapy after a few sessions. I find it best largely to stay out of the way and not do anything stupid, such as trying to make patients out of them. Some of these couples, by the way, came to therapy at the urging of friends who had had a good marital therapy experience; it was "the thing to do."

2. The kind of marriage I feel I can best help is the kind in which each partner is committed to the relationship and each says in some form, "I basically love my spouse and know he/she loves me, but for some reason we can't get along. Will you help us make this marriage work?" Some of these couples are reeling from the impact of their first child ("Why didn't someone tell us what it would be like?"), whereas others are "fight phobic" and afraid to deal with conflict. Some premarital couples, trying to determine whether to marry, fit into this category, whereas other premarital couples belong in the more difficult classifications. Although most professionals agree that premarital therapy is the best way to cut down on the divorce rate, few couples at this stage will come for therapy because they are in love and do not want to examine the relationship too closely.

3. Some partners come in saying that they basically care for each other a great deal but that the zing has gone out of their relationship. They report that there is no excitement, that sex is routine, and that

everything is too damned predictable between them. They will state that their spouse is their "best friend," "like a member of the family," and neither one wants to be married to anyone else. These "brother–sister" marriages have mixed outcomes: some of them do manage to enrich their relationship; others come to accept the status quo; and still others keep searching for ways to recapture the romantic excitement they once had. Therapy techniques for bringing excitement into dull or empty rather than conflictual relationships are not very well developed, at least by me.

This category is probably a mixed one, with masked depression or blocked hostility possibly in the background.

4. Next comes the garden variety type of marital problem where the partners have considerable conflict about a variety of issues. One partner may be having an affair and the couple are fighting over that person's giving up the other relationship. Both partners may be struggling over the issue of having an open sexual arrangement. Couples in conflict almost always have a sexual problem, either an outright sexual dysfunction or, what is more common nowadays, loss of interest in sex in one or both partners. The conflicts may be over in-laws, money, control, children, or, in the case of dual-career couples, whose job should take precedence in determining where they live. In recent years, feminist issues have come up more frequently in marital therapy, ranging all the way from women's retaining their maiden name to conflicts over more even sharing of parental responsibilities and household tasks. In many of these conflictual marriages, the partners may state, "Either this marriage is going to work or let's end it." One client said, in that universal statement about marriage, "When I needed her she wasn't there, and when she needed me, I wasn't there." Some of the divorces that occur in this group seem to be necessary, whereas others are unnecessary.

5. Marriages in which one partner is symptomatic require unique treatment strategies. In these kinds of marriage, there has typically been marked imbalance, with one partner being more overtly dominant, or one partner (usually the wife) wanting more emotional responsiveness from the other, or one partner being the patient and the other the caretaker. Usually the asymptomatic spouse either does not want to come in with the partner or is willing to come in to help you treat the disabled one. Most of the time, it is the wife who has the symptoms and the husband who sees no problem in the marriage. If the wife is depressed, this depression frequently lifts quickly as she begins to express her dissatisfactions with the relationship. When the husband becomes involved

in the treatment, as usually happens, the couple move up into the "conflict" category. Some marriages, however, stay stuck in this position.

6. There are marriages whose problems stem largely from incomplete marital maturation. These spouses never really left home; their primary allegiance is to their families of origin, and there are many complaints about interference from in-laws. The parents are so much in the marriage that it is necessary to involve them in the treatment. Some of these couples do manage to give up their credit cards and make it on their own, whereas others remain bound to their original family. A case description of the treatment of this type of couple is in Framo.[13]

7. Mental health professionals present special kinds of difficulties and challenges. These partners have usually had oceans of psychotherapy; they have been in analysis or individual therapy or encounter groups, have been to EST and have been Rolfed, and have made pilgrimages to see Milton Erikson. Each partner has profound understanding of the mate's dynamics, and each is trying to change the other—which never, never works. The partners have talked over their problems ad nauseum, and their use of technical language and interpretations further befuddles the situation. Often these couples are quite frightened of being on the other side of the therapy fence. The chief therapeutic task is to stop the therapy they are doing badly with each other and to help each to focus on self.

8. Remarriage problems are usually complicated because of the ghosts of the former family and the rearrangements of loyalties. The sequelae of divorce are, in general, more entangled than those following the death of a spouse (e.g., the second wife resents part of the paycheck's going to the former family). Not only does the former marriage create problems in the marital relationship, but there are often problems around step-parenting and children's allegiances to biological parents. I am not reluctant, by the way, to bring both former and present families together for sessions.

9. There are couples who have come too late for marital therapy. These are usually older couples whose relationship problems have calcified and whose options are limited. Sometimes it is the woman experiencing the loneliness of the last child's having left home. Other times it is the man whose career is closing down at a time when his wife's world is opening up. Efforts to help the partners get some satisfaction out of outside jobs or activities are occasionally successful in warming up the

relationship. Some of these couples are tired and beyond fighting, and if you can create some conflict between them, there is hope.

10. One of the most difficult categories to treat is the marriage that is in extremis. In these situations, one spouse may have someone else and wants out, and the couple come to therapy as a last resort before seeing lawyers. Often the partner who is finished with the marriage would like to exit from the therapy and leave the partner with the therapist. Some of these couples can be engaged in divorce therapy.[12]

11. Finally, there is the kind of long-term, chronically unhappy marriage where the partners "can't live with and can't live without." These are the couples who have had many unsuccessful marital therapy experiences; they should have divorced but could not. These marriages have alternated in the past between "agony and ecstasy," but now they are past all that, and some of these spouses are waiting for the other to die. Occasionally couples' group therapy helps these people to separate or come to terms with what they have. Sometimes sessions with their grown children can be useful.

Individual versus Conjoint Therapy

Sager, Gundlach, and Kremer[28] have reported that half of all people requesting psychotherapy do so largely because of marital difficulties and that another 25% have problems related to their marriage. Despite these facts, the overwhelming treatment method used for marital problems in the past has been individual psychotherapy. Part of the reason is that most therapists have been trained in understanding intrapsychic psychology, and the treatment of inner conflict is the one-to-one doctor–patient relationship. There must have been some recognition of the shortcomings of the individual approach to marital problems, as evidenced by the variety of experimentations with many different methods, described by Sager,[27] Greene,[15] Grunebaum, Christ, and Neiberg,[16] Hollander,[18] and Berman and Leif.[1] The following are some of the methods that have been used: therapy or analysis of husband and wife in succession by the same therapist; therapy conducted by two therapists, each of whom sees one spouse, with the therapists periodically conferring about their clients[21]; four-way sessions in which each spouse has a separate therapist and at regular periods the two therapists and two clients have joint sessions; simultaneous treatment of both spouses by the same therapist but in separate sessions; conjoint therapy wherein both spouses are seen together by one therapist or by cotherapists; combined individual and conjoint sessions by the same therapist(s); couples' group therapy[8]; spouses in separate groups; and therapy with spouses and their family of origin.[11]

The foregoing methods of treatment for marital problems reflect, as I see it, the conceptual confusion between the intrapsychic and the transactional models of marriage. As the findings from family therapy began to appear in the literature, there occurred a mixture of models whereby traditional practitioners tried to incorporate systems thinking into their treatment of marital problems, sometimes inappropriately. At the present time, marital therapy seems to be in a transitional phase between the medical model, which focuses on illness and the neurotic features in the individual spouses, and the systems model, which examines the unity of the marital dyad, the interaction between the partners, and the system of the marriage as a part of larger systems. Adding to the complexity are the theoretical differences within the family therapy field, polarizing into dynamically oriented work with families and couples as contrasted with dealing with observable interactions and shifting of sequences of behaviors (often labeled structural or strategic marital and family therapy).

Without going into the merits or disadvantages of either approach, I should lay my own theoretical cards on the table. My experience has led me to believe that it is just as important to know what goes on inside people as to know what goes on between them—that neither dimension can be reduced to the other and that both are important. This is one of the reasons that I agree with Whitaker that when you treat a couple you have three patients—the husband, the wife, and the relationship—and that therapy may focus on any one of those three at any given time. Furthermore, as I stated previously, I think that it is the *relationship* between the intrapsychic and the interpersonal that will provide the greatest understanding and therapeutic leverage, that is, how internalized conflicts from past family relationships are being lived through the spouse and the children in the present. I see a deeper exploration of this relationship by the mental health professions as the number one task over the next century. I predict, further, that conceptual extensions along these lines will result in more sophisticated marital and family diagnostic systems and treatment approaches. In addition to theoretical

Marital Therapy: Initial Interview

advances, we need many more hard data, which will come from the systematic variation of approaches and conditions. Then we might be able to answer such questions as: What kinds of therapy for what kinds of people in what kinds of combinations for what kinds of problems with what kinds of therapists?

In our society, whenever there are problems in a marriage, the one who typically accepts the patient role and goes for psychotherapy is the wife. (In most recent years, since more wives are leaving husbands, it is the male who sometimes becomes the patient). When there is an argument between the spouses, the husband may say, "Get off my back and go talk to your doctor"—which explains why many women cynically refer to their therapists as "My paid friend." In an important and influential paper, Whitaker and Miller [33] have described how the wife, under these circumstances, learns how to communicate beautifully with her therapist; she forms a more intimate relationship with her therapist than with her spouse. These authors stated that treating a married person alone and hoping that the result will generalize into the marriage usually does not work. Furthermore they state, and I agree, that individual therapy with one spouse when the marriage is weak increases the likelihood of divorce (recognizing, of course, that some divorces are healthy steps). I myself only see partners together and I no longer do individual therapy, nor do I see spouses separately for individual sessions. I have found that the advantages of individual sessions (learning about secrets, for instance) are not worth the suspicions of the absent spouse and the conflicts of loyalty and confidentiality in the therapist that such sessions give rise to. Besides, each married person exists in the context of an intimate relationship, and breaking the couple into private sessions negates the context and obscures the collusiveness that goes on between married partners. I have learned that when spouses work on their intrapsychic conflicts in the presence of their partners, the latter develop a more empathic view of the spouse, especially when they come to recognize what their partners have had to struggle with during their lives. The dilution of the transference to the therapist I see as a plus in marital therapy; in more recent years, I have found it more productive to deal with the transferences of spouses to each other.

I recognize that many marital and family therapists do not work as I do; they claim many benefits from having individual sessions concurrently with conjoint therapy. The one time some clients seem most insistent on having individual sessions is during the latter stages of divorce therapy, when some people seem to need the separate sessions to reinforce the reality of the divorce. I do not mean to imply that individual therapy is not useful; indeed there will always be a need for that special, one-to-one confidential relationship. I have referred clients for individual therapy at the conclusion of marital or family therapy, especially when they were motivated to work on inner problems in a more intensive way.

Grunebaum *et al.*[16] have postulated that individual therapy should be done when the marriage does not appear to be the problem of greatest priority (you can't tell that from the initial contact), when one partner has severe psychopathology (I see symptomatic spouses who are seriously disturbed at the beginning of therapy), and when the couple appears to be uncommitted to the marriage (you can't always tell at first who is really committed to whom and whether the couple wants to keep the marriage). These authors' thesis, that one does marital therapy only when the problems arise primarily from the marriage, is not consistent with my own experience. I have successfully treated many couples whose problems initially did not seem related to the marriage (such as the depressed woman who says, "My problems have nothing to do with my husband; they're all in me"). Admittedly, however, there really are not any reliable guidelines on indications or contraindications for individual or conjoint therapy for marital problems.

Marital Therapy Goals and My Philosophy of Therapeutic Change

The average length of time I see couples is about 15 sessions. Approximately three-fourths of the couples I see improve in therapy, defined as mutually agreed-upon termination with agreement that the major goals have been achieved. (Some divorces are regarded as improvement, whereas others are seen as therapy failures.) More technically, from my theoretical viewpoint, I regard as improvement that the partners are more personally differentiated, they have come to terms with the roots of their irrational expectations of marriage and of the spouse derived from their families of origin, they have developed a more empathic understanding of their mate, they can meet each other's realistic needs in the face of their differentness, they can communicate more clearly and openly, they like each other more, they have learned to deal with the issues between them, and they each can enjoy life more. For a more complete account of my conceptual view of family and marital dynamics, the reader is referred to Boszormenyi-Nagy and Framo,[2] and Framo.[7,8,10,11,13]

I once wrote, "Each married person secretly believes that his or her mate is seriously disturbed and cannot love." The majority of people who enter marital therapy do so in order to change their mate. They believe that while they may have some minor adjustments to make in their own personality, it is the mate who needs to make deep, fundamental changes. Some partners have been waiting a long time to have their day in court, where at last they can prove to an objective professional how strange, peculiar, sick, thoughtless, and unloving the spouse really is. One of the first disappointments may occur in marital therapy when the therapist not only does not instantly leap to one's side and begin forthwith to berate, correct, and treat the spouse but has the temerity to suggest that one is expected to take responsibility for change in oneself. (To be sure, there are spouses who take upon themselves all the wrong and badness, but this stance is usually short-lived and, in time, is revealed as an accusation in disguise.)

I believe it is very difficult to change oneself despite the lip service that people give to wanting to change themselves. Some people spend almost their entire lives trying to change someone else (a parent, a child, a spouse), and I communicate to these clients that that is never going to work. The only way I know to change someone else is to change oneself, because when you are different, the intimate other has to change in response to your changed behavior or attitude. That is to say, the other person can no longer rely on your predictable responses. (When I say "change oneself," I do not mean that one can play act at it, role-play the change, pretend or "play games"; the change must be genuine.) But people not only fear change in themselves, they fear change in their intimate other. For instance, spouses are usually quite threatened when their partner goes for individual therapy; they feel that if the spouse gets his or her head together, that person won't want them anymore. This is one of the reasons I insist on seeing spouses together, so they can participate in the process together and their interlocking collusion can be dealt with. (In this connection, a woman once called me to say, "Doctor, I'm having terrible marital problems. Can you see me?" When I told her to bring her husband with her, she said, "Oh, but I don't want him to know we're having problems!") Anxiety about change in the other can be manifested during therapy sessions in many ways, such as protectiveness toward the spouse when the therapist tries to work with that person or anxiety when the other begins to change in the direction originally demanded (e.g., when the formerly sexually cold wife begins to warm up, or when the husband who never talked or expressed feelings begins to do so). There is an old song that goes "I can't adjust to the you that has adjusted to me."

When I first started doing psychotherapy many years ago, I used to spend a lot of time worrying about my clients—losing sleep over whether that lonely, depressed woman was going to commit suicide, whether that teenaged boy was going to run away from home. In those days, I encouraged clients to call me at any time, and I gave the message that I would give of myself ceaselessly. Virginia Satir once told me that when she got out of social work school, she felt she was covered with breasts. (There seems to be something about social work training that communicates that social workers must be self-sacrificing, all-giving.) As the years have gone by, I think I have become more appropriately selfish. Carl Whitaker claims that one of the differences between an amateur and a professional is that a professional learns to cut off at the end of a session. Although there are occasions when emotional transactions in treatment sessions truly move me and carry over after the session is over, I have generally learned to keep separate my professional work and my private life. Once I wrote a paper on the difficulties I had handling this dilemma because the ghosts of my own family came into the treatment room.[6] In any event, I do not do therapy over the telephone; by my manner, I discourage phone calls, communicating thereby, "Let's take it up in the next session." During treatment sessions, I give my all. I am so hyperalert to what is going on that I will hear things being said that no one else hears; when everyone in the room denies it was said and I play the tape back, sure enough there it is. Needless to say, my "third-ear" listening does not work in dealing with my own close relationships; I'm lucky there if I hear with one ear.

Finally, on this question of my philosophy of treatment, I expect a great deal of the people I work with; I push them to their limits, and when they achieve that, I push for more. I want them to get their money's worth. The people who come to see me professionally either change or leave. A family therapist friend, Oscar Weiner, once said, "You can't want more for people than they want for themselves." Believe me, it's true. Some people cannot tolerate prosperity or good things in their lives. One client once said, "I can't stand it. My wife has been nice to me all week, and even my car is working!"

The Initial Interview

In this section, I attempt to describe in concrete terms what I actually do, from the first contact with a couple to the end of the first interview.

Most couples are referred to me by ex-clients, in which case it is the wife or husband who calls me directly. Some couples call who have seen my name in a magazine article; others are referred by family therapists in other cities; and occasionally referrals are made by mental health professionals in my own area of Philadelphia. When a professional is making the referral, I suggest that the client call me directly. I prefer not getting a long history about the couple, not only because about half of the time I never hear from the referred clients but also because I do not want to be biased by the referring source. I never accept a school's, court's, family's, or mental health professional's definition of the problem, unless I know that the referring, uninvolved person thinks in systems terms. Besides, I prefer meeting people where they are now rather than on the basis of their past experience with someone else. As John Rosen once put it, "No one is as sick as his case history."

When the husband or wife calls me, I keep the conversation very short because I do not want a relationship to start with one person; one can be triangled very fast. I don't even go into the problem much except to ask whether the problem is primarily marital or one concerning the kids. If the problem is child-focused, I next ask who is in the family and state that the way I can best help is to see the whole family. If the problem is presented as marital, I state that both partners must come in together. The great majority of clients know I work this way and prefer conjoint therapy, but when the caller insists that he/she or the spouse be seen alone, I will refer that person elsewhere. In the past, when I was asked about my fee, I used to give the standard answer of "We'll discuss that in the first session." Now I simply state my fee. I conclude the call by making an appointment and giving directions to my office. I have been asked by prospective clients about my theoretical orientation and my philosophy of life, and I have been asked to state what kind of person I am, whether I am married or divorced, where I got my training, and how long the treatment lasts. Some of these requests are legitimate ones that consumers have a right to know, but others are strange or frustrating, or make me angry.

I work both as a solo therapist and as a cotherapist with couples; over the years, I have worked with many different cotherapists. My wife and I have worked together for some years, a unique combination that brings a special dimension to the therapy. The great majority of clients are pleasantly surprised that they will be seen by a man and a woman. The topic of cotherapy is complex and beyond the scope of this paper.

I can usually tell something about a couple on the basis of their behavior in the waiting room. Spouses who are talking to each other or laughing seem to do better in therapy than those who do not talk to each other, bury their heads in magazines, or sit there in frozen silence, waiting for the "doctor." I notice how they enter the treatment room, note their appearance, age, the way they are dressed, and the dominant affects. They are, of course, sizing up the same things about me (or us). (Sometimes there is an immediate positive or negative reaction between me and the clients, based on unknown nonverbal cues or on looks. The first statement out of one woman's mouth was "You have one helluva nerve making me walk up those steps to your office." After that, our relationship went downhill.) I bring to their attention immediately the microphone on the table, which is in the middle of a circle of swivel chairs, and I state that I tape all sessions, primarily because I like to lend the tapes to couples so they can listen to the sessions at home.

I then start off with the question "What seems to be the problem?" Usually the partners turn to each other and say, "Would you like to go first?" I have always been curious about the process that goes on between husband and wife that determines who will first state the problem. After one person gives his or her view, I ask the other partner to state the problems as he or she sees them. Following these brief statements of the problems, I get such identifying data as ages, occupations, the length of the marriage, and the ages and sexes of the children. Even if the problem is presented as marital, I ask whether there are any problems in the children. Later I may have family sessions with the couple and their kids. Bringing in the children for sessions, even when the focus is on the marriage, can add much to understanding what goes on between the parents. Children have a way of cutting through adult obfuscations and telling the truth. Furthermore the kids get to be relieved of the burden of being marriage counselors; I tell the children, in effect, that they do not have the training for it and that I am going to take over that job. Children are usually glad their parents are getting help, and besides, the parents do not have to lie about where they go every week. Sessions with the children toward the end of marital therapy can give a reading on how things have settled down at home.

Marital Therapy: Initial Interview

These initial interviews vary considerably in content, activity, coverage, pace, and intensity. I have a general sequence of questions in my head that I tend to follow, but sometimes the interviews go off in unexpected directions, particularly if the emotions are explosive and the crises acute. Some couples talk so freely and rapidly that I can't get a word in, whereas getting others to talk is like pulling teeth. Most of the time, couples start off with cover stories, rehearsed speeches, or stiff, overintellectualized, stilted language. I have learned to ride with those preliminaries, which stem from anxiety about the therapy situation. In the first interview, I try to get maximum information without affecting the flow and process; that is to say, I rarely make therapeutic interventions in a first session. Whenever a spouse says, "We feel," I suggest that things go better if each person speaks only for himself or herself. The partners are acutely aware of my responses to them, I am sure—my facial expressions, degree of interest, my grasp of what they are saying, etc. Most people are unnerved by silent therapists who sit there, staring at them, not giving feedback. It is part of my natural style to be active, open, and direct.

Most couples are fearful when they come to therapy; they feel unusual and different and wonder how "sick" they are. Without necessarily being explicit about it, I think it helps to convey in some form that the therapist has had some life experience, that he or she is no stranger to pain and disappointment, and that marital difficulties are well-nigh universal. In my attempts to decrease the distance between us, I will at times make social comments and even relate something personal about myself when relevant. (This latter can be overdone; some people are offended if the therapist is too disclosing about his or her personal or marital problems.) Sometimes remarks between cotherapists and humor can help ease the tension. It should be remembered, however, that the therapy situation is a professional rather than a social situation.

I try to cover a range of topics in the initial interview: history of previous therapies, previous marriages, what stages of marriage they have gone through, whether they were in love when they got married, whether they ever had a good relationship, what their expectations of marriage were, how the arrival of children affected the relationship, what their fight styles are or how they deal with conflict, and a description of the courtship from each vantage point. I try to evaluate how much the partners seem to care for each other (I always ask the direct question, "Do you love your spouse?"), whether the basic bonding is strong enough to tolerate the pain of change in oneself and in the mate, how motivated each is to do the work of therapy, whether each blames the other or each can take responsibility for himself or herself, whether one partner wants to stay in the marriage more than the other, whether they came too late, what kinds of secondary gains are operating, whether there are factors external to the marriage that would handicap the therapy, etc. As I said in a previous paper, however,[13] it is difficult to predict which couples are going to "make it" in therapy. I have had couples who I was sure would have a successful outcome who got nowhere in therapy, and I have had others whose marriages looked hopeless who profited a great deal. The science of predicting marital therapy outcomes is in its primitive stages. All the while, I am trying to put together pieces of the puzzle that will explain the nature of the hidden agendas in the marriage contract, that is, how they came to select each other as spouses. (Many people have said, "I loved her because she loved me.")

I regard the sexual relationship as a diagnostic indicator in the sense that when the sex is good, other problems can be tolerated, and when it's bad or nonexistent, all other problems get exaggerated. I have learned that you often cannot accept at face value in the first session the partners' characterization of their sexual relationship; couples who initially tell you that sex is "great" or "no problem" later tell you the truth. Since the sexual relationship is uniquely sensitive to feelings of hurt, anger, rejection, disappointment, and so forth, it is not surprising to discover that almost all couples who come for marital therapy have either sexual dysfunctions or diminished interest in sex. Most couples' sexual difficulties disappear as a function of working on other problems. For those sexual problems that persist beyond successful marital therapy, I refer the couple to a sex therapist. The couples who report that the only thing they have going for them in their marriage is exciting sex are rare. I do not pussyfoot about affairs and usually ask directly whether there is a third-party involvement on either side. Although I do not expect that I will always get honest answers to this question, I can usually surmise the existence of an extramarital relationship by the way the replies are given. Long hesitations, reddening of the face, or a quick "no" and an abrupt change of the topic leads me to expect a private phone call the next day. From my practice, I judge that women are having more affairs than they used to.[9]

It frequently happens that one partner, most often the husband, has come to marital therapy unwillingly or is willing to come only as a cotherapist in treating the spouse. These kinds of clients are always a challenge to me, and over the years, I have developed some techniques for "hooking" them into therapy: if a husband brings in a wife with symptoms, I frequently spend most of the session talking with the husband about his own life (particularly his family history). If the questions are not pathology-oriented, these men usually respond to the interest shown in them as persons. Another technique I have used after getting noncommittal or hostile replies to questions is to ignore these men to the point where they feel left out and want to be included. In these circumstances, when I am asked, "How come you always focus on me and not my spouse; am I the sick one?", I use a therapeutic double bind by saying, "On the contrary, you are healthier because I find you more receptive and open to change." The most effective method in dealing with reluctant spouses, I have found, is to put them into a couples' group. Almost no one can resist getting involved in that group process.

To couples who are on the edge of divorce, yet torn up about ending their marriage, I say something like "Let's postpone a decision about the fate of the marriage until later in the therapy. Let's meet for a while, and when each of you knows yourself better and how the two of you interlock, you'll have more information on which to make a decision about the fate of your marriage." Most couples are very frightened of ending even a bad marriage, so this statement relieves most people.

Unless the couple is in a state of crisis that requires immediate attention, I usually get a brief history of each spouse's family of origin. I have found questions like the following to be pertinent: How many were in your family? What was your birth position? What kind of work did your dad do? What kind of person was he as you were growing up? What was your mother like? How would you characterize their marriage? What was the atmosphere in your home or what kind of a family did you come from? Which parent did you feel closer to? How was your relationship with your brothers and sisters? Were there any unusual circumstances in your family (serious illnesses, deaths, grandparent in the home, etc.)? I ask the circumstances under which the person left home, how the parents reacted to his or her getting married and to the prospective mate. After finding out whether the parents are still alive, I inquire into the client's *current* relationship with parents and sibs: how often they see each other, whether the relationship with the parents is fused, superficial, distant, close, or alienated and cut-off. In my experience, unless you directly ask clients about their current relationships with parents and siblings or about problems with the in-laws, that sort of information is not volunteered. Many couples are surprised that the therapist, by this line of questioning, believes that there is a connection between their marital problems and their previous or ongoing relationship with the original family. While relating a family history, some people become upset or tearful. For instance, a man may choke up describing the distant relationship with his father, and I may comment, "That's something we'll have to go into further later on." I always ask about deaths in the family and have found that the old, muted affects can be revived by questioning in minute detail about the actual circumstances of the death (e.g., "Who told you your father was dead? What did you do next? Did you cry? Who picked out his clothes for the viewing? What happened at the funeral? What was left unsaid when your dad died?") Following each person's account of his or her family history, I always ask the spouse to give his or her reaction to that account and also to give his or her own views of the in-laws. Occasionally the mate corrects severe distortions, such as the wife who said, "I'm sitting here amazed. My husband just told you what a normal, average family he came from, and I remember his telling me how he and his sister were always afraid that his parents were going to kill each other. And the police were always called to his home!" Most couples are involved in a web of complex interrelationships with both extended families. A fairly common situation is that, say, the husband works for his father or works in his wife's family business; this arrangement creates all sorts of interesting problems. I tell all couples in the first interview that at some point toward the end of therapy, I would like each spouse to bring in his or her family of origin for a session. My paper on this topic demonstrates the great power of such sessions and also describes how I overcome the strong resistances of clients to this suggestion.[11] I may have sessions with the spouses and extended families or in-laws early in the therapy if there are immediate problems in those relationships, but I consider such sessions different from family-of-origin work, for which adults are prepared to confront and deal with the hard issues with their parents and brothers and sisters.

Simply making the decision to come to therapy starts bringing about changes in the relationship of most partners. For instance, they start talking about topics that could not be talked about previously without much anxiety. Some couples, however, are in a state of euphoria in that first session, not only because they have hope after such long despair but also because, often unrealistically, they expect that they will be made over and achieve ecstasy in their marriage. Everything that has always been wrong will now be made right. When I sense this kind of magical expectation, I tell the couple that after the honeymoon phase of therapy, some disappointment is inevitable once they get to see what's really involved in change. I state that the relationship may get worse before it gets better, and I do not minimize how difficult and painful marital therapy can be.

By the end of the initial interview, I can tell whether the couple will want to continue with the therapy. When they are uncertain, I suggest that they talk it over with each other and let me know; this is analogous to the situation where a couple is making an expensive purchase and the salesman leaves them alone so they can tell each other what they really think. As I stated previously, one-fifth of the couples do not continue with therapy; about half of those who do not return state their reasons during the first session, whereas the others telephone later. I do not try to convince couples or try to change their minds; therapy is difficult enough with motivated people.

Diagnostic interviews usually precipitate strong emotions, not only in the couple but in the therapist(s) as well. Although emotions can serve defensive purposes, I see powerful affects as providing the fuel for change, and I have learned not to be afraid of them. I agree with the statement made by Bryant and Grunebaum[4] in discussing the emotions generated by family diagnostic interviews: "a well run family diagnostic is almost always painful for the leader. It is when we have felt too little that there has been only an evaluation of the surface" (p. 154).

The purpose of this paper was to focus on the beginnings of marital therapy. I have not discussed ongoing techniques in the later phases. I should mention that practically all the couples I see come into a couples' group. I have come to regard couples' group therapy as the treatment of choice for premarital, marital, separation, and divorce problems.[8] To be sure, I have been discussing the easiest part of therapy, which is why these early phases are written about more frequently.[14,17,25,29] One of these days, I'm going to try to describe the part of the therapy process where change takes place, the part that has been called "the dirty middle" of therapy. But for the present, that story will have to wait.

REFERENCES

1. Berman, E., & Lief, H. I. Marital therapy from a psychiatric perspective: An overview. *American Journal of Psychiatry*, 1975, 132(6), 583–592.

2. Boszormenyi-Nagy, I., & Framo, J. L. (Eds.). *Intensive family therapy.* New York: Harper & Row Medical Dept., 1965.
3. Bowen, M. The use of family theory in clinical practice. *Comprehensive Psychiatry,* 1966, *7,* 345–374.
4. Bryant, C. M., & Grunebaum, H. V. The theory and practice of the family diagnostic: II. Theoretical and resident education. In I. M. Cohen (Ed.), *Family structure, dynamics, and therapy.* Psychiatric Research Reports #20. American Psychiatric Association, 1966.
5. Dicks, H. V. *Marital tensions.* New York: Basic Books, Inc., 1967.
6. Framo, J. L. My families, my family. *Voices* (A journal published by the American Academy of Psychotherapists), Fall 1968, *4,* 18–27.
7. Framo, J. L. Symptoms from a family transactional viewpoint. In N. W. Ackerman, J. Lieb, & J. K. Pearce (Eds.), *Family therapy in transition.* Boston: Little, Brown and Company, 1970. (Reprinted in C. Sager & H. S. Kaplan [Eds.], *Progress in group and family therapy.* New York: Brunner/Mazel, Inc., 1972.)
8. Framo, J. L. Marriage therapy in a couples group. In D. A. Bloch (Ed.), *Techniques of family psychotherapy.* New York: Grune & Stratton, Inc., 1973.
9. Framo, J. L. Husbands' reactions to wives' infidelity. *Medical Aspects of Human Sexuality,* May 1975, 78–104. (a)
10. Framo, J. L. Personal reflections of a family therapist. *Journal of Marriage and Family Counseling,* 1975, *1,* 15–28. (b)
11. Framo, J. L. Family of origin as a therapeutic resource for adults in family and marital therapy. *Family Process,* 1976, *15,* 193–210.
12. Framo, J. L. The friendly divorce. *Psychology Today,* Feb. 1978. (a)
13. Framo, J. L. In-laws and out-laws: A marital case of kinship confusion. In P. Papp (Ed.), *Family therapy: Full-length case studies.* New York: Gardner Press, 1978. (b)
14. Franklin, P., & Prosky, P. A standard initial interview. In D. A. Bloch (Ed.), *Techniques of family psychotherapy: A primer.* New York: Grune & Stratton, Inc., 1973.
15. Greene, B. L. Management of marital problems. *Diseases of Nervous System,* 1966, *27,* 204–209.
16. Grunebaum, H., Christ, J., & Neiberg, N. Diagnosis and treatment planning for couples. *International Journal of Group Psychotherapy,* 1969, *19,* 185–202.
17. Haley, J., & Hoffman, L. *Techniques of family therapy.* New York: Basic Books, Inc., 1967.
18. Hollander, M. H. Selection of therapy for marital problems. In J. H. Masserman (Ed.), *Current psychiatric therapies,* Vol. 11. New York: Grune & Stratton, Inc., 1971.
19. Jourard, S. M. Marriage is for life. *Journal of Marriage and Family Counseling,* 1975, *1*(3), 199–207.
20. Kubie, L. S. Psychoanalysis and marriage: Practical and theoretical issues. In V. W. Eisenstein (Ed.), *Neurotic interaction in marriage.* New York: Basic Books, Inc., 1956.

21. Martin, P. A. *A marital therapy manual.* New York: Brunner/Mazel, Inc., 1976.
22. Murstein, B. F. The complementary need hypothesis in newlyweds and middle-aged married couples. *Journal of Abnormal and Social Psychology,* 1961, *63,* 194–197.
23. Napier, A. Y. The marriage of families: Cross-generational complementarity. *Family Process,* 1971, *10,* 373–395.
24. Napier, A. Y. The rejection–intrusion pattern: A central family dynamic. *Journal of Marriage and Family Counseling,* 1978, *4,* 5–12.
25. Napier, A. Y., & Whitaker, C. A. Problems of the beginning family therapist. In D. A. Bloch (Ed.), *Techniques of family psychotherapy: A primer.* New York: Grune & Stratton, Inc., 1973.
26. Patterson, G. R., Weiss, R. L., & Hops, H. Training of marital skills. In H. Leitenberg (Ed.), *Handbook of behavior modification and behavior therapy.* New York: Prentice-Hall, Inc., 1976.
27. Sager, C. J. The treatment of married couples. In S. Arieti (Ed.), *American handbook of psychiatry,* Vol. 3. New York: Basic Books, Inc., 1959.
28. Sager, C. J., Gundlach, R., & Kremer, M. The married in treatment. *Archives of General Psychiatry,* 1968, *19,* 205–217.
29. Skynner, A. C. R. *Systems of family and marital psychotherapy.* Ch. 11. New York: Brunner/Mazel, Inc., 1976.
30. Warkentin, J., & Whitaker, C. A. Serial impasses in marriage. In I. M. Cohen (Ed.), *Family structure, dynamics, and therapy.* Psychiatric Research Reports #20. American Psychiatric Association, 1966.
31. Warkentin, J., & Whitaker, C. A. The secret agenda of the therapist doing couples therapy. In G. H. Zuk & I. Boszormenyi-Nagy (Eds.), *Family therapy and disturbed families.* Palo Alto, Calif.: Science & Behavior Books, 1967.
32. Whitaker, C. A., & Keith, D. V. Counseling the dissolving marriage. In R. F. Stahmann & W. J. Hiebert (Eds.), *Klemer's counseling in marital and sexual problems.* Baltimore: The Williams & Wilkins Co., 1977.
33. Whitaker, C. A., & Miller, M. H. A re-evaluation of "psychiatric help" when divorce impends. *American Journal of Psychiatry,* 1969, *126,* 57–64.
34. Winch, R. F. *Mate selection: A study of complementary needs,* New York: Harper & Row, Publishers, 1958.

6

The Use of Fantasy in a Couples' Group

PEGGY PAPP

This paper will describe a format for a couples' group based on viewing the marital relationship as a mutual programming system in which each spouse programs the other to "play" a reciprocal role. Although each spouse contributes to the shaping of the program with his or her separate personalities, problems, and agendas, the program eventually becomes more powerful than the individuals within it and begins to control their behavior. This behavior becomes rigidified into set patterns that cast each spouse into a specific role. Each spouse is viewed as "playing" a role rather than "being" a certain kind of person, as the program is considered the most powerful determinant of behavior.

The spouses are generally not aware that they are being programmed, seeing themselves as acting independently out of individual motivations such as "fear of closeness," "distrust of men," "hostility toward women," "excessive dependency," etc. (Some therapists also get trapped into defining problems in this way.) These definitions maintain the status quo, as they are states of being determined by the past, rather than reactions to present circumstances.

Since the goal of therapy in the couples' group is a reprogramming of the reciprocal roles, the first task of the therapist is to clearly define those roles and the precise way in which the programming maintains them. This is difficult to decipher, as it is beyond the couple's awareness and they are most often confused and hazy about what is creating the problem. They get bogged down in a morass of irrelevant details and end up in arguments over who should close the garage door. In order to cut through their confusing verbiage in the first session, they are asked to have a fantasy about their relationship and to enact the fantasy with each other before the group. This technique, which I refer to as *couples' choreography*, changes the medium of communication from words to metaphors, movement, space, and physical positioning. Robbed of their familiar verbal cues, the couple are compelled to define their relationship differently using symbolic images. Because the choreography provides a poetic definition of their relationship, rather than a literal one, it is a vehicle for expressing the perceptions that are difficult to express verbally: the expectations, anxieties, projections, fears, and distortions on the periphery of awareness. These are crystallized into simple and eloquent images and projected outward into a living moving picture. This picture caricatures their roles in larger-than-life images and provides a parody of the way in which they maintain them. This parody becomes the artifice through which the mutual programming is changed.

The choreography is introduced in the following manner. The couple are asked to close their eyes and have a dream about one another—not a dream from the past, but a dream in the present. Each is asked to visualize the spouse in whatever form the spouse would take in a dream and to visualize herself or himself in whatever form she or he would take in relation to the form of the spouse. The therapist guides the couple through this "controlled fantasy," asking them to particularize the details of time, place, and movement. They are asked to imagine the movement that would take place between these two forms when they are trying to resolve their presenting problem. This question ensures that the fantasy will be systemic rather than individualistic, as they are asked to visualize themselves in relation to one another and focus on the interaction between the two forms. The images that emerge are invariably complementary: King Kong and Fay Wray, a cop and a criminal, David and Goliath, a log and a fire. The couple are then asked to act out their fantasy in front of the group.

Following is a verbatim example of the manner in which this kind of therapy takes place:

> A wife volunteers to show her fantasy and begins with, "He's a cop and I'm a criminal, like in those old movies, a Keystone Cop—only he's not funny. He's old-looking, not young, with a mustache." The therapist then asks specific questions in order to elicit a detailed picture.
>
> THERAPIST. Where does the dream take place?
> WIFE. It's on a street corner in New York City. It's a hot, sunny

day in summer. I have a gun and I'm about to fire into the crowd, not at anyone in particular, just society at large— I'm a rebel, an anarchist. The cop is defending law and justice, and "protecting other people from me."

The therapist then asks the couple to act out the dream physically, with the wife directing it and instructing the husband what to do.

T. At what moment does the cop spot you?
W. Immediately. I look like a suspicious character. I'm about to fire—he rushes over and lifts my hand so I fire into the air. And then he takes me to jail.
T. How do you react to his taking you to jail?
W. I go willingly. I know I'm guilty and what my husband has done is right.
T. And how do you spend your time in jail?
W. I accept my punishment and just sit and sew. Maybe I'll get out on good behavior.
T. What is the problem for you in this situation?
W. Well—it's that—he isn't something to get close to. There is a wall of good and evil between us. If there was a little evil in him and a little good in me, there would be something drawing us together.
T. Show us the different ways you go about trying to solve this problem.
W. I don't. There is no way out. I just go to jail and wait to get out on good behavior.

In order to test resistance to change, the therapist then asks the couple to change roles, with the wife playing the cop and the husband playing the criminal. In the middle of enacting the reversed roles, the wife suddenly stops and exclaims, "I don't like this. I'd rather be the bad guy. It's easier. To be all good, you have to be—you have to do everything perfect and terrific. You know, people expect a lot of you. To be evil and bad they expect nothing. You can do anything you want."

The husband has an equally negative response to changing roles. After playing the criminal, he states, "It's difficult for me to be the bad guy. I'm frightened—out of control. I have no explanation for what I did. I'm much more comfortable as the cop."

This role reversal provides the therapist with a miniature character sketch of each spouse. The husband's greatest fear is the loss of control; he puts a premium on logic, explanation, and order, and his method of dealing with his fear of losing control, of both himself and his wife, is to police her. The wife's greatest fear is meeting expectations, losing freedom, and becoming committed, and she avoids taking responsibility through "criminal acts."

The couple are then asked to translate these images into daily living, showing how the cop-and-criminal routine is carried out in everyday life. They enact the following scene: the husband is telephoning the wife from the office, interrogating her as to where she has been, with whom, doing what, suspicious of her every move, hoping to control her rebellious impulses through constant monitoring. The wife, on the other end of the phone, is evasive, feeling suffocated by his questions, acting guilty and suspicious. (In actuality, she is having an affair with another man, which the husband knows about.) After the telephone call, the wife becomes depressed, and when her husband comes home, she withdraws from him, because she is so "bad."

This physical enactment of the fantasy has revealed the central emotional issue around which their roles are organized: good and evil. The complementarity of the relationship is maintained by the wife's agreeing to "play" the criminal and the husband's agreeing to "play" the cop. Each person is perceived as "playing" a role in relationship to the role the partner is "playing," rather than "being" that person. This phenomenon is based on the systemic premise that every person has many different character traits and that they overdevelop one in relation to an underdevelopment of that same one in their spouse: "If there was a little evil in him and a little good in me, there would be something drawing us together." It is safe to assume, human nature being what it is, that there is a little evil in him and a little good in her, but it has been negated in the way the system has been organized.

When asked to show his fantasy, the husband presents his wife as a fluttering streamer on a ship, making her maiden voyage. He sees himself as a "huge bird—a kind of superman," flying after the ship and trying to grasp the streamer, but the ship is more powerful than he and keeps pulling the streamer from his hand. When he does manage to catch it, he states, "It's going to be tough holding on, and if I don't do something quickly, I'll lose her." They go round and round in a circle; the tighter the husband grabs, the more the wife pulls away, and the more she pulls away, the tighter she grabs.

Although the metaphors in the two dreams are different, the basic roles of each partner are seen as the same: the husband is pursuing and controlling, the wife is provocative and distancing.

Use of the Group

After the first session, the couples are sometimes separated and seen in separate groups, so that the therapist can give directives without the other spouse's knowing about them. This procedure preserves the element of surprise, which is considered essential to change. Having the husbands in one group and the wives in another also fosters an atmosphere of confidentiality and camaraderie that is difficult to achieve when the couples are mixed. Group interaction is kept focused on the marital relationship and the related tasks and is not allowed to become confrontational or interpretive. Relationships between unrelated individuals are not explored or analyzed as in conventional group therapy. The group is used primarily as a theatrical setting to dramatize the process of change. Since the choreography and the tasks require a shift in conventional thinking, the therapist strives to create a proscenium perspective within which to stage the fantasy and rehearse the tasks. Everything that happens in a group happens for an audience, which heightens the awareness and stimulates the imagination of all the participants. Problems are lifted out of the rigid corridors of the literal and placed in a fanciful setting of "play." This sense of play is of crucial importance to the therapy. The therapist must cultivate it and convey it to the participants.

The pictures that emerge from the choreography provide a blueprint from which to plan strategies for change. The type of strategy that is used is based on a careful evaluation of each couple's particular situation, taking into account their idiosyncratic personality traits, resources, motivations, and, most important, an assessment of the form their resistance will take. There are no set formulas; each strategy is custom-tailored to suit the needs of the couple. Most often, a combination of approaches is used, based on a trial-and-error process. Following is a description of the strategies most frequently used.

Prescribing Roles

If the therapist senses a high degree of rigidity in the roles, rather than attempting to modify them directly, it is better to define one aspect of the role positively and prescribe it.

> In the case of the cop and the criminal, the wife's "criminality" and the husband's "policing" were put to use in a new way. As the wife was a self-defined "anarchist and rebel," the therapist predicted that she would assume this posture in relation to therapy and would resist any direct attempt by the therapist to change her role. Therefore, the therapist began by admiring the devices she had developed to avoid responsibility. Jail was after all a secure place where no expectations were placed on her. She was right in sensing that respectability was burdensome. Why would she want to change her view? She was taken aback by this unexpected attitude and countered with arguments for change. The affair, she stated, was not all that satisfying, as the man really didn't care for her. She wanted to feel closer to her husband, and why did the therapist think they had come for therapy if they didn't want to change? She was then told that it was not her "criminality" that was causing the problem but her guilt about it. Good criminals did not feel guilty and she must learn to become a better criminal. In order to alleviate her guilt, it was suggested that every time she felt guilty she should do something nice for her husband, something very special that would please and surprise him. This reversed the pattern of her becoming depressed and moving away from him. Now, the more she sinned, the more affection she would show toward him.
>
> The husband (in the separate husbands' group) was commended for trying to take such good care of his wife by always watching over her. "Yes," he smiled, "I like to think I have been shepherding her all these years." Using his word, the therapist commented that he had not gone far enough in his shepherding. He had only shepherded one side of her, her moral side, and had neglected to shepherd the other side of her, her desire for pleasure. Her problem was that she didn't know how to experience pleasure without getting into trouble. How could he take care of that aspect of her life? He was stunned by this totally new thought and

had no idea how to go about it. The other husbands in the group came to his aid and began making suggestions with ribald humor.

Two weeks later, in the wives' group, the wife opened the session with "Wow! My husband has gone crazy. I don't know what's happening to him. I don't know if it's because he's coming here or if this was his own idea, but anyway on Friday night he picked me up from work, said, 'Get in the car, we're going away for the weekend.' He had packed my bag and taken Norman [their son] to his parents for the weekend. I didn't even know where he was taking me until we got there. We went to this resort where we had been when we were first married—dinner, dancing, tennis—we had a fantastic time!"—which included her having an orgasm with her husband for the first time in five years.

Rebalancing Roles

The wife began to lose interest in the other man after the husband became more romantic, and she began talking about buying a house and having more children, something her husband had been pressuring her to do for a long time. As could be anticipated, when the wife began to move closer, the husband began to pull back. A crisis often follows a first sudden change, because of the unbalancing of the system. The husband stated ruefully, "I would have given anything for this to have happened a year ago. Now I don't know how I feel about it." In taking charge of his wife's excitement, he found to his consternation that it stirred up his own need for excitement and pleasure, and he began to realize what he had been missing all these years. He became resentful of being the one to take responsibility for the relationship: "What does she give me?" For the first time in their married life, when his wife refused to go to a concert with him, he went with a group of friends from the office, which included an attractive woman: "My greatest worry is I might have such a good time I might want to pull out."

The wife, threatened by his new independence, became jealous and suspicious and began playing the cop.

This temporary role reversal demonstrates the power of the system to shape behavior. A revision of one person's position results in a corresponding revision in the position of the other. As Jung[1] so succinctly described, "Every psychological extreme secretly contains its own opposite, or stands in some sort of intimate and essential relation to it" (p. 375).

The relationship now enters into the realm of the unpredictable, where new reactions and counterreactions come into play. The therapist has little control over this realm as he or she cannot predict or direct spontaneous change. This is a period of personal confusion and upheaval, during which the couple must come to terms with unexpected changes. The therapist can only help them to negotiate their relationship on new terms. In this case, the pendulum of change swung back and settled somewhere in the middle. After contemplating an affair, the husband decided not to abandon ship but to settle in the home harbor.

> During the last session, the couple were asked to have a new fantasy about their relationship as it was in the present. The husband's fantasy was as follows: "She is still a boat but she is in the harbor. It's a sunny day, breezy, blue sky. She is tied to a mooring. I'm not looking at the ship constantly—looking around the harbor more. I'm sitting on a pier—contented." When asked what the problem was for him in this situation, he stated, "No problem now."
>
> The wife stated, "There are no criminals or cops anymore. I don't feel evil and I don't see him as an archangel, the reincarnation of all good. He is just a human being. I see myself as a balloon and he as a peg. The balloon is attached by a long string. It represents my good feelings for him, that I need him, love him, and want to be with him." Were there any problems for her? Yes. Sometimes she still resented the peg, even though she knew she would fly away without it; she sometimes felt it held her down. To which the husband replied, "You are free to go." She would probably need to test this from time to time.

Reversing the Roles

In the above case, a role reversal occurred spontaneously as a result of the therapist's amplifying the original roles. It is sometimes possible to prescribe this reversal directly, simply by instructing each spouse to do the opposite of what he or she is doing. However, because this is difficult

The Use of Fantasy in a Couples' Group

to do, the couple must be cooperative and well motivated. If they are resistant to therapy, the chances of their following directions that produce change are slim. Motivating the couples to follow any directive is a test of the therapist's skill and creativity. A rationale must be given that appeals to them in a personal way. In the following case, the couple was judged to be well enough motivated so that a role reversal could be prescribed directly.

> The wife saw her husband in her fantasy as King Kong and herself as Fay Wray. She portrayed herself as being totally within his power: "He's holding me in the palm of his hand and carrying me to the top of the Empire State Building. If he dies, I go with him, as he won't let me go." She was then asked to choreograph the ways in which she had tried to cope with her predicament. She went through the motions of physically fighting him, throwing dishes at him, arguing with him, hiding from him, leaving him—all of which incited him to clutch her more desperately.
>
> The husband in his dream also saw himself as an ape, but an impotent ape: "I see myself as this huge hulking ape. The bizarre thing is the ape is helpless. It's a dark street and I see her on the ground, but when I try to lift her up, she fights me. It's a total feeling of frustration and not being able to communicate with her."
>
> He was then asked to enact the various ways he had tried to rescue her. He indicated this by lifting her off the ground and standing her on her feet, shaking her, embracing her, pushing her away—all of which spurred her efforts to escape. The more he tried to rescue her, the more she tried to escape; and the more she tried to escape, the more he tried to rescue her.
>
> In the home, he maintained his King Kong position by constantly trying to save her from herself, giving her advice about how she should run every aspect of her life; how to deal with the children; how to handle her mother; how to drive the car; how to plan the future, etc. When she refused to follow this "helpful" advice, he flew into a rage. The wife maintained her Fay Wray position by signaling her husband that she was helpless and then resenting his efforts to help her.
>
> Two coordinated tasks were given to the couple that were designed to reverse the authoritarian role and the helpless role. The

husband was told that if he really wished to help his wife, he must first make her feel important. Instead of giving her advice about how to run her life, he should instead ask her for advice about how to run his. He burst out laughing: "You mean—you mean—I should ask *her* how to run *my* life?" A reversal usually strikes the receiver as humorous, as it unexpectedly changes the premise under which he or she is operating. If the person laughs, it is a good sign that he or she will be able to "play" with the idea and carry it out successfully.

The husband was intrigued by the assignment but felt it would be difficult to do. He anticipated that he might give her advice about how to give him advice. The group helped him figure out ways to avoid the trap. The difficulty in carrying out the task is always discussed in the session as a routine procedure. This discussion acknowledges the strength of the system and provides an opportunity for rehearsing a change in a protected setting.

While the husband was instructed to pull back and resist helping his wife, she was instructed to move forward and elicit help from her husband—but overtly, not covertly as she had been doing. This approach took her out of her defensive position and put her on the offensive. She was to keep asking him for advice about every detail of her life until he got tired of giving it. Moving in counterdirections changed their mutual programming system.

The metaphors provide a road into the private world of each individual and permit solutions to be posed in his or her own language. The central theme of therapy with the wife centered around her learning to "tame the wild beast." It was pointed out to her that Fay Wray actually had tremendous power over King Kong and that she would do well to emulate her. The group suggested that she might one day write a best-seller entitled *My Life with King Kong* for all the thousands of women across the country who might find this information helpful. One of her assignments was to figure out three ways of taming King Kong that neither Fay Wray, the group, nor the therapist could have thought of. This assignment lifted her out of her victim position and made her an authority on the subject of King Kong.

The couple approached the tasks with amusement and curiosity, observing each other's reactions carefully.

The Use of Fantasy in a Couples' Group

The choreography and the tasks add the perspective of humor, which the dictionary defines as "the mental faculty of discovering, expressing or appreciating ludicrous or absurdly incongruous elements in ideas, situations, happenings or acts." There is something absurd about a dysfunctional system as it continues to perpetuate the very dysfunction it is striving to resolve. If a couple can catch a glimpse of this, it frees them to find alternative ways of resolving it.

Prescribing Defenses

A problem that confronts family therapists with regularity is the withdrawn husband who shuts off his feelings and the frantic wife who tries to get through to him by constantly expressing hers. A common therapeutic approach is to attack the husband's defenses directly by attempting to pry open his shell. This approach requires a strenuous effort on the part of the therapist over a protracted period of time, and it usually produces minimal results. It is what family, friends, mothers, sisters, teachers, wives, psychiatrists, and society at large have been trying to do all his life; he has developed ingenious ploys for countering these attempts and uses them to validate his position. A less arduous and often more fruitful approach is to go with the resistance and prescribe the shell.

> In a classic situation of this type, the wife had dragged the reluctant husband to therapy. He sat like a stone as his wife cried, screamed, complained, and accused him of having no feelings, never talking, never coming home, never having sex, never helping her with the baby, never being there when he was needed, etc. The husband endured the attacks with a condescending dignity and stated that he had no intention of making himself over to suit his wife. He had spent his life controlling his emotions, was proud of it, and believed that that was the best way to live. He saw no reason for expressing feelings and looked down on those who did, describing them as "undignified." His involvement in therapy was minimal, since he felt that they had no problems except those that his wife manufactured. In the choreography, he presented himself as a log and his wife as a fire from which he distanced in order not to get burned. She presented him as a rock and herself as a

stonemason, trying to break him into "a lot of little rocks, so I can get close to the pieces." The more she hammered, the more he protected himself, and the more he protected himself, the more she hammered.

The therapist, rather than trying to pry open his shell, advised the husband to close it more tightly. The following is verbatim dialogue from the first husbands' session:

THERAPIST. I really respect the position you took last session about feelings. Everyone is always talking about how important it is to express feelings, particularly in therapy. It's a kind of cult. But I've never heard anyone speak so eloquently on the importance of controlling feelings. I'd like to hear more about your ideas.
HUSBAND. Yeah—well, as far as I'm concerned, it's the only way to live. The only way you get things done in life is not to let your feelings get in your way. I think it's just plain stupid to go around spilling all over—like my wife. And if she had her way, that's what I'd be doing.
T. That's a position that takes a lot of independence and courage to maintain. I admire your determination not to allow your wife to infringe on your right to do your own thing. Not many people can draw boundaries around themselves that firmly. I'm really interested in how you manage to do it. It's not easy to keep one's feelings under control at all times.
H. (*laughing*). You're right, it's not. But I just remain cool. In my line of work, it's important to remain cool. I'm a politician, and my job depends on my outmaneuvering everyone. I'm good at it, too, because I learned it as a kid.

He then went on to describe at length how he had developed control as a survival tactic throughout an embattled life of crisis and danger, both at home and in his neighborhood. During his early youth, he joined the civil rights movement and worked in the South, where his very life depended on his being cool. He ended up with "And I intend to remain that way in spite of all my wife's or anyone else's attempts to change me!"

The Use of Fantasy in a Couples' Group

T. And you should... you definitely should. But you know, I think your real problem is that you don't take a firm enough position with your wife. I may be wrong about this, but I would guess that every once in a while you allow yourself to give in to her.

A look of surprise crossed his face.

H. Well—you know, as a matter of fact that's true. I get feeling guilty and I do something she wants me to do that I don't want to do, and then I resent it.

T. Just as I suspected. You see, you aren't consistent enough in protecting yourself. You're too softhearted and you allow yourself to be influenced by her. Then you lose your independence.

He went on to confess that he actually felt responsible for all the difficulty between the two of them and felt that the problems were all because of him. But he felt helpless to do anything about it because he couldn't change the way he was. The therapist asked him to give an example of when he gave in to his wife. He told of an incident over the weekend. His wife wanted him to go shopping for new clothes for him. He didn't need any new clothes and hated to go shopping, especially for himself, but he felt that this was her way of being with him and he went to please her. The therapist evidenced dismay that he would sacrifice himself in such a way for his wife and urged him to protect himself more by not allowing himself to be persuaded to do something he didn't want to do. He should only do what he felt like doing. He wondered what that would be, since he didn't enjoy any of the things she liked to do such as going to museums, sports events, social gatherings, movies, theaters, and concerts. He always went, but belligerently. The only fun he got out of life was working: "I like to maneuver people and situations in order to accomplish impossible stunts."

T. I can think of one impossible stunt you could never pull off.
H. What's that?
T. Finding a way to have a good time with your wife.
H. That would be impossible.

T. You're right. I apologize for suggesting it. But you said you like to maneuver people. I was just wondering if you could find a way of maneuvering her.
H. It would be a challenge.

Concurrently with the prescribing of the husband's shell, the wife's hysteria was prescribed. The therapist thus avoided the common error of trying to reason with her. To point out to her that what she was doing was making things worse would be redundant. She already knew this but couldn't stop herself. She disliked the image of herself in the position of the witch and had tried countless times to get out of it, only to fail and feel more guilty and incompetent. Rather than compounding her negative feelings about herself, the therapist defined her hysterical outbursts positively as a service to her husband. She was congratulated on expressing all the feelings for both of them.

THERAPIST. Somewhere inside of you you know it would be very frightening for him to express his feelings, so you have taken on the job of expressing them for both of you.
WIFE. I have? But if I don't express them, there is nothing but silence between us.
T. Exactly. And if the silence continued for very long, your husband would have to get in touch with his feelings, and it's probably better that he doesn't do that.
W. I don't understand that. Why is it better?
T. Who knows what those feelings might be? He has a good reason for having covered them up all these years, and he might become anxious or even depressed and angry if he got in touch with them. Your protecting him in this way is a very loving act on your part.
W. Well, I'll tell you one thing. I don't want to go on protecting him, if that's what I'm doing. It's too exhausting for me.
T. I would worry about what would happen to him if you were to become calm.
W. You know, as a matter of fact, I've sometimes wondered myself what would happen if he ever did begin expressing his feelings. I think it might be frightening.
T. Yes, that's why I say I think it's wise for the time being for you

to continue to protect him by expressing all the feelings for both of you.

She left the session in a somewhat pensive mood and came to the next session somewhat perplexed, as her husband had been behaving differently—coming home earlier, spending more time at home—and had asked her to attend a political meeting with him for the first time since they had been married. She was amazed at his having invited her into the inner sanctum of his work. The therapist's having supported the husband's right to resist his wife's pressuring enabled him to move toward her in a way that preserved his sense of control. This move was on his territory and on his terms. As might be predicted, the wife had mixed reactions to her husband's moving toward her. She was surprised and pleased on the one hand, but on the other hand, she was confronted with not knowing what to do with him now that he was home more. She began to realize how much she had enjoyed her privacy. The major therapeutic task at this point was to help the wife adjust to the change in her husband. The therapist left her with the comforting thought that whenever she felt she had had her fill of closeness, she had a surefire way of getting her husband to move away. She could go back to expressing all the feelings for both of them.

Scheduling the Contest

The issue of control is present to some extent in all human relationships. In a marriage, this issue turns into a day-by-day, minute-by-minute negotiation around who defines the relationship and on whose terms. If differences are declared openly, negotiations can take place openly and the terms of the contest are clear, whether they are resolved or not. In some marriages, because one or the other spouse is afraid of stating a need or a preference openly, a hidden agenda is developed and a secret contest is fought around an undisclosed agenda. Unless this contest is recognized and dealt with by the therapist, all attempts to change the relationship will be sabotaged. The secretive nature of the contest militates against therapeutic interventions. One of the most effective ways of dealing with the secret contest is to define it and schedule it. When it is deliberately scheduled, it loses its power to distract and confuse. In order to do this, the therapist must first be able to decipher it and to understand the rules by which it is being played. The choreography will sometimes provide access to these, as the couple is thrown temporarily off-balance.

One couple gave a clue to their hidden power struggle by becoming embroiled in an argument over who should do the choreography first. Neither was willing to reveal himself or herself through a fantasy until the other had. The wife stated, "You go first. My mind is a blank," to which the husband responded, "I just haven't been able to think of anything. You go first." The therapist accepted their resistance, saying that it was better for them not to do the choreography at this time. The precise nature of the contest did not become clear for several sessions, as it had to do with mind reading. Each expected the other to read his or her mind, to know what he or she wanted, and to provide it without being asked for it. The wife expected the husband to know when she needed him to put his arm around her, to visit her mother with her, or to make love to her. She would send him subtle cues, and if he didn't pick up on them, she would get angry and retaliate. The husband likewise sent undecipherable cues to his wife when he wanted her to cook his favorite dish, to sit and watch television with him, or to praise him for his work. When she missed them, he would act hurt and withdraw. The name of the game was "I'll Bet You Can't Guess What I Want."

This game was scheduled but with a change in one rule. During the coming week, they were to think of three things that they wanted from each other. They must not reveal these but must wait for the other person to guess. If either felt he or she had guessed something correctly, he or she should attempt to fulfill the need. Each was asked to write down the three things he or she needed and the three things he or she had guessed the other needed. None of the transactions was to be discussed. In the following session, they were to check their lists with each other and see which one had guessed right most of the time. This procedure changed the game from "I'll Bet You Can't Guess What I Want" to "I'll Bet I Can Guess What You Want Quicker Than You Can Guess What I Want."

When the couple reported back, it was discovered that the

wife had refused to think of any needs for herself, thus preventing her husband from guessing them. But by successfully guessing her husband's, she had managed to win the contest. She innocently claimed that her mind had gone blank and that she couldn't think of a single need all week. The therapist interpreted this claim as her being satisfied with the relationship and instructed her to continue not to think of any needs for another week but in the meantime to continue to try to guess and fulfill her husband's needs. Immediately a dozen needs popped into her mind. "It's amazing," she exclaimed. "As soon as you said that I began to think of all kinds of needs." She was instructed to put them out of her mind and keep them out.

During the following week, the wife grew tired of fulfilling her husband's needs without having any of her own met and defied the therapist by telling her husband what she would like. The husband was then forced to try harder to guess other needs that she wasn't telling him about. The process became ludicrous, with its increasing complication, and they began to laugh at themselves. At the next session, the wife stated, "You know, I'm beginning to realize that we are very competitive with one another."

Their competition was now out in the open, and the couple were encouraged to compete with one another around other important issues. The group kept score and gave prizes to the winner. The competition was changed from a deadly game into an open sport.

Summary

This paper has described a format for a couples' group based on defining and treating the marital problem within the dyadic system through reprogramming the reciprocal roles. Each spouse is perceived as "playing a role" rather than "being" a type of person. The goal of therapy is not to change the roles per se but to help the couple to "play" them differently, thus establishing a workable complementarity. This complementarity is established through the use of action-oriented techniques such as choreography, tasks, rituals, and paradoxical interventions.

Humor, play, and fantasy are considered an essential part of therapy and are used to change the couple's perception of themselves and each other.

Strategies for change are custom-designed to suit each couple based on a careful evaluation of their situation and an assessment of their resistance to change. Resistance is dealt with indirectly, so that a therapeutic power struggle is avoided.

REFERENCE

1. Jung, C. G. *Symbols of transformation.* New York: Bollinger Foundation, 1952.

7

Divorcing
Clinical Notes

DONALD A. BLOCH

The title of this article is intended to convey my intent to put notes before the reader, rather than a fully organized treatise on the subject. The experience on which this material is based includes having been divorced and remarried myself, events that took place in my 50s. There are three children of the first marriage and one from the second. It also includes clinical experience going back over 30 years, first as a psychoanalyst, and, for the last 20 years, as a family therapist.

The article is organized more-or-less randomly and consists of a series of small essays on various aspects of the subject—those that seem to me to be most challenging to clinicians or that seem most to require the adaptation of old clinical skills to the special exigencies of this ever more common pathway in marital life. I hope it will be evident that certain themes consistently run through the material, as to a view of both the divorcing process itself and the clinician's relation to it.

On a simple level, the clinician's interest in divorce lies in the fact that a lot of people are doing it, or having it done to them, and that a good deal of suffering and malfunction seems to attend the process. Despite the legitimacy of the interest, there is risk in generalizing on this subject. Quite clearly, divorce is many things to many people. At the very least, one must consider what is the character structure of the people involved, when in the family life cycle divorce occurs, and what life events preceded it, particularly as to the quality of the marriage relationship and the numbers, sex, and ages of children. The financial situation of the family and the work lives of wife and husband are of great interest as well, both the spouses' immediate circumstances and their near and long-term prospects, since divorce almost always stresses and frequently disorders these aspects of people's lives. Finally, the meaning systems that grow out of the ethnicity and the cultural membership of the spouses must be understood, with particular emphasis on the characteristics of the kin and social networks.

A meaningful typology of divorcing would have to take these parameters into account and perhaps others as well. It should be evident that we are a long way from accomplishing anything like that, although some useful preliminary categorizations have been attempted. Despite this lack of a typology, it is possible to identify what might be called the divorce career line, a common sequence of events that provides one axis along which divorcing families move and their place on which determines some of the issues that concern clinicians.

Social Pressure

During the predecision phase of divorcing, a great deal of affect is often liberated. Couples may be in great agony throughout this period. Children, friends, and kin rapidly become involved as the news gets around and a secondary social process is activated. Perhaps the most important motivation grows out of the identification of other families with the one in crisis. This may take many forms: "If it happened to them, it could happen to us." "Now he or she is on the loose, sexually available, a threat (opportunity) to me (my marriage)." "If he (or she) had the courage to do it, maybe I can get out of my marriage as well."

The most significant set of responses comes from the kin network of the marital pair. As with others, a good part of this response may be the expression of genuine concern at the pain being experienced by loved ones. At other times, it may seem to be gratuitously interfering, often in a damaging direction.

It is important to realize the power of this process, but it is well to realize that it is often isomorphic to the relationship structure of the couple themselves:

> Ginny and George were astounded to find that their brief and apparently happy marriage was in difficulty. The heart of the matter was a debate as to whether or not George should accept what seemed to be a dead-end position on a farm owned by an uncle, a kind of work that he liked to do but that did not seem to

promise much of a future. Ginny liked country living, but she also seemed to be the brightest star in the social agency where she worked and was loath to give up that position. Her family was distressed at the possibility of a breakup but clearly sided with their daughter. The pressure came particularly from her father, who felt she should keep her job, even at the risk of a divorce. The essence of the difficulty, as it developed in the course of the therapeutic work, was that Ginny had chosen George in part because of his low-key, easygoing ways, in order to deal with the ambivalently experienced pressures her ambitious father had placed on her all of her life. To this extent, the social response pattern to the prospect of divorce was isomorphic to the original relationship structure that had led both to the marriage and nearly to the divorce.

Work with this couple went well. They were an attractive and well-endowed pair with good bonding to each other and many strengths that could be utilized in the work. The secondary social pressures were disruptive but also could be used as grist for the therapeutic mill. Working through the inevitably corrupt aspect of their choice of each other as mates enabled them to put the marriage on a much firmer footing than had existed prior to the crisis.

Social Change

It is well established that profound changes are taking place at a rapid rate in the intimate social networks in which people live in the Western world. This is particularly evident in the United States but by no means limited to this country. Inevitably clinicians who are concerned with human dysfunction are required to attend to these issues; at the very least, they need to know the characteristics of formats and careers that were previously unavailable or defined as nonstandard and unacceptable. Divorce and remarriage are high on the list.

Perhaps the most vivid instance concerns the influence of the women's movement on families. There are few households in the United States that have not had to take into account some form of renegotiation of sex roles, although this renegotiation does not necessarily mean that the move has universally been in the direction of more equality and sharing of power or domestic responsibilities. There are certainly large groups that have managed to note these social changes taking place but have been able to define them as irrelevant or indeed, as expressed in "The Total Woman" movement, have emphasized and gloried in the traditional role differentiation. Folks with this sort of orientation are comparatively less common among the consumers of family therapy. More commonly, the impact of the women's movement appears in families such as the following:

> Cynthia and Harold met when Cynthia was a college sophomore and he was graduating and about to enter law school. During his first year as a law student, Cynthia discovered that Harold had not been properly awarded academic honors due him at graduation; she initiated an administrative action with the university to correct this error. One year later, she unhesitatingly gave up a prized assistantship in her chosen academic field in order to spend the summer with his family, so as to smooth out objections in advance of their marriage. He was Catholic and she was Jewish, and she secured his family's approval for the marriage by converting to Catholicism. None of these actions were experienced as dystonic by either of them: Harold was ambitious and career-oriented; Cynthia had as her principal goal in college to make a good marriage. The time was 1962. Their marriage was widely advertised as highly successful, although, retrospectively, Cynthia's intense involvement in cultivating the intellect of their daughter, while remaining comparatively inattentive to similar issues for their son, might have been taken as an early sign of her discontent. Harold became enormously involved in his law firm, became its youngest partner, and then, in a daring, but successful move, left to form his own firm. There was complete agreement that Cynthia's consistent and intelligent support was essential to his rapid rise. The year 1970 found them well established with two children, two homes, two cars, and a bright future. They were generally admired and envied. Reviewing this recently in a consultation around their impending divorce, they both agreed that they would have regarded as "insane" anyone who had raised with them any question about the soundness of their marriage or the general foundation on which their lives were built. Nevertheless the winds of change were blowing. Harold found himself intrigued by the

notion of guilt-free recreational sex and spoke of it casually to Cynthia on a number of occasions, urging that it would be helpful for both of them to have such experiences. He was utterly astonished, when a few months later he reported his adventures along this line to Cynthia, to see her literally shattered by the news. After all, many people were trying it. There were books and popular magazine articles on the subject. An uneasy truce was finally arrived at, and in good time, Cynthia followed suit. Unfortunately Cynthia's adventure did not have the looked-for stabilizing effect; it involved a deeper emotional commitment to her extramarital partner, George, who apparently offered something more than recreational sex. George sponsored Cynthia's awareness of her oppression as a female in the marriage, a point of view for which, again, there was much popular cultural support from the women's movement. A series of changes had been set in motion from which there was no retreat.

The Diagnosis of Irreversibility

The clinician cannot, in good conscience, ever decide what people should do. However, an assessment of the degree to which matters have passed the point of no return must be made. This judgment is critical in matters pertaining to divorce, since an entirely different definition of the life work and therapeutic work devolves according to the estimate one makes of this issue. Matters may not be very clear at the outset, and judgment should be suspended for as long as possible, while its importance is kept clearly in mind.

A simple and exasperating version of the issue turns up when consultation is sought ostensibly with the goal of "saving" the marriage only to have it become apparent that there is no such intention. In these instances, there is, at best, a weak commitment to change in the relationship; in more extreme instances, an irrevocable decision to abandon ship has already been made:

> Fred and Joan were in their early 40s and seemed to be having trouble in a fashion that was not understandable to Joan. She was not a very bright woman, nor was she gifted with extraordinary perceptiveness, but it became obvious to her, as well as to me,

after three sessions that Fred was spectacularly uncommunicative about his feelings and inner life, as well as about his plans. A kindly friend advised Joan that her husband had an additional relationship, that it was of long standing, and that he was committed to it. When confronted with this bit of gossip, Fred acknowledged that it was true and that he had been advised by his attorney to go through the motions of a therapeutic effort so that he could later show in court that he had "tried." Acting valiantly in his client's interest, the attorney had as well advised him to put all of the bank accounts in his name but not to move out of the house, since this could be construed as desertion. It seemed reasonable to entertain a diagnosis of irreversibility at this point.

From another perspective, we can consider the following case:

A young accountant requested consultation growing out of difficulties he was having in his relationship with his live-in girlfriend. They had been living together for about a year and both had been in individual therapy, she in order to assist her to solve problems in her relationship with the 10-year-old son of a former marriage of his. The man found himself quite critical of her way of dealing with the child and was focusing in his individual psychotherapy on issues having to do with his inability to make a final commitment to her and his tendency to be critical of her, particularly as far as her management of the child was concerned. His separation agreement with his wife was still being negotiated, and this negotiation had been going on for an exceptionally long time. Careful review indicated that there were very few, if any, substantive issues, other than child custody concerns that were still needing negotiation. It was noted that an extremely complex arrangement for sharing custody had been worked out that required a great deal of constant telephoning back and forth, so that the arrangements for scheduling and executing the scheduling could be accomplished.

It occurred to me that this case could certainly be classified at this point as an unconsummated divorce. After two interviews with the couple who were living together, I put before them the view that there were issues related to the old marriage that had not been worked through and told them both that I saw no possibility of progress in their relationship if these issues were not resolved. The woman seemed quite in agreement with my view and said that she had felt that the unresolved issues with her lover's wife were standing in their way. As a result, it was then decided that some interviews with husband and wife would be arranged, so as to explore the possibility of completing the separation.

In the course of the interview, husband and wife were obviously under great strain. In somewhat stilted and overly formal terms, he made very clear to her that there were no possibilities of reconciliation, that he did not want to work on the relationship anymore, and that it was over, without regard to whatever else they were going to do. She, on the other hand, seemed to be very upset and not to be at all clear that his view was acceptable. Even though she had a lover, she wanted to consider the possibility of reconstituting the family. The tone of the interview was angry, painful, and stiff.

A second meeting was arranged. On this occasion, things were quite different. In this interview, it was possible to begin some discussion of the nature of their original tie to each other as well as of the nature and patterns of developing difficulties over the years. The interview terminated on the note that they would further explore with a therapist the pattern of their relationship over the years with a view to reducing the possibility that similar difficulties would occur again with other partners, a hint being in the air that they might take up with each other again.

My own view, in this instance, was that there was reason to believe that the pathway to divorce was reversible or, at the very least, that this issue needed to be held in abeyance. Experience indicates that an exploration along therapeutic lines of the problematic aspects of a marriage can be conducted under these circumstances with two possible ultimate outcomes. The couple may very well go on to divorce but can then do so in a climate that permits forgiveness and that makes possible a decent ongoing parental relationship. It is also possible to sail for a certain time under the same banner on a course that ultimately leads to a therapeutically facilitated reconciliation. In this instance, which is unlike those situations where the path toward divorce is irreversible, there is less need for the therapist to be as definite and structured in his or her instructions to the couple to avoid focusing on issues that might raise the possibility of reconciliation. That approach can be very threatening under certain circumstances but is acceptable here.

Money and the Law

When the decision to divorce has been arrived at, the clinician finds that he or she is called on to deal in some fashion with two topics that are often outside the scope of clinical work: money and the law. Therapists often tend to be as squeamish and prissy about money as their lay brothers and sisters are about excretory matters (pace Freud). It is often a simple matter for a therapist to secure anatomical and gymnastic detail about erotic issues and to be totally incapacitated when questions of financial life are to be considered. But if there is one thing divorce is about, it is about money. The marriage contract is a financial document above all else. I have lately been impressed with the large number of new marriages that include explicit contracting. These go into considerable detail as to the mutual financial responsibilities, the nature of the sexual agreement, relations with kin, religion, and the allocation of domestic and child-care responsibilities, among other things. In conducting divorce workshops, I have found it useful to ask the participants to pair off and construct such a contract as an exercise at the beginning of the workshop, in order to highlight the connection between the marriage contract and the issues that need to be decided on in a divorce.

As an illustration of the increasing sophistication of this process, one couple included "maintaining skills in each other" as part of their contract. They meant by that that each would perform functions in areas where they might not have primary skills—for example, cooking, handling finances, fixing the car—so that if they were to go separate ways, neither would find himself or herself handicapped by social-role stereotyping. The reader may wish to conduct such an exercise with his or her mate.

Legal contests about a divorce and about such issues as child custody have a linear relationship to the financial status of the family. The more money the family has, the more they and their attorneys are apt to fight about it. We may talk about money substantively and symbolically; both aspects are clinically important. A detailed understanding of the management of finances provides a map of the structuring of the interpersonal field by the marital pair:

Divorcing: Clinical Notes

A husband and wife were discussing their separation agreement, wanting to modify it to set the stage for a serious try at a reconciliation. In the course of the discussion, the wife persisted in comparing unfavorably with her own the husband's material lifestyle during the separation. She complained that she had no experience in managing money and that she had a desk full of bills, which he would have routinely paid in the past. She argued that he should give her more money in the interim before they started to live together, so that she would be made to feel safe and so that he would show her that he had her interests at heart. This woman had initiated an extramarital affair and some desultory moves toward a career, out of a growing sense of depression and a conviction that her husband's rapid professional rise was leaving her behind. The husband was quite willing to make the adjustment, too willing from my point of view. While on the surface the specifics of her request seemed fair, the therapist interfered, pointing out that they were adopting the same stance in these negotiations that had characterized their complaints about the marriage—a stance that could be described as that of a whining, dependent woman being alternately indulged or restricted by a powerful male figure.

At their best, the law and associated legal procedures can supply much-needed structure, reality testing, and protection for members of families undergoing divorce. At worst, the adversary procedures and inflexible legal codes can fail to help families in need or can even harm them. In principle, the law can forcefully represent the ethical concerns of society; it aims to protect those who cannot protect themselves, to assure fairness to both of the marital pair, and to arrange equitably for future parenting rights and responsibilities. Divorcing is an interpersonal sequence with powerful emotional, psychological, and developmental implications; it is also a contractual event involving the disposition of assets already acquired (houses, cars, bank accounts), the allocation of future earnings (alimony, child support), and a determination of future parenting rights and obligations (custody and visitation).

The need for the law to state the obvious increases with two factors: the tenure of the marriage and the number of minor children. The therapist's interest in the legal issues surrounding the dissolution of the marriage of a young, childless couple may quite rightly be minimal, unless it should happen that a simple matter is being complicated in a therapeutically interesting fashion:

> Two young professionals of approximately equal status, childless and married for less than three years, concluded an informal separation agreement preliminary to an amicable divorce. The husband was permitted to keep their apartment, since his office was located there.
> Weeks and months went by during which they could not (would not) arrange for the wife to collect some valuable art objects and an expensive high-fidelity music system that she had owned prior to their establishing a household together. Envy and competitiveness, together with a deep sense of loss about the terminating relationship, motivated this behavior, generating at the same time a pattern that ensured the impossibility of a reconciliation.

There was no legal problem per se in this instance, although the failure to resolve the emotional issue adequately might eventually force recourse to the courts.

The situation changes drastically when the young couple has children. Under these conditions, the clinician must be fiercely attentive to the arrangements being made for the future. Indeed this is so even when both parties may be in agreement, if the agreement is unfair or prejudicial to the future interests of either party or the children. Admittedly the terms *unfair* and *prejudicial* are value-laden: after all, who is to say? The answer is that in one fashion or another, everyone has a say: attorneys, judges, the parties themselves, to say nothing of kin, friends, and business associates.

It is beyond the scope of this article to argue this issue extensively. The court's ultimate responsibility and authority for these decisions are not in dispute here. But I believe that the clinician should *not* aim to adopt a value-free position. Elsewhere in this article, I have suggested that adopting such a position is neither possible nor desirable; there is no aspect of this issue that, in my opinion, better exemplifies the hazards of so doing.

It is the postdivorce welfare of all parties that must be considered. The clinician, needless to say, is not the sole custodian of that issue and

Divorcing: Clinical Notes

cannot under difficult conditions effectively implemement a plan even though the plan may seem meritorious:

> Some years ago, I was asked by the attorneys for a husband and wife to assist with what seemed to be the unresolvable matter of arrangements for child custody. There were two young children, a boy aged 3 and a girl aged 5. The parents were both mental health workers, and the father insisted on joint custody with a schedule of frequently alternating residence that seemed impractical. During the predivorce period, the couple had expressed the intensity of their devotion to parenting by a novel domiciliary arrangement: they had rented an apartment near their suburban home. Each parent lived alternate months in the apartment, while the children continued to dwell in the original home. As part of the consultation process, I made a home visit to this house; it was an imaginative fairyland for the children, full of interesting walkways, child-sized rooms, peek-through apertures, and, of course, endless numbers of all kinds of toys.
>
> The consultation process did everything it was supposed to do in the way of unraveling the dynamics of the custody struggle. The father had a new lover whose child-caring abilities the wife doubted. The wife's family was wealthy and intrusive, and her husband saw them as capturing the children. Despite my best efforts, and those of their attorneys, it was impossible to reach a final agreement, the sticking point being the insistence of the husband that he take the children abroad for a sabbatical year that was coming up shortly. Quite literally, on the day the case was coming to trial, an agreement was reached, not through my efforts, but through a third attorney appointed by the court as *an attorney for the children.* The power of his position allowed him to insist on a mutual accommodation: it was arranged that the father would take the sabbatical year without the children, but an extended vacation was to take place in the middle of the year, when they would join him abroad; during the following year, they would be domiciled with him in this country, and the wife would have them for a long vacation.

These arrangements were possible because of the ages of the children; schooling would be less interfered with as both parents could see. The plan was practical but involved a measure of trust these folks could not muster under the circumstances without outside and authoritative insistence. In truth, they were all being banished from fairyland, both children and parents. That needed to be faced and endured, a process that would take years and perhaps never be fully accomplished. But the die was cast, and it was better to take up that work than to obscure and fudge the issue under the pretext of litigating a legitimate matter. I tell parents plainly that they can divorce each other but that they cannot divorce their children, adding that I know they would not want to. I am quite authoritative about this, speaking *ex cathedra*, as it were. It is often useful to make the point even more strongly: "If you were never to see them again, they would still be with you, and you with them. Since that is so, we must address ourselves to the question of what kind of parents you both are going to continue to be, not whether you will continue to be parents."

This approach provides a platform for another issue: their continuing responsibility to each other. Each in his or her own way must see that the ex-mate functions in as whole and healthy a way as possible, because both mates' parenting ability for the children they have in common is at stake.

This case is instructive from several points of view: it shows the value of the home visit, for example, as well as the definition of the family consultant role. Most importantly, we can see the law functioning to good ends through its instruments, in this instance, the court-appointed attorney for the children.

As a prelude to the following section, it seems appropriate to display two prejudices. The first prejudice is that I am convinced that raising children requires two pairs of hands, preferably but not necessarily of opposite sex. The second prejudice is that I consider myself a committed feminist, committed insofar as a somewhat superannuated male can hold himself so to be. The change in mores has in no way changed the psychobiological requirements of the growing child nor the logistics of providing for them. At this point, the single parent is more often female, and the single female parent is at an even greater economic disadvantage. She is competing in a job market where women are still paid less than men for comparable work, fighting the frictional drag of her child-care responsibilities, and struggling to clear enough space to carry on an adult life that includes some sexual experience and companionship.

The polemic point I wish to make is that by my definition, the single-parent family is shorthanded, seriously "underpersonned," logistically crippled. Courts and clinicians alike often tend, in my view, to be light-headed and vacant on this subject. Divorcing parents themselves are rarely in possession of the relevant facts, that time, money and energy are about to be in dreadfully short supply and that this scarcity will have immediate and painful consequences. When there is less to be generous about, generosity of spirit and emotion may be rapidly eroded.

The above can be read as an antifeminist position. It is not, although I regard as shortsighted the tendency of a few leaders in the women's movement to encourage others to have babies without a reliable partner in sight. Nor am I suggesting that women stay in destructive relationships simply in order to share child-rearing responsibilities. Finally, I am not prejudging the merits of alternate lifestyles, communes, homosexual marriages, or matrilineal families as suitable child-rearing environments. I dilate on this point for an entirely different reason; there is an important population at high risk whose needs cannot be neglected: the young family with children who are divorcing.

It is impossible in a short review to spin out the practical expression of this point of view. Indeed, the point of view is hardly novel in its general purposes; my concern is to alert the clinician to the matter and to provide what I believe is an effective stance from which to launch an appropriate advocacy, the advocacy of the family.

The family therapist is in a position to say to the family, and to attorneys and the court as well, that despite divorce, the family endures in some of its critical functions, most particularly parenting. This point is not debatable; it is a biopsychosocial fact. As advocates for the family in its enduring existence, our concern is to optimize these potentials and reduce the associated hazards.

It flows from this position that spouses must continue to care for each other, even when it can be assumed that they have ceased to care about each other. An ex-mate needs to have, if it is at all possible, peace of mind and financial flexibility so as to be able to resume a sexual life, to have adult companionship, and, most particularly, to carry on a satisfactory work life. Given the sexist nature of society, males are most likely to be poorly served in regard to their emotional needs (indeed frequently to have been acculturated so as not to recognize them), while females are most likely to be inequitably dealt with financially in relation to their educational and vocational needs and in an unfair distribution of child-care responsibilities.

Donald A. Bloch

The Therapist's Self

There are few clinical issues that so deeply touch the person of the family therapist. The motivation for undertaking this sort of work is almost always born out of some profound and painful interest in family, a subject on which there is rarely neutrality. It is hard to catalog the full extent of possible interactions between the place of the therapist in his or her own life cycle, as well as the direct personal experience that he or she has had with these matters. It seems trite to say so, yet the matter is often glossed over. My own divorce altered my clinical attitudes, principally by intensifying them and by increasing my empathic involvement with divorcing families. Prior to this unexpected turn of events in my own family, I would certainly have considered myself concerned and sensitive but essentially neutral as to the outcome, leaving the final decisions as best I could entirely to the couple. In candor, I do not think that that assessment had been really accurate in the past; I certainly do not take it to be accurate now.

Based on the usual imponderable mix of clinical and personal experience, I find myself more often with an explicit opinion on the matter. While there is no question that the decision must be made by the people involved, I am now much more aware of my own judgment that some people *should* divorce and, equally, that others *should not*. There are particularly painful experiences—the reduction of direct fatherly contact with children, for example—that I could assess before only in general terms but that now are extremely vivid, palpably so for me, and I am certain that this vividness colors my work. I knew it before, but I know it differently now.

On a less emotionally intense level, it is possible for me to understand the effect of the legal and economic issues in a divorce quite differently. One may speak about the impact of the adversary stance of the law; it is quite a different stance from that operating in a divorce proceeding, such as the one in which I was involved, where both participants aim to be humane, fair, and ethical with each other:

> While supervising a colleague in his treatment of a couple whose relationship seemed to be characterized by continued paranoid assaults by the husband on a confused and compliant wife, I realized that certain options for the wife had not been considered. These mainly had to do with her inability to establish an economic

and social base for herself outside the relationship. Inquiry led the therapist to say that such moves might ultimately lead to divorce and that this was an outcome he did not favor as a family therapist. His general view of marriage was that it was a permanent, irrevocable contract; interestingly this was not a view based, for this man, on religious grounds but one that seemed to align with the kinds of choices he had made in his own marriage. Because divorce could not be considered, certain interpersonal moves and associated clinical strategies were ruled out as well. There is no end to discovering the ways in which our personal and professional lives intertwine. It is usually important to keep such issues in our awareness in work with divorcing families.

A Note on Forgiveness and Growth

The divorcing sequence properly begins with marriage. It is an exquisite psychosocial truth that people often marry for exactly the same reasons they divorce. This truth has been put in various ways. The version that appeals to me most is that affiliation leading to marriage grows out of the complex of unresolved issues that each mate brings from his or her family of origin. (We speak here of marriages in the Western mode, that is, where the individuals involved must carry the proper valences for affiliation and generate the necessary energies as well. Arranged marriages in other cultures deal with these matters through other mechanisms.)

The elucidation of this issue, the multigenerational reasons for marrying and divorcing, is, I feel, the central human concern about divorces at all stages of marriage. It figures prominently in all family therapy considerations and cannot be elaborated here. The relevance to the divorcing process appears particularly at two points.

Often we console ourselves in the midst of dreadful experiences with the notion that at least we have learned something. An associated idea also designed to relieve present pain is that things are bound to get better. To both the answer might be "Well, yes and no." If divorce, even for those married a short time, is not to be a trivial event, some part of the experience must contribute to personal growth. There is a paradox evident here: a couple that can adequately deal with the divorcing process ought, in principle, to have an excellent marriage.

The interconnection of these issues can be seen most easily as one considers how the clinician can relate to a young, childless couple, perhaps married for less than five or six years. Commonly such a couple come for consultation in an extreme state of conflict and indecision. Having courted each other well, they have married for love and now, only a short time later, find themselves in despair. Not only is the bloom off the rose (they knew that that state of freshness and excitement could not last forever), but the damn rosebush seems to be dying. What to do? What stance can the clinician usefully take?

My custom, after a preliminary inventory of the situation has been carried out and after the couple and I have created a working therapeutic relationship, is to set before them my sense of the possible goals of the work in some sequence such as this:

> "I have no notion as to whether the two of you should stay together or not. In any case, that cannot be my decision, and eventually you will go in one direction or the other, or continue in a perpetual state of indecision. I suggest we meet together for a few sessions in order to try to come to an answer about that."

Obviously a couple may be at any point in the decision-making process, and this statement must take that into account. I make a point of including all elements even when there is no expressed question about divorce, since I believe, as noted above, that a good marriage must always include full awareness of the possibility of termination. The obverse, that the decision to divorce includes the possibility of reconciliation, must be kept in mind as well. The statement continues:

> "Should the eventual decision be to divorce, I am sure you both are wanting to be part of a couple, to live with another person on some sort of permanent basis." (Time for thought and questions here.)

> "In order to do that, I think it is very important for you to understand what has gone right as well as wrong. In a funny way, it is as important for you to understand why you got married as to understand why you will be divorcing."

The doors are being kept open. A couple ostensibly committed to terminating their marriage are frequently unable to begin any kind of serious therapeutic work unless they are guaranteed that the therapist will *not* try to "save the marriage." Still, the therapist should be genuinely open to the possibility that things may not go in that direction and should make every effort to protect the self-esteem and credibility of the couple while carrying on a line of work that might lead in a different direction than that to which they have committed themselves.

Couples in therapy are always very sensitive to bias in the therapist. That sensitivity is heightened when they are in the early stages of deciding two delicately interrelated questions: Shall we stay together or divorce? and Shall we go through that with the help of this therapist?

Speeches on the subject are of little use; the therapist must demonstrate by his or her conduct that the decision genuinely belongs to the couple, that the therapist does not hold a strong bias in either direction. It is also essential to be scrupulously fair about and attentive to issues of sex bias. Questions of the therapist's values have been dealt with more extensively elsewhere in this report. It is worth emphasizing that they are most critically visible in the work.

Finally, the following thoughts are put before the couple, although the timing will vary:

> "If you divorce, there is work that you must do so as to have a good divorce. No matter how much this may be a wise decision, you will have some regrets about it and real losses as well. In order to be free to go on to another relationship, you must be able to mourn for each other and to forgive each other."

It is at this point that the matter comes full circle, because, finally, to forgive one's mate requires that one be able to forgive oneself. It requires a genuine understanding of the basis for choosing each other and for the more profound complementarities of the relationship.

As in all of the other aspects of the divorcing progression that we have described, the nature of this phase, too, will depend on the age of the partners and the quality of their time together. Whatever the circumstances, though, my view is that it is essential for the therapist to pay attention to achieving genuine forgiveness. If one cannot in sadness and understanding bestow forgiveness on an ex-mate, my belief is that one cannot bestow it on onself and that one is therefore endlessly committed to a residue of guilt and blame. To be married, in the best sense of that word, requires that one forgive one's mate for having married one. In the same spirit, a similar act must be performed when people part.

8

Treatment of Sexual Disorders in a Community Program

ILDA FICHER

On a nightly television news show in Philadelphia, the popular anchorman, who usually concerns himself with matters like rising real-estate taxes, recently devoted a week of special reports to the theme of human sexuality. The segments I watched were very explicit, touching on such things as female orgasm, masturbation, homosexuality, and extramarital relations. The presentation was open, direct, permissive, and quite frank in its approach. Several sexual myths were discussed and "exploded," among them the belief that males are more knowledgeable than females about sex; the concomitant belief that men are more interested in sex than women and must therefore always initiate sexual activity; and the pervasive opinion that all single, and most married men are always interested in and ready for sex.

These sexual matters were discussed with a frankness that would have been unthinkable 20 years ago. Philosopher–humanists may ruminate at length over the actual dimensions of the sexual revolution, but there is little question that there has been a vast explosion of sexual information in recent years. As is evident from the television presentation, norm-shattering information is now widely disseminated to every segment of the population through the media. Television, radio, films, advertising, popular music—all carry the message of sexual freedom and accessibility. Satisfaction is acclaimed the right of all free people; expectations of men and women rise only to be satisfied.

SOCIOCULTURAL FACTORS

Informational fallout of this kind settles over a wide range of people, some better prepared to accept its unfamiliar message than others. Although the impact of today's sexual revolution is great on all social classes, the ease with which attitudes change is mediated by many factors, including education, cultural background, and socioeconomic status.

In working with men and women of the lower socioeconomic classes, one is struck by their varying responses to widely available sexual information. The old norms, standards, and "myths" of sexual behavior may shatter explosively, but the message must filter through generations of values and traditions. Vast changes in sexual attitudes make demands on all, but my own experience suggests that middle-class couples have the least difficulty in adapting to today's changing sexual attitudes. Better educated and possibly exposed to more sexual freedom, men and women of the middle class express their comfort with today's standards in a variety of ways.

Working-class people are not so well prepared to accept the sexual freedom of today. For generations, the double standard of sexual behavior has governed the relations between men and women. Several early studies[8,9] pointed out that sexual enjoyment of the male is emphasized in lower socioeconomic groups. Both initiation and control are seen as the man's role; his satisfaction is believed to be more significant than the woman's. Premarital sexual activity is condoned, if not encouraged, for young men of this culture, while it is severely condemned for young women.

For this reason, young women of the lower socioeconomic classes receive very little in the way of sexual instruction. Modesty, prudishness, and sexual ignorance are highly valued, lower socioeconomic class husbands often expressing great pride in their claim of teaching their wives everything they know about sex. It is not surprising that several investigators report that married women of the working class express little or no positive feelings about sexual relations.[9,12]

Relatively isolated from college and other potent sources of new ideas, the young people of the lower socioeconomic classes tend to accept and repeat parental values to an extent not seen in comparable groups of middle-class individuals. The mother's limited knowledge of sexual matters is usually passed intact to the daughters; when questioned, working-class women have far less accurate information than other women.[3]

It has been observed, clinically and anthropologically, that many of the middle-class assumptions concerning the sexuality of the lower socioeconomic classes are myths. Studies of these couples show them to have less frequent sexual relations during marriage; they hold more conservative views about nudity and reach orgasm less often than middle- and upper-class populations.[8]

These findings would seem to bear out Kinsey's[5,6] early observation that the sexual enjoyment of married couples is influenced to a large extent by their social status. Other reports point to the traditional separation of men's and women's activities among the lower classes as a factor that hampers sexual development. In their working life and in recreational activities, working-class men tend to congregate with other men, usually outside of the home. Women tend to remain at home, usually in the company of female kin or other women whose sexual attitudes are shaped by the same constraints.[11]

Rainwater[11] suggested that the relatively exclusive social networks of the lower classes greatly complicate individual adjustment to today's changing sexual morality: "The legacy of socialization directed toward a system in which men and women orient themselves to different social networks and sharply segregated conjugal roles makes change difficult, and reduces the frequency with which couples develop sexual relations involving mutual gratification."

Changing Treatment Modalities

The sociocultural factors that shape the sexual behavior of men and women in the lower socioeconomic classes have considerable influence on treatment planning for sexual dysfunction in the context of a community-based program. Although Masters and Johnson[7] stated that half of all married couples experience sexual difficulties at some point in their lives, the number of working-class people seeking or referred for treatment remains minimal.

On the other side of the coin is the finding that the number of sexual problems recognized by health professionals is directly related to their own attitudes toward the subject. In practical terms, this often means that any existing sexual problem is overlooked, and couples in the lower socioeconomic classes are not referred for sex therapy as often as would be indicated. Underdiagnosis or misdiagnosis of an existing condition is a problem in the mental as well as in the physical health field; depression, for example, may be overlooked or wrongly evaluated.

Moreover this population does not easily talk about sexual problems. Sexual matters are especially difficult to share with a professional who may know little of the client's cultural and ethnic background. The aura associated with sexual dysfunction would inhibit any mass influx to free or low-cost sex therapy clinics, even if they were to exist in ample numbers. Clinicians also observe that working-class men and women who present for treatment often have expectations that vary widely from those of the traditional therapist, who is usually trained to serve a middle-class clientele.

Through the Hahnemann Community Mental Health and Mental Retardation Center, I have been involved in the supervision and training of and informal interaction with mental health workers affiliated with a variety of professions. I observed that the working-class client or couple was usually referred for sex therapy only if the sexual dysfunction was associated with somatic symptoms, with reaction to medication or illness, or with marital discord severe enough to have generated a request for treatment. Either the husband or the wife might appear without the partner, most usually the wife, unless the husband was clearly the identified patient suffering from critical symptoms such as impotence. There were often insuperable problems in just getting the couple to appear together for counseling.

I also observed that sex was almost never mentioned in the case notes of the mental health workers dealing with their clients. This observation suggested several questions. Was sex not a factor in the clients' concerns? Were the clients unable or unwilling to trust the therapist with their feelings about sex or other very personal concerns? Were the therapists themselves creating a barrier to the discussion of sex? Was the absence of discussion of sex a facet of socioeconomic communication barriers between client and therapist?

My impression was that the intellectual–emotional barriers to communication established by the therapist determine whether, or how well, the sexual problems of our client population were treated. In order to test this assumption, a special training program was developed. Its goals were to develop the therapists' levels of self-awareness of sex, to broaden their attitudes and knowledge of human sexuality, and to increase the therapists' understanding of this population's attitudes and behavior concerning sex and marriage. Although we focused on the sexual attitudes and patterns of the specific culture of the patient population, we also hoped to develop in the therapists a heightened awareness of their own sexuality. This greater understanding of the patients' problems would allow therapists to respond appropriately to the sexual difficulties presented.

Treatment of Sexual Disorders

The training program and the statistical results of our study are presented elsewhere, but in general, the results were positive in every regard. Mental health workers who completed the training program showed significant changes in their sexual attitudes, knowledge, and behavior. Increased referrals of lower-socioeconomic-class clients for sexual therapy provided evidence that some basic shifts in attitudes and behavior had occurred.[3]

As a result of my close supervision of the counselors who participated in the program, I was able to observe other behavioral changes as well. A sexual history became part of the patient's chart in a number of cases. The therapists appeared to have increased understanding of the impact of their culture on the sexuality of our working-class clients, insights that freed them to try less conventional sex therapy approaches.

Clinical examples derived from our experience in working with clients from the lower socioeconomic class will illustrate some sex therapy approaches used in the community program.

Case 1: Treatment of Erectile Dysfunction in the Community Clinic

This 35-year-old black male was referred to the clinic by a male friend. The client is next to the youngest in a family of six children. His parents had been married for 30 years but had separated several years earlier. The client dropped out of school in the 11th grade. He had had several odd jobs in the last few years but was unemployed at the time he was seen in the clinic. He reported no incidence of psychiatric illness in the family, although a brother and a sister are both stutterers and he himself had stuttered at one time.

The patient was married at age 19 but had been legally separated from his wife for six years. He had dated his wife for several years, and they had married after she gave birth to their first child. Following his marriage, the patient reported that he drank heavily, was involved in some drug usage, and was arrested and sent to jail on several occasions. Four years after his marriage, while he was in jail, the patient's wife became involved with another man. Soon after his release from prison, his wife left him for the other man.

The patient's presenting complaint was his difficulty in getting and maintaining an erection when attempting intercourse, especially with a new female partner. He also reported the same difficulty with one of his two steady girfriends.

He presented as an attractive, well-dressed, and physically fit young man. At first, he seemed fairly uncomfortable in discussing his sexual difficulties and sweated profusely, but gradually he became more relaxed and was able to express himself without difficulty. No signs of depression were observed, and the patient appeared to have average intellectual functioning.

The patient dated the onset of his sexual problems to an incident that occurred about six months prior to his coming to the clinic. He was in a bar with a male friend who suddenly suggested that the patient go upstairs and have sexual relations with a woman he had arranged for him. At first, the patient reported, he had been reluctant, but he eventually went to the room above the bar, where he found the girl lying naked on a bed waiting for him. During the half hour he spent with her, he was unable to get an erection; the patient remembers thinking to himself, "Will you be able to deal with this, or will you get laughed at?"

Since this incident, the patient had experienced increasing difficulties in getting erections, especially with the one steady girlfriend and with new women he met. He reported particular difficulty when he met a new woman "with a head on her shoulders," one with whom he might really wish to form a relationship. The one woman with whom he could perform successfully, and did so once or twice a week, was 20 years old, considerably younger than he, and he considered this relationship mainly a sexual one. The girlfriend with whom he had the erection problem represented a relationship with a potential for greater emotional involvement. But since meeting her four months earlier, the patient reported only several successful encounters. She appeared to be understanding about his problem, but the patient imagined that she considered him "all dried up."

Three years earlier, the patient had also experienced some erection problems toward the end of a relationship with a girl he had been dating for several years. He attributed these difficulties to being "run down" physically and started taking vitamins, which he felt solved the problem. A year before that, he had experienced periodic erection difficulties but attributed them to a muscle relaxant he was taking for back pain. He stated that he attributed the cause of his current impotence to being "run down" again, and he had begun to work out regularly at a spa. He had also started taking vitamins again, his only medication.

From the information collected in the initial interview, it seemed likely that the patient's impotency was related to his unresolved feelings about his wife's leaving him and his fear of further emotional attachment and subsequent rejection. He reported feeling shattered after his wife left him, and he stated that he had had no sexual relations for about four months after the breakup. It was difficult for him to discuss the separation, and when asked to describe his feelings, he would quickly change the subject.

The patient reported that during the year after the separation, he had decided to "stay out of trouble." He stopped drinking heavily and tried to make something of himself. He had not been arrested since then, denied any drug usage, and reported only moderate current alcohol intake.

The difficulty the patient had in discussing his wife or their separation indicated that this was still a very live issue for him. The first time he experienced impotence after the separation occurred toward the end of a long-term relationship with a woman with whom he had lived for three years. He reported that the relationship broke up gradually when the woman became interested in another man.

At the time he was seen at the clinic, the patient was having erection difficulties mainly with women he perceived as potential candidates for a long-term relationship, the one steady girlfriend and any other woman with "a head on her shoulders." The patient stated that his main concern was that his impotence was keeping him from forming any relationships with women he really liked. The therapist treating him noted that "as long as his penis wouldn't function, he had a perfect excuse not to become involved."

The therapist's treatment plan involved two main approaches. He was to be seen weekly for individual therapy designed to help him understand the origins of his problem, to talk about and deal with his unresolved feelings concerning his wife, and to come to see what purpose the impotency might have for him. The therapist also planned to prescribe specific behavioral techniques.

In terms of the treatment process that followed, this turned out to be an inadequate formulation of the patient's problems. In the early therapy sessions, the discussion revolved around his two girlfriends, the differences he saw between them, and his feelings about being abandoned by his wife and the other woman four years earlier. The therapist noted in the patient's record that "in fact it became clear that his impotency was serving to keep him from further involvement and hurt"; she also reported that the patient seemed confused from the very beginning. The patient said that he could not see how talking could help him solve his problem but went along with it because "you're the doctor and know best."

Throughout the therapy sessions, however, the patient wondered whether there might be something wrong with him physically; he was unable to grasp the connection between the life events that were discussed and his sexual problems. He also expressed concern that his difficulties meant that he was getting old and might never be able to perform sexually again.

At the first therapy session, he was asked not to have intercourse during the following week in order to break the cycle of attempt and failure. He was also asked not to drink because that would make the treatment more difficult. The patient followed both recommendations and came in the next week anxious to report how things had worked out. He seemed relieved that there had been no pressure on him to perform sexually during that week, but he also expressed the fear that he might become accustomed to not having sexual relations.

At the end of the second session, the therapist asked him again to refrain from intercourse and suggested that the treatment would be even more effective if he could come in with the steady girlfriend with whom he was impotent. He rejected the proposal at once, stating that he did not want her "to know my business." During the third session, his reluctance to include his girlfriend was discussed. The therapist suggested that he tell her that because the problem was physical, the doctor didn't want him to have intercourse for several weeks but had directed him to engage in foreplay without an erection as part of the treatment. The therapist specifically stated that he was not to try to have an erection.

During these sessions, the patient found it difficult to discuss his feelings concerning his ex-wife and how these might relate to his impotency. When the patient failed to keep the next appointment, the therapist called him on the telephone. The patient was evasive but finally said that he had broken one of the rules. Another appointment was made, and at this fourth session, the patient began by saying that he didn't think the talking was helping him and that he was beginning to think his problem was "mental."

He stated that he had broken the rule concerning having an erection by successfully having intercourse with the girlfriend with whom he had been having problems concerning impotence. The patient placed no importance on this success, stating, "It was no big deal, I can get an erection with any girl if I wait long enough." He emphasized that he was still not successful with new women, and he failed to keep the next appointment.

The therapist, a white female, made the following assessment of the treatment:

At the beginning of treatment, the patient was highly motivated and closely followed all instructions. Trying to help him look at some of the dynamic conflicts connected with his problem, however, fell on deaf ears. In fact, the more it was focused on his gaining some understanding, the more reluctant he became to continue, until eventually he dropped out of treatment. One could say that the treatment has been a partial success because he was able to function sexually with the one woman he had had difficulties with. He did not see it as a success, however, and still very much felt himself to have the problem.

In several ways this case illustrates the difficulty of treating the sexual problems of people of the lower socioeconomic class in the context of a treatment program based on middle-class value orientations. Although the therapist assigned to this patient was well trained, she was unable to appreciate the patient's perception of himself as an unsuccessful black male. The image of the hypersexual black male may be a stereotype, but there is little doubt that it compounds the difficulties of an individual who may feel that he fails even to approach these unrealistic standards. The patient's complaint that he didn't feel like a man, his belief that he was physically unwell and "run down," should have drawn the attention of the clinician to his underlying feelings of inadequacy. The myths that black males are always ready for sexual activity and always able to satisfy their partners add considerably to the anxieties of a black man who is not performing adequately.

Moreover, in this instance, there was an incongruence between the patient's expectations concerning his treatment and those of the therapist. Unfamiliar with or insensitive to the demands of the patient's culture, the therapist evolved a treatment plan to provide insight-oriented therapy. The patient, on the other hand, quite clearly wished a specific prescription for cure, probably a medical one. His goal was to fulfill his expectations of himself as a functioning black male; in failing to grapple with the impact of these deeply rooted social and cultural myths, the therapist unwittingly sabotaged her own treatment plan. Nowhere is this clearer than in her statement that the treatment was a partial success because the patient was able to perform with one woman; the patient, of course, saw this treatment as a failure because he was not confident that he could perform with all women.

Although there was no question that the patient had personal intrapsychic problems, he indicated in a variety of ways that he was not willing or ready to deal with them. Therefore the therapist's effort to work through his problems and to provide insights was a misguided one. Like many lower-socioeconomic-class males, this patient was concerned mainly with his sexual performance. The psychogenic background of his dysfunction was of little or no interest to him and may, in fact, have been a source of added anxiety.

Another factor that may have been overlooked by the therapist was this patient's lack of success in the job world. Since he had achieved very little satisfaction in his work, the patient's sexual dysfunction was even more significant to him than was probably recognized. The low self-esteem associated with failure as a wage earner cannot help but exacerbate any existing personal problems.

Case 2: Treatment of Premature Ejaculation in the Community Clinic

Mr. and Mrs. B. were referred for treatment by a urologist. They had been married for six years. Mr. B. was a 29-year-old laborer. Mrs. B. was an attractive 28-year-old woman who had been caring for their little girl since her birth three years earlier. She had worked as a secretary from the time she was graduated from high school until she became pregnant.

The couple reported having an excellent marital relationship, except for Mr. B's problem with premature ejaculation. Both husband and wife reported that he ejaculated as soon as he entered Mrs. B's vagina, sometimes after only two or three strokes. This pattern had existed throughout their marriage, and Mr. B. reported that he had been a premature ejaculator since he had begun to have intercourse at age 16 or 17.

No major pathology was observed during the psychiatric evaluation. The couple appeared to enjoy a loving, caring relationship. Mrs. B. did not report sexual dysfunction, stating that she was orgasmic on clitoral stimulation, although she considered the use of "only" this form of sexual activity "abnormal." She reported being orgasmic during coitus with an old boyfriend before she had met her present husband. It was Mrs. B. who had taken the initiative in seeking treatment.

Although there were elements in the psychiatric history of each of the partners and in their relationship that could be interpreted as indicative of intrapsychic conflicts, these issues were not taken up during therapy sessions. The therapist's feeling at the time was that they had no immediate relevance and could be bypassed without undermining therapy.

In this case, the treatment appeared to be relatively simple. The therapeutic contract included the understanding that the focus of treatment was to be the husband's prematurity. Mr. and Mrs. B. were told of the importance of their following all instructions given if success were to be obtained. The couple was also informed of the rate of success in the treatment of premature ejaculation by these methods. It was emphasized that the procedures used were the only ones found to be successful and were widely used by urologists, family physicians, and sex therapists. The intention was to create an ambience in which the systematic prescription of sensuous and erotic experiences would be seen by the clients as similar to prescriptions given by a doctor to treat physical illness.

The couple were seen together during the first session to determine the quality of their relationship and communication patterns. During the next two weeks, each partner was seen separately. These early discussions centered on their individual past histories, their perception of the sexual problems, the quality of the relationship with the therapist, and their evaluation of the effect of the problem on the marriage. The therapist also supplied accurate sexual information, in this way dispelling some of the mistaken beliefs held by both husband and wife. During the subsequent sessions, the couple were seen together.

From the beginning, the treatment focused on the male's perceptions of the sensations preceding orgasm (point of inevitability). The method used was the stop–start technique.[4] Although in general the couple followed the prescribed tasks, there were sessions in which one (usually the wife) or both partners would admit to failing to follow the instructions. Resistance to responding to the sexual task usually indicates the presence of intrapsychic conflict or dyadic problems that must be worked through, to a certain extent, before treatment can continue.

In this case, the technique used to handle resistance was simple confrontation. No attempt was made to interpret unconscious material. The couple were merely confronted with the consequences of their reluctance to participate in the exercises. It was pointed out that they were the ones responsible for conducting the therapy; if they wished relief for their condition, the therapist emphasized, they could not resist filling the prescription.

Treatment consisted of eight consecutive weekly sessions, and two final visits one month apart. The couple reported overall success in the treatment. Mr. B. attained good ejaculatory control, and his wife reported frequent orgasms during intercourse. They reported no difficulty on follow-up six months later.

In this case, several different counseling techniques were used to treat the couple effectively. First, the problem was defined, and the treatment contract was directed toward this specific problem. By limiting the therapy in this way and by assuring the couple that success was indeed expectable, the clinician was able to set the stage for their cooperation. This approach also assured a considerable degree of congruence between patients and therapist concerning the goals of therapy.

It should also be noted that the therapy was simple, direct, and task-oriented. Although some intrapsychic conflicts were present in both partners, the therapist chose to focus on the presenting complaint only. From the outset, it was clear that patients and therapist had the same expectations of treatment and were working toward the same goal.

The therapist also emphasized the need for both clients to follow the directions that were given, just as they would a medical prescription. The specific tasks assigned were structured to yield easily achieved successes, allowing the patients to experience progress. Behavioral modification techniques, used in this way, provided the therapy needed by the couple. This open, permissive, and supportive approach also appeared to provide as much insight as was comfortable for the patients.

Conclusions

The cases presented emphasize the need to adapt therapeutic techniques to the lifestyle and value systems of the lower-socioeconomic-class patient. Further clinical observations and extensive experience with this population suggest that several methods can be utilized to provide effective marital and sexual counseling in the context of a community clinic.

It is clear that therapists and clinic personnel require specific training if they are to deal effectively with men and women whose lifestyles and values differ considerably from their own. With some knowledge of the cultural background of the working-class and minority-group client, the therapist can avoid employing methods that are clearly contrary to the patient's expectations, goals, and traditions. Education of this kind also helps to dispel some of the preconceptions and sexual myths that are held by even well-trained mental health workers.

In order to avoid the resistance that has kept lower-socioeconomic-class patients from fully utilizing community-based clinics, therapists must handle the psychogenic causes underlying sexual dysfunction very carefully. As we have seen, this population does not readily accept psychological interpretations as a possible basis for sexual dysfunction. For this reason, successful therapy usually revolves about a simple, direct prescription that helps the patient to achieve an easily recognized goal. Accurate sexual information is also effective, as is insight counseling to the extent that seems acceptable to the client. Counseling must be permissive and supportive, directed always to the therapeutic goals as conceptualized by the patient.

In practical terms, flexibility concerning clinic hours and the setting in which clients are seen has proved to be very helpful. If only one partner appears for treatment, the therapist must adapt his or her skills to meet this individual's needs. Sometimes a therapist must provide to the client more than is usual in terms of professional flexibility. While it may seem self-evident that the treatment of sexual disorders in this group is extremely important, there have been very few attempts to investigate treatment modalities with this population. My suggestions and findings are based only on a pilot study and clinical observations. Further study and systematic research are certainly needed.

REFERENCES

1. Devanesan, M., Tiku, I., Massler, D., Calderwood, M. D., Samuels, R., & Kaminetzky, H. A. Changing attendance patterns to sex therapy programs as a function of location and personnel. *Journal of Sex and Marital Therapy*, 1976, 2, 309–314.
2. Ficher, I. V. Sexual communication in marriage within different social and economic groups. Presented at the Ninth Annual Conference, Family Institute of Philadelphia, Philadelphia, Nov. 18, 1977. (a)
3. Ficher, I. V. Sex counseling: Opening the system for minority counselors and disadvantaged patients. *Doctoral Dissertation*, Union Graduate School, Cincinnati, Ohio, 1977. (b)
4. Kaplan, H. S. *The new sex therapy*. New York: Brunner/Mazel, Inc., 1974.
5. Kinsey, A. C., Pomeroy, W. B., & Martin, C. *Sexual behavior in the human male*. Philadelphia: W. B. Saunders Company, 1948.
6. Kinsey, A. C., Pomeroy, W. B., Martin, C. B., & Gebbard, P. H. *Sexual behavior in the human female*. Philadelphia: W. B. Saunders Company, 1953.
7. Masters, W. H., & Johnson, V. E. *Human sexual inadequacy*. Boston: Little, Brown and Company, 1970.
8. Rainwater, L. *And the poor get children: Sex, contraception and family planning in the working class*. Chicago: Quadrangle Books, Inc., 1960.
9. Rainwater, L. Some aspects of lower class sexual behavior. *Journal of Social Issues*, 1966, 22, 96–108.
10. Rainwater, L. *Behind ghetto walls*. Chicago: Aldine Publishing Company, 1970.
11. Rainwater, L. Marital sexuality in four cultures of poverty. In W. C. Sze (Ed.), *Human life cycle*. New York: Jason Aronson, 1975.
12. Rubin, L. B. *Worlds of pain*. New York: Basic Books, Inc., 1976.

SCHIZOPHRENIA

9

Family Communication and Social Connectedness in the Development of Schizophrenia

Albert E. Scheflen

Introduction

We have recently gained some new leads about the nature of schizophrenia. There is evidence of a disorder in neurotransmission in the limbic system.[6] And there is a problem of "torque" and cerebral dominance, for instance.[4] In addition to new leads, we have had a revolution in neurophysiology, we can describe the actual behavior of family communication, and we have an exciting new hypothesis about the relations of cognitive organization and social attachment. So it is time to put these new leads and concepts to work in the hope that we can gain a less hazy picture about the nature of schizophrenia.

Here is how I will try to do this in this paper: I will tell my view of how schizophrenia develops, putting in some new and some old data as I go along. I will focus on the family perspective. I will also make a distinction between schizophrenia as a lifelong problem in neural organization and relationships, and episodes of psychosis that occur in schizophrenia under particular circumstances. Because of this distinction, my story will have two parts: one on schizophrenia and the other on psychotic complications.

On the Development of Schizophrenia

We know almost nothing about the prenatal development of schizophrenia. Our best evidence indicates that genetic transmission plays a role in schizophrenia but that genetic mechanisms are insufficient alone to explain its occurrence.[11] Possibly the catecholaminergic disorder is inherited, but there are other explanations of it.

Possibly some infants who will be schizophrenic are so unresponsive at birth that no mother can make contact with them. Conversely, it seems, some are so hyperkinetic and spastic that it is almost impossible to engage them. On the other hand, some newborns who will become schizophrenic may be quite normal, but no one forms an interpersonal contact with them even though they are fed and otherwise not grossly neglected. And there are probably intermediate instances in which contact could be made if a mothering figure could be helped to make a dedicated and knowing effort. This is quite a spectrum of possibilities, but the accounts of mothers years later indicate such a range.

There are two things we can say with some authority about nature–nurture problems of this kind. Human infants who do not have interpersonal experience do not even acquire the ability to sit up, smile, focus gaze, and speak.[20] Furthermore it is not so, as we used to believe, that the nervous system is anatomically complete at birth. We are born with our adult complement of neurons, but there is a marked proliferation of dendrites and glial cells during childhood, and this proliferation seems to depend upon learning.[17] With the proliferation of dendrites, there is a geometric increase in the number of synaptic junctures in the nervous system, and accordingly there must be a sharply increasing metabolism of neurotransmitters, such as the catecholamines. It is possible, then, that a failure of interactional experience and learning does not stimulate the development of neuronal, synaptic, and neurotransmissional capacities. All in all, we can postulate that in some instances, schizophrenia may be primarily a problem of genetic deviation, while in others it may be a consequence of experiential deficit, but for *the class of* schizophrenia, we can no longer hold to an archaic dichotomy between organic–genetic and functional–acquired, for these terms represent complementary processes.

The Problem in Family Communication

We have a little information that allows us to pin down the early problem of interactional contact, whatever its origins. The interactional failure is not usually a matter of gross parental neglect. On the contrary, the mothers of most schizophrenic people seem to be inordinately devoted. There is a specific deficit in those instances we have carefully examined *in gaze, touch, and probably in smiling.* And the deficiency in these behaviors of contact *is shared by mother and infant.*

Masse[14] reported an instance in which the father had made home movies of the mother–infant relationship from the time of birth until the child had become clearly autistic. A communicational analysis of these films showed that the mother had repeatedly prevented the child from looking at her face from the earliest weeks of life. She also avoided touching it with the palms of her hands. Birdwhistell[3] has also reported a film analysis of a mother with an older autistic child who avoided gaze and tactile contact with her new infant. Stern[21] filmed the interactions of a mother with her identical twins. The mother and the infant who was judged normal employed a usual pattern of mutual gaze; the other twin was autistic in the first year of life. This child and the mother showed a persisting pattern of mutual gaze avoidance. In another publication,[19] I have described other such instances and given more details about this deviant mother–infant interaction.

In cases of marked autism, the child does not relate to the mother at all. Such children do not gaze at, touch, or otherwise attend to other people.[15] Condon[7] has shown that autistic infants move in relation to outside noises instead of with the mother's speech or body. There is a lack of smiling, adequate speech, and psychomotor development. It seems likely that children with a less serious problem do not become obviously autistic and are not perceived as clinically abnormal. Yet they show problems with gazing, smiling, and touching. Some scream when they are left alone. Others scream when they are held. Some are so flaccid or hypertonic that it is difficult to pick them up or hold them.[8]

Infants with difficulties like this may elicit protective responses and the special attention of the mother or of some other older person. In some of these relations, the child follows the partner about, clings, refuses to relate to anyone else. The mother or mother surrogate may devote herself to this child in an exclusive way. A symbiotic relation forms.[13]

If the symbiotic pair is increasingly alienated from other family members, a vicious circle is established. The mother's preoccupation with the child separates her from the others, and their alienation turns the mother and the child back to their dependency on each other. As the child gets older, the symbiotic bond is more and more unacceptable and constraining. The partners blame each other, argue, and avoid each other. Eventually there is little interaction between the schizoid child and its mother, and both of these partners have little to say to or to do with other family members. The bond is now covert.

Yet we can actually *see* this bond on a videotape of a family session even though there is minimal interaction. What we see is an unspoken affiliation. The schizophreniform child and the protective parent come to look more alike. They dress in similar styles and colors and may wear similar hairdos and insignia. Their vocal qualities, facial sets, and postures are remarkably alike. And they change facial expressions and postures *at the same time.* They move in synchrony like ballet dancers.

It seems that the partners share mood changes like the legendary Corsican Brothers. They also have a communality of styles, positions, and tempos. As their story unfolds, we usually find that they share the same beliefs, fears, and institutional memberships. Both are locked into a tie, but they rarely interact.

Clinicians have made abstrations about these family relationships in schizophrenia. For example, Bowen[5] has said that the family members lack differentiation and are caught in a common "emotional field."

At first glance, the observations seem paradoxical. There is alienation *and* overaffiliation. But the problem is resolved if we distinguish between interactions, like conversation and courtship, and the unspoken, synchronous behavior I have just described. In the schizophrenic family, *there is a dearth of interaction and an excessive measure of affiliation.*

It is now common to claim that at least some other members of the family of a schizophrenic person are borderline; that is, they too have schizophreniform traits. Kernberg[10] has described such traits in psychoanalytic terms. There are many reports in the literature of schizophrenic disorders in speech, which are sometimes called *schizophrenese*. In my experience, these styles of speech are also shared among some family members. Wynne and Singer[22] have also described these and other cognitive deficiencies that are shared by members of the family. So speech, cognition, and body movement are deviant, and in some measure, these deviancies are shared in the family.

The problem in family relations has been conceived of in other terms. The double-bind hypothesis holds that the child is subjected to persistent, contradictory messages.[2] It is claimed that the contradictions lead to a psychotic degree of confusion about messages and instructions. In another publication,[19] I have argued that the contradiction is built into any situation in which an infant is insufficiently and symbiotically attached. The child is "bound" to the attachment with the mother. But the child is also expected to mature and become independent in a Western society, so it is bound to dependency and "bound" to a course of self-realization. Hence the child with schizophrenic inabilities is double-bound.

From the standpoint of communication theory, then, the childhood problem in schizophrenia is a marked, often covert dependency upon an affiliative tie *and* a dearth of interactional contact. The affiliative tie is necessary because of the relative incompetence of the psychotic-to-be, but the affiliative tie in turn limits further interactional experience and maturation. So a vicious circle is established. By late childhood or adolescence, the child is likely to be classified as "schizoid," "borderline," "latent schizophrenic," or "at high risk" for psychosis.

The number of film-recorded cases of a lack of contact between mother and infant is small, but it is probable that this lack of contact is a significant finding *because much the same deficiency of interactional participation is seen later in life in schizophrenia.*

Usually the bodily states show a picture that we observe in people who are relatively uninvolved in a human interaction. The speech is flat, monotonous; the body is flaccid and relatively immobile. In clinical terms, there is a "flat affect." In everyday language, we can say that the person lacks animation or involvement. Sometimes schizophrenic people show the opposite picture. There is endless overactivity, hypotonicity, easy irritability, and a tendency toward fight-or-flight reactions.

In clinical circles we look at low or high bodily, facial, and autonomic reactivity from a psychodynamic or physiological point of view. We look at these behaviors as expressing something that is going on *in* the person. So we say the szhizophrenic person has a flat hypoemotionality or, less often, an excited hyperemotionality. In physiological terms, we attribute these affective behaviors to a failure of the cortex to modulate the activities of the corebrain, that is, the septal areas, the lateral hypothalamus, and the reticular activating system. Thus there is a disturbance in autonomic and vegetative functions, such as sex, sleep, appetite, and the fight–flight reaction.

But we can also look at the "emotional" disturbances in schizophrenia from a social perspective. We can ask what they mean in a social interaction. If one is detached or uninvolved in a social relationship, the face is held in a deadpan expression, the body is flaccid and immobile, and there is little attention and animation. So a picture of "flattened" affect is also a picture of social detachment or uninvolvement. The hypoemotionality seen in schizophrenia is quite like that of a lack of courtship, charisma, or confrontation. So we can attribute this "hypoemotionality" *to a failure of interactional participation* as well as to a failure of cerebral modulation.

By the same token, excitable, overly animated, garrulous, and hyperkinetic behavior is sometimes seen in an anxious overinvolvement. So one could attribute the hyperemotionality of some schizophrenic people with paranoid characteristics to a hyperengagement, albeit a pathological and highly ambivalent one. In my experience, these sorts of schizophrenic people do desperately seek some involvement, even though they avoid it and escape from it at the very same time. So the overaffectivity of some schizophrenic states could be viewed as a desperate, though highly deviant, search for involvement. But whatever the purposes of such facial and bodily behaviors, their effect is to make it very difficult for these people to form and sustain a human relationship. It is most difficult to converse with someone who is totally inert or else crazily hyperactive.

We have a similar problem in conception when we focus upon the more voluntary motor behavior of the schizophrenic person. We notice that speech is circumstantial, discontinuous, and wandering, so we say there is a thought disorder. We also notice that the schizophrenic person has difficulty in putting his or her actions in an appropriate relation to the context or situation. On the basis of these observations, we say that the schizophrenic person has a cognitive deficiency, or in the terms of contemporary neuroscience, we say there is a lack of "dominance" by the speech-related (usually the left) cerebral hemisphere.[4,16] But these behaviors are also evident in an interaction. The ability to maintain a narrative, for example, is a prerequisite for acceptable participation and so for an ability to take one's part at a usual time and in a usual form. The relative inability of the schizophrenic person in this area makes interactional participation difficult.

I am not arguing that the schizophrenic deviance *is* interactional *rather than* psychological or neurophysiological. On the contrary, it is interactional, cognitive–emotional, cerebral, *and* limbic.

There is a third kind of interactional difficulty. The schizophrenic person often declines to form contact when required to do so. On this account, we are inclined to overlook an important aspect of prepsychosis.

Family Communication and Schizophrenia

It is not only that the schizophreniform person declines to participate; it is also that *he or she does not know how to do so in an adequate way.* This becomes clear to us if we closely observe schizophrenic people in circumstances in which they avidly wish to engage and wish to learn how to do so. Commonly this is the case with young patients engaged in therapy programs as they are recovering from the first psychotic episode. Here are some observations on this score:

Sometimes the gaze is evasive. Sometimes there are fixed stares, or the gaze is held too long for the comfort of a partner. Or the prepsychotic tries to make eye contact by turning the head away and looking at the other person with peripheral vision, or vision is focused *in front* of or *in back* of the person being looked at.

In these cases, the schizophreniform person does not make use of foveal vision and perceives blurred outlines and gross motion. If one has used the eyes in these ways since childhood, a serious deprivation in fine discrimination and pattern recognition can accrue. It may then be impossible to catch the subtle cues of face, eye, and hand behavior that are so critical for adequate participation.

The schizophreniform person is also likely to have deviations of touch: the touching of other people may be avoided altogether, or else it is carried out with fingertips, knuckles, or the back of the hand. Analogously the palms are not displayed in greeting or courtship as they normally are. In fact, many prepsychotic schizophrenic people do not use gesture at all. And there are marked deviations in the use of personal and interpersonal spacing. I have described these deviations of contact in more detail in another paper.[18]

In short, then, the schizophrenic person—even before the psychotic episode—shows a triad of behavioral deviations; that is, in some degree, there are disorders in the modulation of bodily states, in the organization of actions and roles, and in the behaviors of social contact.

We can only guess how these disorders develop. Possibly an early life deficiency in the behaviors of social contact makes it impossible to learn adequate participation in more complex interactional forms, and this inability in turn hampers all types of learning. As the schizophrenic child grows older, a spiral of vicious circles occurs. The problems of interactional participation result in many social failures. These in turn result in a psychology of seclusiveness or defensiveness or else in grandiosity. These reactions in turn make social relations even more difficult. And an inability to form relationships with other people turns the schizophrenic child back to dependency on a symbiotic parental partner. This dependency in turn further deprives the child of social experiences and learning opportunities. Schizophrenia does not have *a* cause; there are cycles of them.

Psychosis and Social Isolation

A failure to participate in social interaction does not necessarily mean social isolation. One can refrain from courting, conversing, and confronting yet have very strong affiliative ties and a marked dependency on these ties. This is the case in the prepsychotic stages of schizophrenia. A rupture of these affiliations seems to precipitate the psychosis.

Field Dependency in Schizophrenia

Consider a usual state of affairs that precedes the first manifest episode of psychosis. The schizophrenic person has few social ties and little ability or inclination to form them. Yet there is a marked dependency on the partner in symbiosis and on a field of impersonal cues as well. With increasing maturation, this dependency involves more and more constraints and more and more loss of pride. The attachment comes to be denied and then hidden. The partners spend less and less time in discourse. They often stay home together, but they avoid close contact and they often argue. As this happens, both partners may withdraw into themselves. The psychotic-to-be substitutes an impersonal world of place, thoughts, and symbols.

We discover this world if we make home visits. There is a gestalt of memorabilia, letters, old toys, real or stuffed pets, and a montage of pictures on the wall. Some of these are bizarre. There may be rubber suits, costumes, deformed toys, or a montage of human eyes. But these objects are not simply the forgotten residue of the past life. They are vital for sanity. A few days away from them may be followed by a panic and the threat of cognitive disorganization. The prepsychotic person stays put there or hastens back there when there is a warning attack of anxiety. One of my patients could ward off a psychotic attack if he could get to his bedroom and put on a French Musketeer's costume.

The schizophrenic person is now in a precarious position. There is a lack of sustaining relationships, the tie to the old partner is strained and ambivalent, and there is a need to stay in the familiar field of symbols. Alone the psychotic-to-be has difficulty in maintaining the neural or cognitive organization of sanity.

Jaynes's View of Hallucinations and Social Ties

The idea that neuropsychological integration can depend on intact social ties has been dramatically elaborated by Jaynes in a well-documented thesis about Neolithic societies before about 1000 B.C.[9]

Jaynes first described the concept of a "bicameral mind" as a lack of self-awareness or self-differentiation; a lack of a sense of time, space, and order; and a dependency on the vocal commands of superiors or elders in order to carry out a complex sequential task or plan. Jaynes dealt only with language and hence with vocal cues, so he overlooked the possibility that this dependency could be upon nonlanguage cues as well. But in any event, Jaynes's concept of a bicameral mind is quite like that of the cognitive–affiliative problem we now attribute to schizophrenia and to the neurophysiological concept of a lack of cerebral dominance and a failure of the limbic system.

Jaynes went on to document evidence that these late *Neolithic people with "bicameral minds" would hallucinate when their parental figures or superiors died.* They would hallucinate the eyes, bodily images, and vocal commands of these authority figures. Jaynes interpreted this hallucinatory behavior as a need to reestablish the cues on which these people were dependent. Nowadays we might say that these people became psychotic when their affiliative tie was broken.

We should note that at that time in Eurasian history, the old tribal societies had given way to very pyramidal chiefdoms. Serflike armies of soldiers and workers did the bidding of clan heads and conquerors, who in turn claimed to be commanded by gods. Democratic states, dialogues, and dialectics and linear forms of scholarship had not yet evolved.[1]

Jaynes's bold hypothesis leaps the old-fashioned gap between individual-centered and social thinking. It points to an interdependency between neurocognitive and social organization. On this account, we cannot speak in old dichotomous terms such as *psychological* or *social*. We cannot say a condition has a biological *or* a psychological *or* a social origin. To be sure, nonschizophrenic people have a relatively greater ability to act without continuous cues and commands, but the difference is relative rather than absolute. In short, the problem of schizophrenia is a bio-neuro-psycho-social one. So is human development in general.

I suspect that we will eventually find a relative dendritic, glial, and catecholaminergic deficiency in schizophrenia in—at the least—the entire frontal–temporal–limbic region. But if this is found to be the case, we will not on this account have discovered *the* cause of schizophrenia. A complex system of events or dysfunctions does not have a cause. Schizophrenia is an unstable system of interdependent processes at all levels, from molecular to social.

If any link in the chain is broken, there is a disorganization or entropic collapse. The broken link may be a dopamine depletion, a tie-breaking rage, or a forced separation.

Isolation and Schizophrenic Psychosis

In my view, there is a less hypothetical reason for taking Jaynes's work quite seriously. I think the idea fits our clinical experience with schizophrenic people. *A psychotic break begins to escalate when the schizophrenic person cannot get back to the symbiotic partner and/or the field of symbolic and iconic cues.* The disorganization and panic or sensory isolation ensues.

The separation may occur when the symbiotic partner dies or takes another partner. It may occur when the psychotic-to-be leaves home for college or military service or attempts to "go it alone." Not only do these separations involve the loss of a symbiotic partner. They involve as well a separation from the familiar habitat and the field of impersonal signs and symbols. Suddenly the psychotic-to-be must function in a strange and alien environment.

In the case of highly seclusive or isolated people, the psychosis may follow only a separation from place and symbolic memberships. Sometimes psychosis follows the renunciation of a hero, a mystical leader, or a religious affiliation. I have known psychosis to occur immediately after a parent threw out a treasure house of keepsakes or when a montage of pictures was stripped from the bedroom wall. I once knew a schizophreniform man who would hallucinate whenever he was away from a huge plastic eye on his bedroom wall. His father had placed it there during his childhood to keep him from masturbating.

The psychotic episode is ameliorated with phenothiazines and sometimes with hospitalization alone. But it is my experience that *this amelioration is most rapidly and effectively brought about when these measures are accompanied by a social reaffiliation.* Sometimes a reunion with the symbiotic partner is facilitated by the very occurrence of the psychosis. The psychotic member gives up an effort to be independent in the face of the psychotic panic. A defecting partner returns in guilt and concern at the occurrence of psychosis. Sometimes a reunion is deliberately or automatically engineered by the hospital staff. I have not been able to find statistical data on the relation between improvement and reunion, but the prognosis of psychosis is significantly better when the family members agree with and participate in the treatment program.[12]

A generation ago, it was well known in psychoanalytic circles that an improvement in psychosis followed a transference reaction in psychotherapy. Some psychotic patients do not seem able or willing to affiliate with anyone other than the original symbiotic partner. They also lack the interactional skills to form new attachments easily, and they often irritate or otherwise dissuade the ward staff members from entering into a personal relationship with them. In such instances, the psychotic patient may accept an impersonal dependency on the hospital milieu. Then the psychosis may become less florid, *but it settles into a chronic phase.*

There are obvious clinical implications to this point of view. We can often terminate the manifest psychosis by a combination of reaffiliation, psychotherapy, and phenothiazine medication. *But we have not therefore radically changed the schizophrenic problem itself.* The methods of psychotherapy can sometimes enable the schizophrenic patient to develop a new dependent tie. The psychosis is then ameliorated, but unless further measures are taken to help the client gain cognitive and interpersonal skills, the basic deficiency remains. And if psychotherapy simply breaks the symbiotic tie to the parent, it may increase the alienation of the schizophrenic person and make the psychosis more chronic.

So it is clear that we must develop better and more explicit ways to enhance the ability of the schizophrenic to make contact, establish interactional abilities, and reinitiate the developmental process. It is not clear whether or not neural fields, neurotransmissional metabolism, cerebral organization, and an increased autonomy can occur if these processes have been arrested in childhood. But we will not know until we make a systematic effort to arrest them. Now is the time to begin.

Similarly, if we can learn to spot an interactional deficit in infancy, maybe we can learn how to overcome it and thus develop our first preventive programs.

REFERENCES

1. Ashcraft, N. Personal communication, 1978.
2. Bateson, G., Jackson, D. D., Haley, J., & Weakland, J. Toward a theory of schizophrenia. *Behavioral Science,* 1956, *1,* 251–264.
3. Birdwhistell, R. L. *Kinesics and context.* Philadelphia: University of Pennsylvania Press, 1970.
4. Blau, T. H. Torque and schizophrenic vulnerability. *American Psychologist,* Dec. 1977, 99–1005.
5. Bowen, M. A family concept of schizophrenia. In D. D. Jackson (Ed.), *The etiology of schizophrenia.* New York: Basic Books, Inc., 1960.
6. Carlsson, A. Antipsychotic drugs, neurotransmitters and schizophrenia. *American Journal of Psychiatry,* 1978, *135,* 164–173.
7. Condon, W. S. Multiple response to sound in dysfunctional children. *Journal of Autism and Child Schizophrenia,* 1975, *5,* 27–56.
8. Ferber, J., Yorberg, L., & Welsh, M. Forced hugging therapy for autistic children. Presented at Workshop at American Orthopsychiatric Meeting, San Francisco, March 1978.
9. Jaynes, J. *The origins of consciousness in the breakdown of the bicameral mind.* Boston: Houghton Mifflin Company, 1976.
10. Kernberg, O. Borderline personality organizations. *Journal of the American Psychoanalytic Association,* 1968, *15,* 641–685.
11. Kety, S. S., Rosenthal, D., Wender, P. H., & Schulsinger, F. Mental illness in the biological and adoptive families of adopted schizophrenics. *American Journal of Psychiatry,* 1971, *128,* 302–306.
12. Klein, H., Person, T., & Ital, T. Family and environmental variables as predictors of social outcome in chronic schizophrenia. *Comprehensive Psychiatry,* 1972, *13*(4), 317–334.
13. Mahler, M. S., & LaPerriere, K. Mother–child interaction during individuation–separation. *Psychoanalytic Quarterly,* 1965, *34,* 483–498.
14. Masse, H. Personal collaboration, 1972–1973.
15. Ornitz, E. M., & Ritvo, E. R. The syndrome of autism: A critical review. *American Journal of Psychiatry,* 1976, *133,* 609–621.
16. Ornstein, R. E. *The psychology of consciousness* (2nd ed.). New York: Harcourt Brace Jovanovich, 1977.
17. Pribram, K. L. *Languages of the brain.* Englewood Cliffs, N.J.: Prentice-Hall, Inc., 1971.
18. Scheflen, A. E. On teaching communicative skills. In J. Meislin (Ed.), *Rehabilitation medicine and psychiatry.* Springfield, Ill.: Charles C Thomas, Publisher, 1976.

19. Scheflen, A. E. Double-bind theory and schizophrenia. In M. Berger (Ed.), *Beyond the double bind*. New York: Brunner/Mazel, Inc., 1979.
20. Spitz, R. A. Anaclitic depression. *Psychoanalytic Study of the Child*, 1963, *18*, 361-366.
21. Stern, D. N. A micro-analysis of the mother-infant interaction. *Journal of Child Psychiatry*, 1974, *10*, 501-517.
22. Wynne, L. C., Singer, M. T., Bartko, J. J., & Toohey, M. L. Schizophrenics and their families. In J. M. Tanner (Ed.), *Developments in psychiatric research*. London: Hodden and Stoughton, 1977.

10

Add Craziness and Stir
Psychotherapy with a Psychoticogenic Family

DAVID V. KEITH
CARL A. WHITAKER

Schizophrenia emerges through the baptism of the sacred one. The pattern is insidious, resulting from a biopsychosocial hormone secreted out of the family's living. It colors the family socially, interpersonally, and intrapsychically. Treatment involves each of these levels. This complex job is like major surgery and requires more than one surgeon. We work as cotherapists. An important part of our teaming has been our effort to depathologize human experience through the interpersonal components of schizophrenia. The task is complicated by the depersonalizing component of schizophrenia. Our first battle is with the depersonalizing chain reaction in the family.

For most therapists who work with schizophrenics, the treatment demand comes from the community and the family must be enticed into the clinic. However, if the treatment demand comes from the family, it is usually to protect their status quo in hope of improved adaptation. When the demand stays at this level, it is unlikely that psychological growth or family creativity will advance. In order to bring the family alive, the therapists need first to confront the family's chaos. In this instance, and it is unusual with schizophrenics, the treatment demand came from the schizophrenic. This paper summarizes 20 months of therapy with a family.

Bill Deacon called Carl Whitaker with the following introduction:

> I dropped out of Hammond College last winter. I could not study and was not doing as well as I think I should be able to do. I was a disappointment to my parents. After I dropped out, I saw a psychiatrist because I wanted to find out what was wrong. He told

> me that I had a passive–aggressive personality. I saw him about six times. It did not help me at all. I thought I must have something much worse than passive–aggressive personality and asked him to refer me to someone else. I saw another psychiatrist who talked with me and gave me some psychological tests. He said that I was a schizophrenic and that if I were going to do better, I would have to be put on medication. I forget which one. He said I would be on medication for the rest of my life. Now I am confused. I don't know what to do. I went back to the first psychiatrist and asked him to refer me to someone else for a third opinion. He said that you are an expert on schizophrenia and schizophrenics, and I would like to come to you to find out whether I am a schizophrenic or not.

Bill's phone conversation could have been the beginning of a Woody Allen movie. While his predicament and concern with it was genuine, there was also a sliver of the absurd. The absurdity involved not only him but the psychiatric profession as well.

Dr. Whitaker agreed to see him: "You'll have to bring your whole family. I will have a cotherapist so that we will charge you double and we will videotape the evaluation." The absurd component of the chief complaint had activated Whitaker's response. Mr. Deacon's experience with psychiatrists had been brief, and useless. We usually demand full power at the outset. But power is funny stuff. It has no person in it. We use it early in therapy, but we are soon involved with the family in a way that prevents us from using it arbitrarily. The play therapy for real started on the phone.

We met with the family as planned. Bill was their nervous spokesman. He took charge of the family and of the situation. He was tense and hyperalert. His face wore an overplayed, agonizing mask. As he talked, he puffed as if in a wrestling contest with himself. He stammered and became confused, his voice cracked as he explained why he had called Whitaker and sought the evaluation. The family listened carefully to every nuance, correcting mistakes and filling in words when he could not find one. He explained that he was nervous about having his family there. It was "terribly inhibiting" and he did not think it really necessary. It was his problem and they were too busy and had more important things to do. He spoke clearly, his vocabulary was stilted and grotesque.

As a family, the Deacons were stiff and proper, but witty. The

Add Craziness and Stir

family consisted of father (Fred), age 50; mother (Doris), age 48; Bill, age 20; Karen, age 19; and Tim, age 13. Their physical and emotional formality combined with the tendency to huddle together and to shriek as their affect mounted gave them the feel of a flock of birds: cocking their heads, ruffling their feathers, and strutting on stiff legs. The family were disturbed that Bill stayed at home all the time and was so shy socially. They had expected him to flower into a genius with unusual personal adequacy. He was the one in the family for whom the parents had always relished the highest aspirations. Their chief hope now was that he would at least leave home and begin to live independently, schizophrenic or not. His father had offered him $5,000 to leave the family. We suggested that they could spend the $5,000 on psychotherapy instead.

We then asked the parents to talk about the family. Next we reviewed their impressions with the younger generation. The whole family were careful and nonsubjective. The family history was like a musical score that had been written out beforehand. Each family member was intellectual and had a large vocabulary. There was no concrete evidence of troubles elsewhere in the family. The main trouble, which was hard to put into words at the time, was the lack of intimacy. In this first interview, Bill played a comic Hamlet who asked us to decide if he was schizophrenic or normal. We spontaneously evolved into a parody of a psychiatric team and hinted at all sorts of pathological behavior; heterosexual and homosexual incest, imminent divorce, and bilateral affairs with the neighbors. We predicted that young Tim would become a paranoid schizophrenic. The family were surprised by our failure to be more discrete but were simultaneously comforted by our mixture of gentleness and acceptance. By the end of the first two-hour interview, we had the impression that Bill's psychosis had never really coalesced. We pronounced him abnormally normal. He was not pleased with this diagnosis. He acted as though he hoped to be found possessed of a terminal illness. We wondered if the family wanted to come back, so we could help save him from this paralyzing normality. We warned them of danger. It could become worse. They were indecisive, so we insisted they not make a return appointment. Whitaker asked them to say nothing to one another about the appointment until 48 hours had elapsed. Then they should meet and decide whether or not to return.

We think of our work with families as a form of play therapy with three generations. Psychotherapy is play. It certainly includes real events, but the frame of psychotherapy qualifies the impact. In play, primary and secondary process are mixed.[1] This mixture is an important component of healthy family living. Grandiosity is the result of the lack of any primary process counterbalance in the family. "Play is universal. It belongs to health and facilitates growth."[4] When a family is unable to play, our effort is to guide them to the place where play is possible.

Therapy moved slowly at first. The family separated the appointments by four to eight weeks. In the early interviews, we were constantly absurd, burlesquing psychiatrists at work, making fun of the family. "You charge so much." "Well," said Whitaker, "I still have one kid in college and Keith here has three little ones at home." We used humor to increase interpersonal stress: to increase tension, not to diminish it. The humor, blended with our obvious caring, created a sticky double bind. We would not allow them to discuss it. They could respond by exposing their own patienthood or by becoming different. This work is delicate. It is difficult to do alone. The process looks casual, informal, and crude, but there is a great deal of structure. The structure is implicit in the therapist's personhood and in his or her caring. Peggy Papp described the process of early work with schizophrenic families. She said it was "like removing the drumstick from a turkey. The process takes a combination of strength and delicacy."[2]

In the first phase of therapy, we take the family on as a whole. This family was a bees' nest. Outside it looked smooth and seemed airtight. We could only guess at the internal structure. Bill was the only visible patient. We invaded his fantasy life with gusto. He was no longer sacred. He lost his omnipotence. The family joined in on the teasing. Bill, who had initiated the therapy meetings, became opposed to them. He did not think it right that his family should have to experience so much inconvenience. Besides, the thriftiness in him could not stand the idea of paying so much money to see us. He took a firm stand against continuing. His wish to end treatment acted as a lovely paradox. The family had agreed implicitly to do the opposite of whatever Bill wanted, and so we continued. The father had developed a strong transference to Carl and became the strongest advocate of the return appointments. Karen, at 19, was in the early stages of an individuation process, and she was interested in returning. The mother would not go against the father's wish to return. She was not an enthusiastic participant but was unwilling to take issue against the father. Her restraint was a surprise; it looked to us as though the father would have been a pushover.

Add Craziness and Stir

The End of the Beginning:
The Family Stumbles into Therapy

We videotaped almost all of our interviews. At the fifth meeting, which occurred five months after the first interview, the family protested that they had yet to see any of the videotapes. After the meeting, Keith took them to the viewing room and arranged for the family to watch the fourth interview, recorded three weeks previously. When he returned an hour later, the family was gone. The video machine was turned off. They had looked at only a small portion of the interview.

When they returned for the sixth family meeting, the mother was tense and furious. The father was jittery, like an apologetic old shepherd: "She doesn't want to be here today. She was verrry upset after the last meeting." The mother took her cue: "Yes, I think it was an awful thing that you did." We were uncertain as to what it was that we had done. "You shouldn't do that to patients. You shouldn't show them pictures of themselves looking absolutely horrible. Why, I couldn't believe the way I looked on that television. That *can't* be me. I can't stand the idea that I am such a shrieking, unpleasant shrew. No wonder Bill is like he is." She was upset and angry, blaming us for perpetrating a trick on her. She perceived it as a crude practical joke. At the same time, she was more vibrant than ever. As her anger poured out, her tenseness diminished. We tried to reassure her: "We really didn't want to upset you." She had a new access to herself. She had caught a glimpse of herself that could be important to growing. Keith said he was glad that she could be so upset about the scene instead of staying cool as she had in the past and told her so. "What do you mean?" she asked. "I think you had a new look at yourself. And you have enough anxiety about it so that it may lead you to change. You are tapping into the part of yourself that leads into being a patient. I hope that you will let us help you with it." At last, they had permitted us to scratch the surface a least bit. We proceeded carefully, treating the mother like a fragile china teacup that would break if held too tightly, and yet we did not want to risk the danger of dropping her. This was a delicate moment and our teamwork at this point was important. The mother was exposed, and if we went too fast, we risked losing the family. On the other hand, we didn't want to block the possibility that she might get more of herself into the psychotherapy.

Young Tim, the 13-year-old pompous one, reacted to the mother's vulnerability: "Oh, come on you guys, you don't know what you're talking about. This is just a lot of psychiatric nonsense. You're just making all of this up to make my mother feel better. You're just a couple of quacks." He broadened the *a* to increase the superciliousness of his observation. Whitaker made an illusion to castration. "You know, it's interesting," turning to Keith, "when you cut them off, they sometimes grow back twice as big." Little Tim panicked. Tears came to his eyes, and he jumped up: "I won't take any more of this! I won't take any more of this!" He shot out of the room. The family was dismayed. The mother was completely forgotten and so was her anxiety. She started being motherly and wondered what had happened to her son. "You better go get him, Dad," Keith said. The father said, "You think I should?" and off he went. The other three family members remained in the room. The mother thought it strange that Tim had become angry. She had not realized that he was so disturbed by all this. He was known as the coolest one in the family. She could not believe that he would be so upset. We suggested that she go off and help Dad bring him back. She did. This is where the therapy began in earnest. The parents had joined to do something about their family.

We always assume that the whole family is crazy. The patient is only the cover for a variety of struggles in the family. We are very careful, however, to avoid developing a new individual scapegoat. The scapegoat must be the family group, usually a three-generational group. Sometimes it is even worse: it is the family in juxtaposition with the culture. The double bind in the nuclear family may even be a response to a double bind initiated by the grandparents or by the culture. One method of dealing with the problem of the individual scapegoat is to be direct and to reorganize the family with power and strength. We are more likely to do this when there is an acute psychosis with its attendant load of chaotic anxiety and despair. In this family, we did not do it that way. Most of the struggles in the family were covert. We felt more like facilitators, making it possible for other family pathology to emerge. This family's troubles were so implicit and culturally invisible that it would have been difficult to go at them with too much force without bursting bubbles and causing them to disappear before our eyes. It would be like trying to catch fish bare-handed.

SISTER UNMASKS HER PSYCHOSIS

At the next interview, daughter Karen emerged as patient. Bill had been appointed at their preplanning caucus to start the interview. He said that

Add Craziness and Stir

he wanted to find out how to stop being crazy. Whitaker said, "Craziness is always a joint venture, between you and your mother or you and a girlfriend or you and your family. I suppose the worst one is marriage. The problem for you is how to make use of your craziness." He continued, "The reason that I am so high is that I just got through seeing a woman I went crazy with ten years ago, and now she is in the full bloom of creativity."

Bill looked morose: "I've always used my craziness to my detriment." Whitaker stretched back in his chair, his hands sliding forward on the arms, "That's because you're stupid, but you can get over that. You've just been doing dumb things." Fred, who had been listening to the exchange attentively, interrupted, "Dr. Whitaker, you are always talking about craziness, but is that the same as psychosis?"

"It's a kind of packed-together craziness, like a snowball," said Whitaker. "The family and the community expect them to be crazy and they can't get out of it."

"The family gets saner and the patient gets crazier," Keith added. Then he turned to Doris, "That's why I thought it was helpful when you got so upset last week. Your craziness could drive Bill sane." Karen joined the conversation: "Do you think that people are crazy because they want to be? I had some troubles last winter that I don't know how to think about. I suppose you would say I was crazy. Sometimes I thought I was very ill, but I just don't know. I don't think I was sick, but I was very upset and it went on and on. It's all behind me now, but I'm afraid it could happen again and I would be terrified."

Karen had been away at college. Over the course of the year, she found herself becoming more reclusive and more and more preoccupied. She had been spending much time in her room and was unable to study. Messages on the television told her that the Russians were going to take over the country. She interpreted everything in the news in this manner. She developed a delusion that winter would never end. The cold would go on and on. Karen was unable to watch television any longer because these messages upset her so. She tried to talk with friends to test her reality, but it didn't work. They laughed at her, and then her isolation increased. She spent more time in her room crying. The college physician sent her to see a psychiatrist. After two visits with the psychiatrist, she was put on trifluoperazine. She took two doses, found it intolerable, and at that point decided to return home. There she gradually began to feel better. Four weeks later, Bill had called Dr. Whitaker to make an appointment for the family to come and see us.

At the end of Karen's monologue, Whitaker rubbed his chin and said, "Did you lose a friend or gain a friend in all this? We go crazy when we are all alone and come back when we discover someone."

"No, I don't think so," said Karen and, contradicting herself, added, "It wasn't till after that that the boys were interested in me."

"Have you turned it all off or can you turn it back on?" Karen looked puzzled. "You ought to have access to it. Real life consists in always being surprised by yourself."

This interview had started something cooking in the family. They wanted to return for another interview one week later. The effect of this interview seemed to have been an increase in the family's warmth toward us—and simultaneously, a breakthrough into the nonrational side of their lives.

When they came back, the father had been reflecting on his growing up. He told some stories of his isolation as a college student. Doris said that she had been aware of episodes where she felt disorganized and unable to do things, but she couldn't be very specific about it. She assumed that they happened to everybody.

Again they decided to return after one week. The interview was an exciting one. The afternoon and evening prior to this interview, the father and Karen had a loud fight about a date that Karen was going to go on with a boyfriend. They had shouted at each other and carried on and on. It sounded like a great incestuous lovemaking scene that had gone all the way to orgasm. Both the father and Karen were relaxed about it, joking and talking about how much they had enjoyed their fight. Doris, however, was very uptight and misinterpreted their feelings. She had a completely different perspective on what had happened. She was angry that the fight had occurred at all and did not understand that it was over and done with. She said that the scene reminded her of her own family, where her father had always yelled and shouted at her, and she found this frightening.

Thus we had our first glimpse of her panic over craziness. She did not sense that she was describing her own panic. She became very concrete and forceful. Doris was like an irritable general trying to organize her sluggish troops. The use of power also seemed like a mask for her profound personal insecurity.

The family's roles were emerging. Karen was very much into the psychotherapy experience. She was the most present patient. Her experience was existential. The father tended to examine his own experience historically. He was *learning* a lot, but not changing much. He talked about himself in the past. He was like a psychoanalytic patient. The mother was not a patient. She expressed her feelings with a kind of outrage, acting as if it was our fault that these things had happened and were being unmasked. The videotape experience was a prototype. We saw very little evidence of change in her, although she had softened some. Tim was not directly involved with the therapy. He enjoyed us and liked to play in his smart-ass 13-year-old way. Bill continued to be a caricature. We teased him about his voice and his sparse beard. It was our intent to continually invade his private fantasies. By this point, the family had developed a ripeness. There was a whisper of excitement about them that was not specific. They were more colorful and warmer. Karen saw herself modeling her mother and started to squirm. Little Tim continued to be grandiose, and we teased him about being headed for a Ph.D. by the time he was 21. We warned him, however, that if his brother Bill got less crazy, there was a good chance that he would have to replace him as the family freak.

They made an appointment for three weeks hence after the family vacation. They postponed that appointment, so that 10 weeks elapsed between sessions. They made no mention of the previous sessions. Things were back to normal; cool and safely impersonal.

A Fight for Intimacy

Over the years that we have worked as cotherapists, it has been interesting to note how patients respond to Whitaker's narcoleptic episodes. Keith is envious of Whitaker's capacity to fall asleep in therapy sessions. Several members of the Atlanta Psychiatric Clinic had developed the capacity, but Keith has not had success. Boredom in an interview does not cause him to go to sleep. His response to boredom is to work a little harder, to induce the family's confusion and thereby heighten their availability. He is likely to become drowsy when he is having a good therapeutic experience with a patient. Drowsing is a way for him to gain more access to his unconscious. He feels drowsy when there is a significant tension in the family that does not include him. With Whitaker, it is a much more profound experience. He suddenly goes to *sleep*. His head lolls, his mouth falls agape. The patients are clearly aware of it. The message is always quadribiguous. Very few people confront him directly about it. The Deacons became troubled by his falling asleep and always made a thing of it. The anger was most overt in young Tim. He would protest vehemently and lob things at Whitaker. The mother would call Tim's attention to Whitaker's sleep, and the whole family would hoot and call and make noises to bring him out of his trance. One day, the father protested earnestly. "Dr. Whitaker," he said, "I must say that I am very disturbed by your falling asleep when we are here. We may be boring. God knows we don't intend to be. I don't know why you fall asleep. At first, I thought I was boring you, but it happens even when we are talking about things of *great* importance to us. We pay good money to come here and we travel a long distance. We come here because we have been finding this experience to be important to us. I wish you would *please* not fall asleep." At times in the past, we had puzzled about why Whitaker seemed to fall asleep so much with this family. It was more confounding because they protested so much.

When the father confronted him directly, it clarified the situation for Whitaker. "I think the trouble is that I miss the intimacy," he said. The family reacted to this remark. They discussed intimacy and said that as a group they were intimate, with the exception of Bill. They said we probably missed it because it was expressed in "subtle ways." And Bill was so cold that it was difficult to get close to him. Whenever they made overtures, he would duck away, sometimes hitting at them, but never was he warm and accepting. At one time in the past, he had in fact broken the father's collar bone. Karen complained that any time any twosome in the family tried to be cozy, he would make fun of them and that made it all the more difficult. "He is just impossible to get close to," said his father. With that, Whitaker bounded out of his chair and with a hoot said, "I'll show you how to get close to this bird!" He sat down on a surprised Bill, who squirmed and wormed and tried to get away but to no avail. "I'll teach you guys how to cuddle with this lumpy old character. Hey! You're much softer than you look." Whitaker was sitting on top of Bill, who was rolling and bucking and trying to get out from under Whitaker. "Get off me, you old homosexual!" Whitaker reached under Bill's shirt and tickled him. "Didn't your father tell you that we queers have all the fun?" said Whitaker. "Look at that family of yours. They won't even come and help you. They must enjoy seeing you get squashed. No wonder you feel like such an outsider. They don't even care what happens to you. They'll let an old psychiatrist like me jump all over you and they'll sit back and enjoy it." This acted as a paradoxical goose to the family, who said,

Add Craziness and Stir

"We've got to help him." Young Tim came after Whitaker first, grabbing him by the upper arm and tugging without success. Then the rest of the family joined in. They fought with their fingertips: poking, pecking, and pinching, fearful, tentative rescuers. The 19-year-old daughter pulled at Whitaker's foot, squatting down in front of Keith with her back turned. He reached around her waist and picked her up and pulled her onto his lap. The shrieking increased, and so did the fun. Then Bill escaped and ran around the couch to hide. The room was not quiet but alive as we kidded the family about their cautious fight style. Young Tim stayed provocative and said that he could beat an old man like Whitaker without any trouble. Whitaker said, "Oh, yeah?" grabbed him and pulled him over onto the couch and thus started another wrestling match in which the family got Whitaker down. Keith stayed in his chair. He was jealous of the fun and shortly dove into the melee. We had a good round of play roughhouse. A real body-to-body wrestling match with the family. The father was the one who was most in on it. Finally it quieted and we all separated.

The mother became thoughtful and pensive. She said she didn't like this kind of noise and fighting. She wasn't sure why: "Do you have any idea why Bill is like he is? What do you think causes it?" Carl said, "I think that it's a phobia. Usually there's somebody else in the family who's afraid of going crazy."

At the time we started work with this family, Whitaker was just finishing a paper entitled "Co-therapy of Chronic Schizophrenia."[3] In the paper, he developed a model (model = myth without divine characters) for the evolution of a schizophrenic offspring in a socially adapted family. He suggested that one component in the development of schizophrenia is a phobia about craziness in one of the family members, most likely the mother.

Mrs. Deacon's demeanor changed. Her lips were pursed, her head tilted slightly back, her voice soft: "You know, that's a funny thing that you say. I used to have the idea that my whole family was crazy. I mean, nobody was in the hospital and nobody ever went to see a psychiatrist. We would all work on each other, pushing the other one to go crazy, especially my mother and father. Whenever one of us kids would get in trouble, they would not come to help, they would come to push us further. I decided a long time ago that I was never going to let them win. I swore I was never going to go crazy." From his corner of the couch, Tim laughed: "Ha, ha, ha. It's the craziest thing in this family. Whenever anybody has a real strong feeling against anything, you can be sure that it's going to happen. Whenever anybody says I'm *not*, I'm absolutely *not* going to do this or that, it is almost for certain that this or that will happen. Mom, I remember once when you said no matter what happens, I'm *never* going to see a psychiatrist. And here we are, a whole family sitting here talking to not one but two psychiatrists."

From there the mother went on recounting the time when Bill was born. At birth, his toes were missing. Her family had all come to see her. She was certain their interest was not supportive but an attempt to make her more vulnerable and push her further into madness. As she talked, she wandered into guilt feelings related to her concern that she had done something to Bill. She wasn't certain what it was. But she feared that the something had resulted in his disturbance. She was exploring her own feelings with involuntary honesty. At the end of it, she looked more rigid and chilled than I had ever seen her. She said she did not want to return to our clinic again.

This was not a new pattern with Doris. Each time she experienced some part of her subjective self, she would withdraw. She was like someone who had experienced a horrid fright. Her vegetative nervous system left her drained but still tense. There was no relief for her. The father was consoling toward her but in a cool, cautious way; impersonal and ineffectual. Part of him was glad to see her finally open and vulnerable.

The process went flat again. The family complained about being stymied, and we unfolded more double-binding humor. Appointments were spread out and low-key. We assumed that the family was digesting the massive bolus of experience they had received in that single stress interview. We found it difficult to measure what, if any, change was taking place in the family. They had learned to make fun of themselves, but unfortunately, it did not go anywhere. It seemed that they laughed at themselves as an adaptation to us, but not to permit themselves more interpersonal freedom. The parents had gained a little courage to play with each other, but it was scant.

Bill initiated reapplication to college. He asked Whitaker to write a letter on his behalf. The following is the content of the letter that Whitaker wrote to the director of psychological serivces at Hammond College:

> Dr. David Keith and I have been working with William Deacon and his entire family since April of 1977. We think he has made considerable progress in getting past his preoccupation with his

family stress and that the family stress itself has been considerably modified. Mr. Deacon's capacity to carry on meaningful, studious work had been badly impaired by his concern with maintaining the family image of him; the family's dedication to excellence had become an obsession in his thinking. We have no way of predicting whether he is capable of taking on a full university load but would certainly be willing to trust his judgment, since that responsibility is one of the things he takes very seriously. We will hope to continue working with the family and with William until such time as they feel they have no further need of us. The amount of therapy and the duration we leave to their considered judgment, which we trust.

Whitaker Breaks into Bill's World

In February, Keith brought his children into an interview. Their ages were 4, 3, and 1. The Deacons dropped most of the metatype talk and there was a lot of active play. In the beginning of the hour, the activity centered on the children. Everyone but Bill played with them. The family's willingness to drift in this purposeless way exposed a healthy understructure that we had not seen before. At some point, Whitaker got into a wrestling match with Bill, but it was scarcely noticed because of the activity with the little kids. Whitaker sat on Bill, removed Bill's shoes and socks, then massaged his absent toes, saying they really weren't so weird after all. Keith had a flash and said that maybe the toes were still inside his mother's uterus and that explained why he seemed to tickle her innermost feelings and thoughts.

What was so peculiar about this interview was that it was thoroughly outrageous yet casual. Whitaker lay on Bill, who was face down on the floor, holding him with a half nelson. The family milled back to watch, singly and in groups of two or three. They kibbitzed a bit, then returned to play with the kids. Children in the therapy room humanize what we do and change the categorizing of behavior into pathological and normal.

On the way home after the interview, I said to the kids, "That is what I do when I work like a psychiatrist. What do you think about it?" The 4-year-old said, "I thought it was kind of dumb." So much for trying to impress the kids.

Bill left the interview room in a different way. It was our sense that he had been hooked that day. He had fallen in love with Whitaker. They parted with a warm handshake. Bill had never allowed himself to be touched before, let alone offering his own hand.

Measuring change in psychotherapy is a problem. Keith did not even catch the small difference in Bill's farewell. Whitaker did. It was small, the offering of his hand, a warmth in his eyes replacing terror. If Bill had filled out a questionnaire, what would he have said? Did he like himself better? Did he like Whitaker better? We think he *experienced* a change.

Karen Seeks Relief from Her Isolation

In March, the interviews began much as they had in November. Bill and the mother, Tim and the mother, or just Bill would complain about how they were getting nowhere in therapy while the father and Karen or the father and the mother or just the father would justify why they had come.

They usually had rehearsed the night before to be certain they would cover the important topics. They had now been in therapy 11 months.

Bill began, "Why are my dependency needs so important?" "Just because you are such a freak," Whitaker replied in a flat, matter of fact tone.

Bill took on a look of comic disgust that said, "Here we go again, no straight answers." "But what's so important about my dependency needs? If I want to be alone, I'll be alone." Whitaker went after him: "Look, if you really wanted to be isolated, you'd go away from your family. You'd go out west and get a job on a dude ranch or go south and sell used cars. But you don't. You stick around and bug your family about it. You are playing both sides of the fence. You won't let them touch you, but you still live at home. You make your parents feel as if they have failed. It's like marrying and not sleeping together to avoid losing your independence."

Mother enjoyed Whitaker's jokes: "So why would anyone want to do that?"

Karen was listening on a different level: "I can see where that would happen. I can see where people would be afraid of being close. I have lots of dependency needs and I don't get to touch anyone."

"Maybe you could get Dave to cuddle up to you," said Whitaker, referring to his partner. Karen laughed: "Oh, no! I mean sometimes you just want to talk to someone and cuddle up."

Add Craziness and Stir

Whitaker's tone changed, "Do you dare?"

Karen's voice became squeaky: "No! I'm really kind of afraid of it, with men or women." A chorus rose from the parents: "It is scarier, it is scarier when you're younger, but it gets easier when you're older, it really does." The mother said, "I mean I always was careful, especially with men. They might get the wrong idea." The family chorus was murmuring, "It's okay to be like you are: you are like us."

Karen continued, her voice still very high and squeaky: "Oh, I don't mean I can't *stand* to be touched. I mean, it's okay if you're in my room and somebody lays on the sofa and puts their stocking feet against my leg or something. If it isn't supposed to *m-e-a-n* something."

At this point, Whitaker moved his chair over, removed his shoes, and put his stocking feet against Karen's leg. She was embarrassed and in mock disdain said, "That's not what I had in mind."

The mother continued with her recitation on the advantages of being older. She was saying in essence that you could touch and not be viewed as being sexual. Whitaker countered with a bit of trivia, one-upping the mother, but it was so indirect that it was scarcely noticed. He turned to Keith and said, "Did you see that article on psychogeriatrics? It said that even older men needed to be careful about whom they touch in old folks' treatment homes."

"What do you mean?" said Doris. Whitaker replied, "There's the danger of becoming sexual, even with old folks." The conversation moved on. Karen was squirming and looking uncomfortable about Whitaker's feet. "Move away," the mother said to her. "I can't get over any further," said Karen.

"Why that's the nicest invitation I've had all day," said Whitaker. He moved over next to Karen on the couch and took her hand. She fought to get away. Whitaker leaned against her and she could not get up. The family became excited and restless. Tim was nervous and offered to protect his sister. He had on a large pair of mittens. He waved his dukes like a prize fighter, challenging Whitaker. "You sir, get away from my sister or I shall have my *men* do you some harm," he said in a gruff voice with pseudogallantry. "Take your hands off or I will put you in a body cast for six weeks." "With or without your sister?" Keith offered. Tim went on, "I'm going to lay you up in the hospital."

Whitaker looked insulted: "I don't want to be laid—I'm heterosexual."

Karen was making a crying sound: "What can I do?"

Keith encouraged Whitaker to continue his efforts, saying it looked as if Karen's face was softening and she was beginning to relax. "What can I do?" repeated Karen.

"You could put your arm around me," said Whitaker.

Keith tried to be helpful: "Why don't you try talking your mother into trading places with you?"

"I'm perfectly comfortable here," the mother said, straightening her skirt. "But I suggest that you tickle him, Karen."

Whitaker lapsed into schizophrenese. "Is your mother propositioning me?" he said to Karen.

At last, Karen bolted free in a clumsy way and sat down close to her mother on the couch. As she settled in, Whitaker said, "Now I know where your brother got it. He stole it from you."

"What?" asked Karen.

"The isolation. He picked it up from you." Then Whitaker said, "Dave, if you go and cuddle Bill, maybe he'll go and sit in Dad's lap, then we'll have this family getting somewhere."

"Great idea," Keith said and moved over toward Bill, who got out of his chair and hopped away awkwardly. He circled the room with Keith in steady pursuit. "Can't we just have an intellectual discussion?" he said. "You start and I'll try to stay interested," Keith said. Bill bolted out the door. Keith followed him a short way, but he disappeared. Keith returned to his chair, and the interview stopped until Bill returned. When he did come back, Whitaker said to Karen, "Being serious—it was a surprise to me that you were so personally afraid." Karen said, "But you are a man and I don't like that."

"That's not what I'm talking about. I started to play something just for fun and suddenly it became frightening for you."

The father joined in: "Doris is like that whenever she's around men. She gets so uneasy."

"This isn't a social situation. This does not have implications or is not misbehaving. I moved over because you have a real fear about touch, it's not just discomfort. It's like there's something about touch that's a real fear to you."

Karen agreed, "It is. It's very hard for me."

Whitaker was firm: "Then for God's sake, let's work on it. It's ridiculous for you to go through life in some kind of undercover panic about how little control you have over other people."

This was much more than a teaching session. Whitaker's tone was warm but very firm. He was saying, "Look, I love you." The impact was

Add Craziness and Stir

strong and comforting, like the pressure of kind hands in a moment of fear. The family were confused. We expected silence, but they kept chattering. Each tried to explain some bit of what had happened in an effort to get an intellectual hold on their feelings. They were reassuring Karen and themselves, saying in effect that we are not cool, we aren't really afraid. They tried to shore up their image of themselves. Doris reached around Karen's shoulder to comfort her, but instead of hugging, she touched her on the ear with the tip of her index finger, patting her there several times. The father stayed back from the interaction. He appeared to be gloating a bit about the fact that this coolness in his family was being uncovered. Now and again, he appeared cheated by the coolness, perhaps it involved a nostalgia for his own mother. He was too terrified to say anything about it, anything that would further alienate him from his wife.

The treatment lumbered on like a Brechtian caravan; the comic mingled with the tragic, the fantastical with the real. Karen's experience with Whitaker of hugging and struggling and worrying about intimacy increased the momentum of her move for individuation. When the family started treatment, Karen was the mother's close associate and admirer, a deeply identified apprentice. She now became aware that she was an even cooler version of her mother. The symbiosis was uncomfortable. Karen began to fight free, but her mother would not fight back. Her mother's ability to stay cool simultaneously suggested power and the ever-present danger: the fragmentation of her Self. Several times when she felt exposed, she panicked. She guarded against the reexperience of her nonrational side. The father continued his duplicity, fearful that his wife would be upset, yet gratified by his daughter's courage.

Every family therapist knows that the scapegoat must be made detumescent early in therapy. When this effort is successful, the family readjusts as a whole or finds a new scapegoat. One of the ways the change process continues to evolve is when another patient emerges with an existential concern. It works best when the new patient is a healthy sibling. His or her change is not threatening to the family in the way that a change in the mother or the scapegoat can be. In this family, the interest in therapy increased when the family saw how upset Tim was. Their interest deepened when, later, Karen began to make her demand for psychotherapy.

Here is another example of the way in which treating a healthy sibling activates the impulse for health in the whole family. A family came to the clinic with a 15-year-old anorexic daughter and a 9-year-old daughter who was viewed as normal except for being a tease. At the third family interview, the 9-year-old became furious with her mother. Tearfully she accused the mother and father of not loving her: "All you care about is if Lorraine eats or not. Nobody cares about me." The family therapist then began to do a form of play therapy with the whole family present. The family came alive around the issue of the 9-year-old's feeling of isolation.

As our work with the Deacons continued, some lusty warfare emerged between the mother and Karen. The lust was provided by Karen in her growth spurt. She was openly a patient and took advantage of the family meetings to talk about herself and her struggles with her mother. All the initiative was Karen's. Often the mother would not fight back. Karen would carry the battle to her anyway. She was clearly not trying to change the mother's mind. She was moving her own growth along.

When the family therapy was 15 months along, Bill's application for readmission to college was accepted. He was very tense about the upcoming new experience. What a relief it would have been to be turned down and go on being a nobody. He called us up several times because of his anxiety about returning to school. We had too much unwarranted confidence in him, he said.

The Family Goes Existential

Bill's anticipated return to college loosened the family up considerably. At an interview in August, Karen sat on a couch, clogs off, wriggling her bare feet. Keith accepted the nonverbal invitation and moved to sit on the couch between mother and daughter. Karen put her bare feet in his lap and he massaged them. She was relaxed and enjoyed it, a lovely contrast from several months earlier. Tim had eyed Keith with combined admiration and scorn during the course of the treatment. Now that Keith was being openly personal with his sister, he decided to intervene. He stood over Keith and said he wasn't going to tolerate anybody fooling with his sister in public. His tone was a mixture of playfulness and irritability. He wanted to know something about Keith. He seized Keith's wrist to pull him away. Keith took Tim on his lap and wrestled him. He held him though Tim tried to squirm away. When Keith did not let Tim go, he became forceful. The family started to talk about coming to Tim's aid. Cautiously they moved over to tug on Keith, hoping to free Tim. The

Add Craziness and Stir

mother led the campaign. Suddenly, and for no clear reason, Tim went into a panic and tried to escape. Keith controlled him easily, then let him get away. Tim was crying and agitated. He had banged his mother's shoulder and thumb in his escape and she was upset.

From Keith's perspective, things were out of control. The mother was angry at Keith and scolding. Keith felt slightly scared. Whitaker was across the room from him, relaxed, a small smile on his face. His relaxation rescued Keith. That is exactly what a cotherapist is for. The havoc of the moment was comfortably held in their relationship.

Tim left the room for a drink of water. Five minutes later, he came back. He looked refreshed and rosy cheeked, like an 11-year-old kid. His hair was wet and slicked down. Tim said he didn't know that Keith was so strong. He was relieved by his loss. It is interesting how these struggles go in therapy. Tim is only 14, but he is rangy and in good athletic condition. Keith was surprised that he had handled him so easily. It was the transference that tipped it in Keith's favor. Tim helped him to stay in control. To Keith, the struggle was like a dream in which he was powerful, an astronaut on the moon easily lifting and moving Volkswagen-sized boulders.

By the time we reached the next interview, Bill was back in college. The family said little about him. Karen wanted help with her troubles at a commune where she was living. The father was quiet. He looked depressed, even haggard. He said that he missed Bill, more than he had ever noticed before. The mother was her usual matter-of-fact, nonsubjective self. We assumed the father's depressed demeanor to mean that Bill had been detriangulated.

The last interview to be reviewed in this ongoing treatment case occurred 20 months after therapy began. Bill had been in school for 3 months, and the family dated the interview to coincide with his autumn vacation. As the interview began, Bill was criticizing us for having too much confidence in him. He felt depressed. He was discouraged about a paper that he was unable to finish. In the week before coming home, he had made two long-distance phone calls to his parents on consecutive nights. The mother noted that this was most unusual for Bill. He had previously suffered in silent isolation. Whitaker congratulated Bill on his unusual extrasensory perception of their loneliness and his willingness to interrupt his work at school to phone his parents. He commended Bill for his unusual ability to notice the covert upset in his parents' voices the night of his first call and complimented his willingness to further interrupt his work in school to call again to prevent conditions from deteriorating at home.

That was a neat twist of the therapeutic screw. We had worked to help Bill be more openly dependent on his family, and when he was, Whitaker made fun of him. There are several reasons for doing this. First, it prevented Bill from changing to please us. When families accomplish what we are pushing them to do, we disown the push so that they can end up with the feeling that it came out of their initiative; they must decide for themselves about the value of such a shift. Thus the change in the family belongs to them. Second, this kind of reversal frustrates the family's natural tendency to turn Bill into the patient when he was really a visiting dignitary at this meeting. Whitaker's comment established Bill as the family therapist. Third, it readdressed ever so gently the parents' marriage, the shyest patient in this family. It had remained comparatively silent throughout the whole course of treatment.

Bill persisted in his demand to be acknowledged a failure. He complained that his progress in school was not what he had hoped it would be. It evolved that he was getting B+ when he had expected to get A+. His hand flailed as he talked. His face contorted. His eyes blinked and he tossed his head about. His voice was high-pitched, his manner affecting a sweet Keatsian agony. "Look," said Whitaker, "will you stop acting like a freak? When you toss your head around like that and then blink your eyes, you look absolutely silly. How can I take you seriously when you talk like that?" Whitaker's directness short-circuited Bill, and he fell silent. The rest of the family was quiet.

Then Bill started again: "This is a difficult time for me. I feel very depressed. I don't know what to do about it." His manner was much different. Whitaker's comment had stopped him and straightened him out. He was considerably more real in his statement of his concern about himself. His omnipotence had melted away and there was only a remnant of his comic disdain. The grotesque grimaces were erased.

The father began talking about himself. He had wanted to say some things for a long time but had found it hard to do so: "Why is it that I cannot remember any of my life before I was twenty-five? Perhaps it is because I didn't have much of a life." He continued to talk about how sick he felt when he went to work mornings and how desperately he did not want to go to work some mornings. Several times in his professional life, he had been promoted, and then he had given up the higher-level position because his anxiety remained so devastating. Karen and Tim talked to each other on the sofa, not interrupting, but on the other hand, oblivious to their dad. Bill was preoccupied with his own thoughts. Doris sat across from Fred and nodded approvingly like a high school speech teacher listening to a student's recitation. Fred described how tired he had been lately. He found himself unable to do light physical work without feeling exhausted. He described himself, however, in a self-mocking way so that his family would not have to listen. Simultaneously he protected the mother from her panic about her insides and short-circuited the possibility of criticism for self-pity. The father was depressed. He was stepping up to take his turn as a patient, struggling to open up the parts of himself that had been long hidden. We assume that the family ignored him because of a long-standing, unconscious agreement in the family. The old myth was that father needed protection.

As the interview came to an end and the family stood up to leave, Bill said, "What am I going to do about my depression? It's very difficult for me." Whitaker told him that the depression was what happens when a person begins to emerge from his craziness and told Bill to take it seriously. It was the way out of his madness. Bill said he had no sense of himself as being any different from the way he had been before. Keith's immediate response was "You are different from when I first met you. You feel much more available than I've known you to be."

Closing

We still see the Deacons at four- to six-week intervals. Bill may or may not make it in college. We assume that he will. Our assumption is a leap of faith that enables the family to believe in themselves and allows them room for their own creativity.

Our first project in family therapy is to restore the belongingness of the family members. With some families, restoration occurs as a rescue from the stony abyss of individualism without individuation. Other families are aware of the group consciousness and want to explore it further. The Deacons started out as a rescue, but now work with them is becoming an adventure, albeit a cautious one.

The family has regained a sense of themselves as a group. They see Bill reflecting the family. He is not a genetic aberration. Each family member can then face the fact that he or she is also a reflection of the family. In this way, creating a group initiates the differentiation of each person from the family.

The second problem is what to do about the sacred one. The schizophrenic is perplexing. We think his or her job in the family is to watch. He or she should not become a patient until later. Treatment success is measured by the extent to which he or she rejoins the family. It is difficult for him or her to do so, however, for his or her problem is similar to that of an ex-president attempting to become a citizen, or of a priest who attempts to rejoin the flock. It is impossible to entirely disown his or her previous position. We think that the therapist can be helpful in the task by *ignoring* the schizophrenic.

The third part of treatment is to find an existential patient inside the family. In order to do this, the therapist needs to be aware of the culturally invisible pathologies: overfunctioning, never having failed, the impersonal square, obesity, loneliness, or as in Karen's case, fear of physical touching. We think it is best to treat the healthy siblings because their change is usually much less threatening to the family unity.

Finally, it is time to work with the parents. But as we saw in this case, they come to the front cautiously. The family will try to prevent their entry into patienthood either by scapegoating one of the parents or by protecting them. The therapist must not push; treatment must come out of their initiative.

The last patient, the most tough yet the most tender, is the marriage. That family litmus paper turns pink with the acid of scorn and blue with the base color of sadness. If we are lucky, this marriage will not die.

The authors express their appreciation to Noel Keith for her criticism and suggestions and to Cyndi Hackett for help in completing the manuscript.

REFERENCES

1. Bateson, G. A theory of play and fantasy. In *Steps to an ecology of mind*. New York: Ballantine Books, Inc., 1972.
2. Papp, P. Personal communication, 1978.
3. Whitaker, C. A. Co-therapy of chronic schizophrenia. In M. Berger (Ed.), *Beyond the double bind: Communication and family systems, theories, and techniques with schizophrenics*. New York: Brunner/Mazel, Inc., 1978.
4. Winnicott, D. W. *Playing and reality*. New York: Basic Books, Inc., 1971.

11

Why a Long Interval between Sessions?
The Therapeutic Control of the Family–Therapist Suprasystem

MARA SELVINI PALAZZOLI

This paper offers a theoretical explanation for our practice, which has proved empirically profitable, of interrupting our connection with the family after each session for a period of about one month.

The focus of this analysis is the family–therapist suprasystem, meaning the resulting system of interaction between the two subsystems in the treatment context.

We shall describe the successive hypotheses that we pursued in trying to understand the empirical data as our research was progressing.

Our present hypothesis, suggested by a great number of clinical observations—particularly by some peculiar resistance patterns of the families—derives from the cybernetic model, and in particular from some hypotheses formulated by Ashby in his *Design for a Brain*.[1] We have been convinced that the greatest danger to the goal of change threatening the family–therapist suprasystem is that it may organize itself as a too richly joined system. The practice we have applied seems to us to counteract this danger effectively by means of two concurrent operations on the part of the therapists: (1) introducing into the family system therapeutic inputs that, never varying, act as continuous disturbances of the ongoing organization; and (2) interrupting the family–therapist interaction during a longer interval, indispensable for accumulating observable reactions.

At the beginning of 1972, our team drew up a research plan for therapy on families with anorectic and schizophrenic identified patients.

Having adopted the systemic model, we made it our chief aim to apply it rigorously. We were determined to avoid at all costs any eclectic contamination by other conceptual models. As to the rhythm of the sessions, we did not consider this a methodological problem. For some time, we went on with the practice of weekly sessions.

It was only by chance that we were confronted with a highly interesting phenomenon: some families, which out of necessity were invited to meet us less frequently, were showing from one session to the next markedly greater changes than the families attending weekly sessions. They were families living in southern and central Italy who could not frequently undertake long and expensive journeys. This observation required an explanation.

The most obvious explanation was the greater motivation these families had for changing: the discomfort of the journey (which sometimes meant traveling by night on crowded trains where no sleeping cars were provided) was the test of an unequivocal motivation that appeared to explain the results.

With the intent of testing the validity of this hypothesis, we decided to prolong the interval between the sessions with families living in Milan as well. The results were similar and forced us to eliminate the first explanation. The fact of having to submit to an uncomfortable journey did not at all coincide with a particular motivation for the families to change.

We then proceeded to formulate a second hypothesis: we had reached better results because we had worked better. Confronting a family we were about to leave for a comparatively long period of time, we obviously felt obliged to concentrate more on observation and to call more on our imagination so as to devise original interventions.

This was the starting point of a phase in our work that I shall call *interventive:* we had to devise increasingly "powerful" interventions. It was during that period (1972–1975) that we devised family rituals and systemic paradoxical prescriptions.

However, as we later realized, there was a conceptual error underlying this effort. Although intellectually we knew perfectly well that in the therapeutic treatment context, family and therapists cannot be considered independent entities, underneath we *actually* continued to maintain a separation. We were working only with tightly interlocked and mechanically autocorrective families, and we believed that the long intervals required in order to obtain a change were specific conditions for treating that type of family organization.

Long Interval between Sessions

Finally certain phenomena, occurring repeatedly with less rigidly organized families as well, compelled us to reconsider the matter. These phenomena were the following:

1. If, after a paradoxical intervention at the end of a session, we did not immediately take leave of the families but lingered on, allowing the members to discuss it with us, the intervention was compromised and lost its efficacy.
2. If, instead, after "the bomb had been dropped," we took leave immediately, fixing the date of the following session, quite often we were called on the phone a few days later and were asked, on this or that pretext (for instance, a worsening in the condition of the identified patient), to grant a session at an earlier date.
3. If, giving up for once our "interventive fury," we terminated a session without making any comment or imparting any prescription—just setting the date for the following appointment—this unexpected and cryptic termination stimulated the family to important changes that could be observed in the following session.

Such a sequence of empirical verifications helped us to reconsider the treatment context as a suprasystem, the control of which—for the purpose of change—must be kept firmly in hand by the therapists.

First of all, we had to explain why the families' resistance was expressed either through the attempt to prolong the *direct interaction* with the therapists or through the urgency to go back to it as soon as possible. Clearly, we thought, in this way the family was aiming at *suppressing* the effects of our intervention; and, in fact, they had been successful when, after one of these phone calls, we naively agreed to name an earlier date for the appointment.* *We had realized that to grant an earlier session was tantamount to our disqualifying our intervention.* The tactic of the family that succeeded in obtaining an earlier appointment was actually that of meeting us again in order to raise completely different problems from the one focused upon in the preceding session. But even when the family did not go as far as that, another form of redundant behavior emerged. Families that, on first negotiating the

---

*Later, experience taught us to exploit the phone calls so as to gain clarifying elements, which mostly evinced the idleness of the pretext hidden under the urgency to see us and enabled us to avoid getting involved in the family maneuvers.

treatment contract, had shown relief at the prospect of 10 monthly sessions only and had commented on how expensive the sessions were, after a therapeutic "uppercut" suddenly inverted their attitude: very graciously they begged us not to be concerned about them . . . they would be pleased to come to many more sessions and they did not care a bit about the expense!

In order to clarify the problem we were faced with, we started again, in a sense, from the very beginning: during several team meetings, we reexamined the therapist's peculiar position in the treatment context. It was clear to us that the therapists, if they are up to their task, must enter the suprasystem as accepted and accepting members. But, as we had ascertained, it was equally essential that they should firmly hold in their own hands the control of the context and of the definition of the relationship. They must discover as soon as possible certain rules of the ongoing family game without submitting to them, avoiding being caught up in the same organizational pattern. The family's game, on the contrary, was that of getting the therapists mixed up, subjecting them to its own rules so as to establish *with them too* the same prevalently homeostatic, tightly interlocked, autocorrective system.

An interesting article by Lynn Hoffman,[3] published in *Family Process* in 1975, offered new hints for our theoretical elaboration. In this article, going back to Ashby and particularly to his classic *Design for a Brain*, Hoffman suggested that dysfunctioning families are too richly joined systems, which, in a way, reproduce the mechanism and the slowness of adaptation of the homeostat's functioning. Still, in therapy, these families may change, and even rapidly:

> Adaptiveness to change in such a system will depend on the possibility for the joints between parts to become temporarily inactive. This observation supports maneuvers in family therapy that emphasize the creation of boundaries between sub-systems differentiating individuals from one another, and blocking customary sequences of interaction.

In our case, such a hypothesis must include the therapists, too. Since we had come to regard the family–therapist system as a suprasystemic unity, we were bound to explain in cybernetic terms both our therapeutic maneuver and the family's countermaneuvers.

The hypothesis was supplied by Ashby. As is known, he had devised his homeostat as a model: a starting point for understanding how

Long Interval between Sessions

the human brain functions. Yet the homeostat, as an ultrastable fully joined system, requires a period of adaptation, and therefore of learning, that is infinitely longer than that required by the human brain. In order to explain the enormously quicker adaptation of the brain, Ashby formulated two hypotheses:

1. that there may be moments during which a partial dynamic disconnection between parts of the brain occurs. In these temporarily disconnected parts, partial changes take place, with possibly an accumulation of these changes;
2. that such disconnections are obtained by introducing in the interactive sequence constancies or *null-functions,* designed to temporarily interrupt the flux of information. This may be exemplified by a device used in experimental neurophysiology: the congealing of a segment of the spinal cord acts like the introduction of a constancy or null-function, since the congealed segment, by not interacting with the upper segment, prevents the passing on of information to the lower segment. Thus the spinal cord becomes temporarily disconnected, separated into two independent subsystems, each compelled to undergo independent adaptations.

If, provided with these hypotheses, we go back to the problem of family therapy mentioned above, we must first of all regard the family–therapist suprasystem as a cybernetic apparatus *in which the chief danger, in connection with the aim of change, is that of organizing itself as a too richly joined system, making it difficult, if not impossible, for the therapists to maintain a metaposition of control.*

We shall now try to explain our therapeutic maneuvers on the strength of these hypotheses.

The first maneuver consists of introducing into the family system some information, or input, having a negentropic effect. Such input, in fact—though it is shaped, as we shall see, in different modalities—always represents *alternative* information and therefore a possibility of learning. See, for example, the prescription of family rituals that tacitly substitutes new rules for the rules that perpetuate the dysfunction. The family that performs such rituals is experimenting on the action level with *behavioral alternatives* that were formerly excluded from its learning context. In the same way, the concluding move of a session that reverses the punctuations in order to paradoxically redefine beliefs and relationships establishes itself as an *alternative epistemology* that overturns the ontological and perceptive universe of the family.

The *second therapeutic maneuver* consists in the therapists' withdrawing immediately after the intervention, cutting off for a longer period of time their direct interaction with the family.

Let us try to analyze the effects of these maneuvers, keeping in mind how difficult it is to describe separately what, in reality, are concomitant phenomena. The effect of the first maneuver, as information, while having an impact on the totality of the system, *cannot* possibly fail to produce a different effect on the various members. Why is this so? Because each member inevitably holds a different position in the network of systematic relationships. Haley[2] first stated this principle: *it is impossible for two members of one system to occupy an identical position at the same moment.* In this sense, the input introduced by the therapists, by conveying a different meaning to each member of the family, causes each to react in a different way. These different—and differentiating—reactions are merely partial adaptations in answer to the information received. But there is more to it: each partial adaptation of one member becomes for each of the other members of the family a new information, to which it is impossible not to react. Thus an accumulation of partial effects will be reached, provided, as Ashby states, "we allow time for the effects to work round the system," which means that such a sequence of feedbacks to the therapeutic input requires a certain lapse of time to develop and become conspicuous. Consequently, if after a therapeutic input we leave the family alone for too short a time, the change will not have developed enough to be observable. See, for instance, the case of an anorectic who, after an intervention, suddenly drops her symptom: the depressive reaction of one or both the parents becomes apparent only after some time has elapsed. Let us consider a more complex case, that of a family of four with an identified schizophrenic boy of 16 and a daughter, aged 13, docile and childish in her behavior. If the girl is the first to react to a therapeutic intervention, starting a stormy teenager's rebellion phase, some time will pass before the mother develops an anguished reaction, to which the identified patient in turn reacts unexpectedly by running away from home.

If the family is left alone for a suitable delay, the whirlpool of reciprocal reactions will have resulted in a conspicuous change. And this change, obviously, happens in connection with the passing of time.

Translating these theoretical reflections into clinical experience, what phenomena are mostly observed in a family left to itself for a month after a therapeutic impact?

Long Interval between Sessions

Very frequently the family *does not say* there has been a change, and therefore the evidence that there has indeed been a change is expressed by one of the following behaviors: the outstanding depressive attitude of some member, mostly of one or both the parents; discouragement and mistrust toward the therapy; loss of outward control; and intense aggressiveness toward the one who has changed most of all. If the identified patient has dropped his or her symptom, the parents may admit it almost incidentally as something of minor importance and disqualify it by a jeremiad of reproaches for other of his or her behaviors. A number of families, with a psychotic member who had been chronically ill for several decades, have gone as far as to declare that they were deeply discouraged because the identified patient, at the fourth session, had not yet recovered!

But the therapeutic process does not operate only in this manner. I have mentioned above how language, because its linear and descriptive nature, compels us to describe separately what in reality is concomitant. Everything I have described up to this point, in fact, seems to be entirely a function of the family's subsystem. This is not so, inasmuch as our analysis also concerns the family-therapist suprasystem. Thus we realize that the therapists—by withdrawing immediately after the intervention and breaking off interaction with the family for a period of time determined by the therapists—perform a fundamental operation involving them too: they disconnect themselves materially from the suprasystem.

Thus the therapeutic intervention—which by itself has already disconnected the members of the family from their customary connections through the different positions assumed by the various members with the family system—is strengthened by an additional disconnection, this time of a material kind: the therapists cease to interact with the family and exit tangibly, for a time, from the system.

How does this disconnection of the therapists operate?

We may say with Ashby that this material disconnection alone is not sufficient to break the system if, at the same time, we do not introduce constancies that are nonfunctional for the former circuit. *These constancies are supplied by the quality of our interventions*—for example, a repetitive ritual, a paradoxical comment delivered in writing, or a systemic prescription, which remains unvaried in the therapist's absence. Constancies, according to Ashby, can cut a system to pieces.

The feedbacks described above offer to the family subsystem a terrific risk to its homeostasis. Disconnected from the therapists, the members of the family are acutely aware of the danger implied in a change of the reciprocal connections. Suddenly nobody knows anymore how the others will react to the "disturbance" introduced by the therapists. Everyone feels alone, separated from the others by a sort of fence. Beyond, there is the unknown. No one, in the meantime, dares to metacommunicate with the others on what has happened. Experience, in fact, has shown us that the members of the family do not discuss among themselves—or, if they do, only perfunctorily so—the therapists' comments or prescriptions. When asked, they will show embarrassment and confess that silence has been kept persistently. At most, someone will retell some disqualifying comment or sarcastic remark about us uttered by one of the other members. Therefore, once the risk of change has been registered, resistance rises to meet the danger, which means reentering as soon as possible into direct interaction with the therapists, disqualifying, confusing, and neutralizing their intervention.

I am now ready to formulate a few concluding reflections.

The first concerns the length of time necessary for the family–therapist suprasystem to develop a change. We think we may state that this lapse of time, in the first place, varies with the quality of the therapeutic intervention. When interventions "hit the mark," they can shorten enormously the time otherwise required by a family system to develop change.

Nevertheless there is another aspect that precludes haste. A system requires a certain lapse of time in order to develop, in answer to a well-aimed intervention, that whirlpool of feedbacks that forms an observable change. And on the other side, only an observable change provides the therapists with the information that is necessary to the building up of a further hypothesis and, consequently, of a further intervention.

However, we are still far from being able to establish exactly, case by case, the optimal interval between a therapeutic intervention and the following session.

In practice, we generally employ intervals of about a month between the sessions. We have shortened this interval in only a very few cases. Conversely, and always after we had flung a paradoxical challenge to the family, we have prolonged the intervals for several months, sometimes even for a year, registering positive results. We are gradually reaching the conviction that a very prolonged interval is indicated and perhaps even essential with families presenting chronic schizophrenics as identified patients. The results seem to validate the hypothesis we have formulated.

REFERENCES

1. Ashby, W. R. *Design for a brain.* New York: John Wiley & Sons, Inc., 1954.
2. Haley, J. Towards a theory of pathological systems. In G. Zuk & I. Boszormenyi-Nagy (Eds.), *Family therapy and disturbed families.* Palo Alto, Calif.: Science and Behavior Books, 1967.
3. Hoffman, L. Enmeshment and the too richly cross-joined system. *Family Process,* 1975, 14(4), 457-469.
4. Selvini Palazzoli, M., Boscolo, L., Cecchin, G., & Prata, G. *Paradox and counterparadox: A new model in the therapy of the family in schizophrenic transaction.* New York: Jason Aronson, 1978.

12

Interaction in Rigid Systems
A Model of Intervention in Families with a Schizophrenic Member

MAURIZIO ANDOLFI   ANNA M. NICOLÒ
PAOLO MENGHI   CARMINE SACCU

This is the first comprehensive presentation of work in progress on a five-year research project on intervention in rigid systems with particular reference to families with a schizophrenic member.

Work on this project was initiated two years ago as a part of the research program of the Italian Society for Family Therapy and has been carried out at the Family Therapy Institute in Rome.

FLEXIBLE SYSTEMS AND RIGID SYSTEMS

The hypotheses presented in this article are based on the postulate that the family group is an *open interactional system* that interacts with other systems.[3] Family processes, like those of all intrinsically active organisms, can be modified. The family's inherent capacity for change enables it to achieve *self-regulation* by means of rules that it develops and modifies over a period of time and *to adapt* to the varying demands posed in different phases of its life cycle.[7] The family system ensures both continuity and growth through a dynamic equilibrium between two functions common to all systems: a tendency toward homeostasis (H) and a capacity for transformation (T).

Therefore, to achieve change in a family group, the existing relationship between homeostasis and transformation has to be modified in favor of the latter. On the other hand, to stabilize and maintain the new structure, the H/T relationship has to be modified in favor of the former. Consequently every change or adjustment is preceded by a temporary state of *imbalance* between H and T. The degree of imbalance depends on the importance of the change and subsequent stabilization that take place.

The capacity to modify an existing equilibrium between homeostasis and transformation differs from one family system to another and can be measured objectively. Some systems can easily alternate between their capacity for change and their ability to maintain the status quo, whereas other systems find it particularly difficult. Family systems can therefore be described as *flexible* or *rigid* according to their position on a scale that goes from a maximum to a minimum degree of flexibility.

We describe a family system as more or less rigid according to the degree of difficulty it has in attaining new equilibria in response to developments that occur during its life cycle. The situations that are potentially disruptive to its equilibrium—such as individual growth, marriage, birth, aging, and death—coincide with the normal developmental processes of the family system. Therefore, flexibility and rigidity are not intrinsic characteristics of the structure of a given system; they are relative to variations in the state and the dynamics of the system at a particular *time* and *place*. For example, a system that is flexible in State A may become rigid in State B, and so forth.

While the evaluation of a system in a longitudinal perspective provides information concerning the system's evolution, a spatial parameter enables us to evaluate the relationships existing here and now among the members of the system as well as their respective levels of individual growth and differentiation. In the course of time, the family should be capable of modifying the equilibrium between the *functions* of its members (the state of cohesion) and the *growth* of each individual (the state of differentiation).

A family system becomes rigid when an accumulation of functions or the inability to modify these functions in the course of time interferes with the members' needs for differentiation. When opportunities for self-expression are reduced because of increased demands at the level of function, the group structures rigid relationships that progressively compress the energies existing within the system, and communications with the extrafamilial world become impoverished. The family group then creates a complicated network of functions that become mutually reinforcing and crystallize relationships in stereotyped roles. Consequently, the members lose opportunities for new and differentiated experiences and information, which are perceived as threatening to the family's equilibrium. There is a growing confusion in each member between *personal space* and *interactional space*, or between the locus of the individual's definition of his or her self and the locus of his or her negotiated transactions with the outer world.* This kind of confusion is usually attributed only to a mentally disturbed individual. In reality, it is the system itself that presents a serious psychiatric symptomatology, permitting each member to intrude into the personal space of the other members—for altruistic or even "therapeutic" motives. Such behavior ultimately leads to an impoverishment of personal space (although this is invariably denied) and to a massive reduction of free interaction (interaction not motivated by one member's "mental illness"). As the individual self becomes increasingly impoverished, interpersonal matters and needs gradually replace personal ones. Individual emptiness is then filled in by a role, determined by the family's preconceived image of each member's function.† Thus, personal space is reduced further, and interactive space becomes even more rigid, setting up a vicious circle.

This kind of situation is particularly evident in families with a schizophrenic patient, where the kind of limitations to flexibility that we have described are clearly present.

A Model of Intervention: The Formulation of a Strategy

We differentiate between rigid and flexible families for therapeutic purposes and because we assume that rigidity is a component of family pathology and an obstacle to treatment. Our evaluation is based on the specific manifestations of rigidity observed during therapy.

We should note, however, that the system under observation in therapy is not the family itself but the family in interaction with the therapist. This *therapeutic system,* composed of the family plus the

---

*All space, including personal space, is created and defined in relation to others.

†The term *role* is used to indicate the system's codification of the function of each member.

therapist, evolves dynamically; it creates its own structure, whose rules are defined gradually during the course of the therapy.

Some families, more effectively than others, interact with the therapist in ways that tend to *enmesh* him or her in the family's transactional rules. The enmeshment of the therapist leads to the formation of a therapeutic system that is just as rigid as the family system. It will be equally incapable of modifying its H/T relationship, or its own equilibrium, during the course of therapy. Our objective is to prevent the formation of a therapeutic system of this kind.

When intervention takes place in a family whose capacity for transformation is easily activated (that is, when the tendency toward homeostatic rigidity is not preponderant), the T of the therapist and the T of the family integrate, potentiate each other, and facilitate a rapid solution of the problem. On the contrary, if the therapist's T activates a family system whose T has been suppressed by rigid internal rules, the family will perceive the therapeutic T as threatening and will eventually neutralize it by assimilating it in its own homeostasis.[4] The more the therapist openly opposes the family's H, the more the family system will respond by reinforcing the status quo. Even if the existing equilibrium is a source of intense suffering, it will be defended at any cost because it serves to maintain interactional solutions that the members believe to be the only ones possible. After years spent in carefully selecting acceptable transactional modalities through an arduous process of trial and error, the family sees the present situation as the best that it can achieve.

The therapist can promote change in families of this kind by disguising the therapeutic T as H, thereby supporting the H of the family system. He or she can even prescribe or suggest ways of reinforcing the existing homeostatic equilibrium. Since the family will not be able to oppose the therapist's T, which is now syntonic with its own H, it will be forced to change. It will have to liberate its own T in order to demonstrate that the therapist is making a mistake in confirming the family's tendency to resist change.

We have utilized this methodology in the interventions carried out as part of our research project. The diagram on page 175 differentiates four basic phases of intervention. Each phase will be exemplified by excerpts from sessions held with rigid families (a member of each family had previously been diagnosed as schizophrenic). Longitudinal studies have also been carried out on each family.

The diagram on page 175 indicates the successive modifications

Interaction in Rigid Systems

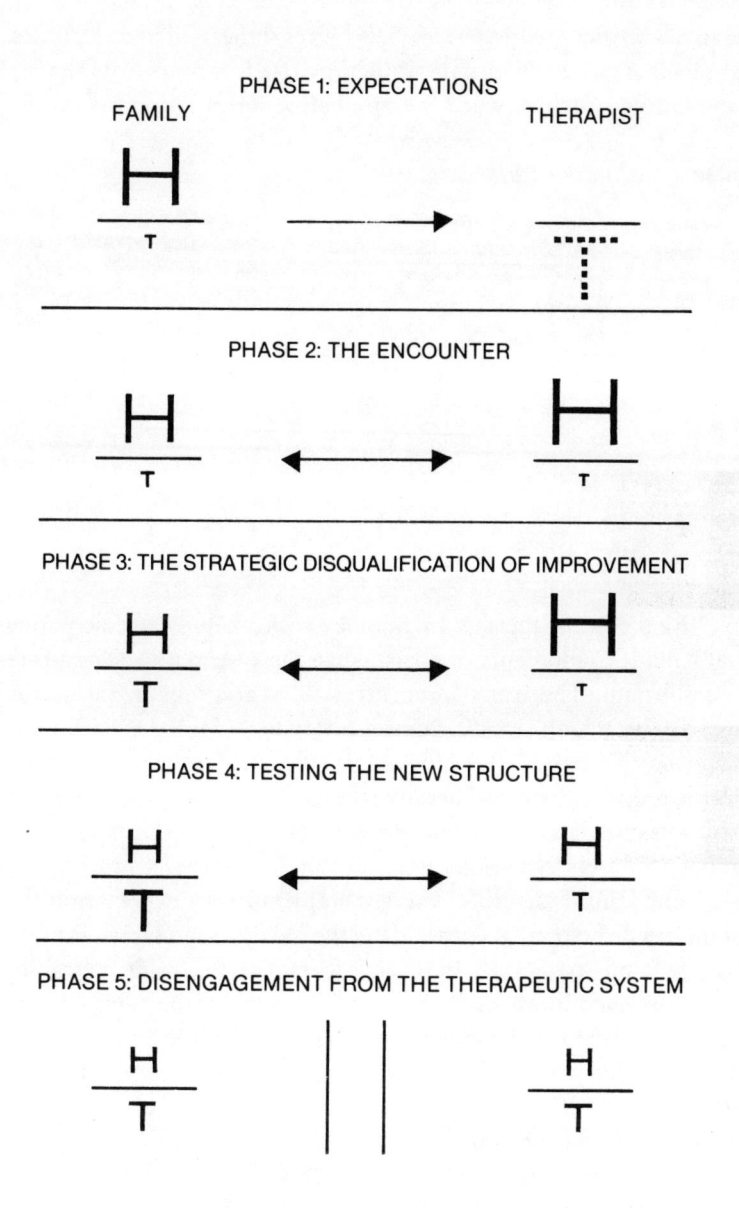

PHASE 1: EXPECTATIONS

FAMILY — THERAPIST

$$\frac{H}{T} \longrightarrow \frac{}{T}$$

PHASE 2: THE ENCOUNTER

$$\frac{H}{T} \longleftrightarrow \frac{H}{T}$$

PHASE 3: THE STRATEGIC DISQUALIFICATION OF IMPROVEMENT

$$\frac{H}{T} \longleftrightarrow \frac{H}{T}$$

PHASE 4: TESTING THE NEW STRUCTURE

$$\frac{H}{T} \longleftrightarrow \frac{H}{T}$$

PHASE 5: DISENGAGEMENT FROM THE THERAPEUTIC SYSTEM

$$\frac{H}{T} \quad || \quad \frac{H}{T}$$

175

of the relationship between homeostatic tendencies (H) and tendencies toward transformation (T) in the family–therapist relationship during therapy. The therapeutic process has been synthesized in five phases. The first phase is not really a part of therapy itself; it represents the attitude of the family system toward therapy before intervention begins.

Phase 1: Expectations

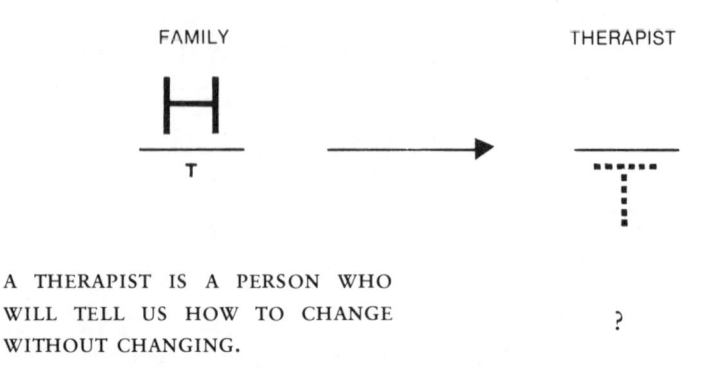

FAMILY   THERAPIST

$$\frac{H}{T} \longrightarrow \frac{}{T}$$

A THERAPIST IS A PERSON WHO
WILL TELL US HOW TO CHANGE   ?
WITHOUT CHANGING.

Requests for therapy by families with a schizophrenic patient are usually made in moments of crisis, when the system perceives a threat to its equilibrium. The fear of uncontrollable variations in the status quo coexists with a long-standing desire for change. However, although real change may be desired, it is blocked by all of the family members because it seems too threatening. Therapy is regarded in the same way: it represents the same danger as other potentially disruptive situations that the family encounters at various times during its *life cycle.*

The family therefore enters therapy with the expectation that the therapist will help to reconsolidate the system's previous equilibrium. Since the family requests help when it fears that it is losing its stability, its behavior is even more rigid than usual. Basically the family wants the therapist to perform an impossible task: *to change a situation while adhering to the same rules of interaction that have served to maintain that situation in the past.* Clinical experience has shown that these contradictory expectations on the part of the family often create a situation in which the therapist attempts to cure a family group whose members unite to demonstrate the futility of his or her efforts. As a result, a rigid therapeutic system is formed in which family–therapist interactions tend to crystallize in increasingly static and predictable roles and functions.

Phase 2: The Encounter

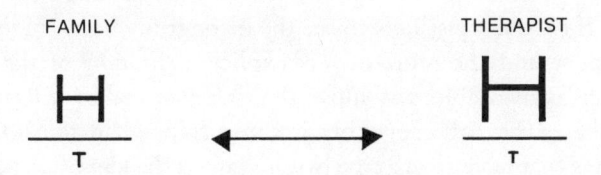

FAMILY	THERAPIST
H̄	H̄
T	T

← →

PROVOCATION

HELP US, EVEN IF IT IS IMPOSSIBLE TO HELP US.

The family requests the therapist's help to produce change in the identified patient. All of the family members, however, including the patient himself, define him as incapable of changing—because he is crazy.

Since all previous efforts have failed, change is impossible.

COUNTERPROVOCATION

YES, I WILL HELP YOU BY NOT HELPING YOU.

The therapist indicates that he is willing to initiate therapy, and at the same time, *he or she denies his or her role as an agent of change.* The therapist agrees with the family that it is impossible to change the situation and even emphasizes the need to maintain the status quo. He or she challenges the family system's homeostasis by redefining the patient's symptomatology positively and *reinforcing its function.*

All differences and conflicts among the members of these families are disguised by their unanimous agreement on one issue: that the only one who needs treatment is the identified patient. The patient is invariably *brought* to therapy by the others. Since the patient is considered crazy, he or she is not conceded the right to make decisions, nor does he or she claim this right. The patient's behavior in the sessions tends to underscore three basic characteristics of all family transactions: the patient's symptomatology is of central importance to the system, apparently filling the family's entire world; all of the patient's communications (even those that are fully appropriate) are denied any validity; consequently all efforts made by the family or by outsiders to modify the patient's behavior are doomed to failure.

The family's request, based on these premises, can be formulated as follows: "Help us to cure him by telling us what to do to make him normal." If the therapist fails to see the incongruity between the request for treatment and the more-or-less explicit definition of the patient's disturbance as incurable, any move the therapist makes will prove ineffectual. She or he will inevitably become trapped in the homeostatic mechanisms that have so effectively maintained the identified patient in a passive yet central role as the crazy member of the family.

How can a person unanimously considered incurable possibly be cured? If the therapist ignores the paradoxical message transmitted by the family system and openly accepts a therapeutic role, the question of the patient's curability will eventually become a battleground between the two factions. On the one hand, the therapist will try to force the system to effectuate real changes; on the other hand, the family members will engage in a collective campaign to demonstrate its own good intentions and the failure of the therapist.

The identified patient will be completely excluded from the whole process, and his or her inadequacy will thus be reconfirmed once more.

Our approach consists in regarding the message transmitted by the family as a *provocation* and trying to formulate a therapeutic strategy that constitutes a *response* to this message.

We immediately respond with a *counterprovocation*, using the identified patient as our entering contact to breach the defenses of the family system. The therapist directly confronts the member who is defined as incapable of behaving adequately or autonomously. This constitutes an explicit challenge, for the therapist *strategically denies the abnormality of the identified patient's behavior.* If the therapist successfully creates a context in which the patient's illogical and involuntary behavior appears logical and voluntary, the system will begin to destabilize and will become less rigid.

If this strategy is to be effective, the therapist must immediately discredit all attempts by the system to present the situation as pathological. Since the identified patient's mental illness regulates the entire family system, and all familial roles and functions revolve around it, the therapist has to present the idea of change as something to be feared. A struggle will still be inevitable, but paradoxically it will be a struggle in which the therapist maintains a more rigid position than the family, so that the family's habitual transactional style will enter into a state of crisis.[8]

Interaction in Rigid Systems

In this first phase of therapy, the therapist attacks the system by depriving the identified patient of his or her power to control family relationships by behaving "crazily."* By redefining the patient's behavior as logical and voluntary, and by supporting his or her function as the acknowledged, indispensable, and irreplaceable leader of the family (no other member could perform this function as well), the therapist destroys the family's alibi for playing its usual transactional game: maintaining a scapegoat so that the members can avoid open conflict.

The therapist's counterprovocation serves a twofold purpose: it divests the identified patient of his or her *power to control* the family, and it reevaluates him or her as a person capable of autonomous behavior. By simultaneously *attacking the patient at the level of function and supporting him or her at the level of self,* the therapist encourages the identified patient to accept the challenge of presenting himself or herself in a more authentic way within the family.

As she or he redefines the patient's "crazy" behavior, the therapist also warns the family that any modification of the present situation would jeopardize the family's hard-won equilibrium. The therapist's position represents a *strategic negation of therapy.* Since the family expected the therapist to try to change the unchangeable, his or her effort to reinforce the family's homeostasis—expressed as "Don't change anything"—will come as a surprise. At this point, the family's difficulties will probably become more severe, although in many cases the deterioration of the situation will be more apparent than real, and it will be flaunted by the family to demonstrate that the therapy is a failure. However, if the therapist adheres to his or her strategy consistently, defining even the deterioration of the situation as confirmation that the patient's behavior is logical, voluntary, and useful, he or she will gain entrance into the family system, and its members will be able to begin exploring new areas and functions.

The following excerpts from sessions with a family with a designated schizophrenic member illustrate what has been said. Therapy with

---

*Although symptomatic behavior is usually considered an expression of suffering on the part of the individual and the other family members, it is clear that this behavior also has positive advantages for everyone concerned. Frequently we make the mistake of underestimating the enormous power—due in large part to its "involuntary" nature—that the symptom bestows on the identified patient to control relationships with others. The symptom is simultaneously a prison and an instrument of power.

this family was carried out by a team composed of the four authors, one of whom worked directly with the family in the therapy room while the others observed through the one-way mirror. Twenty-three sessions were held. Initially, the meetings took place weekly, and later, every two weeks. All of the sessions were recorded on videotape.

The Fraioli family asks us for help after many years of trying various kinds of treatment without success. The nuclear family lives in a small city in northern Italy. Their social and cultural level can be described as middle class. The father is a doctor with a strict Catholic upbringing. He is sexually repressed and a generally stern man. The mother, an apparently conventional and dutiful housewife, surreptitiously controls the organization of family life. There is a large age difference between husband and wife, who became parents of four children late in life. The three oldest children are boys; the youngest is a girl. Only Giuseppe, the youngest boy, lives at home with his parents. He is the identified patient.

Giuseppe is 28 years old. He has become progressively more isolated in the past few years. At present, he no longer goes out of the house at all. His detachment from outer reality, his depression, and his aggressive behavior at home culminate in crises of psychomotor agitation and, at times, in serious attempts at suicide. Giuseppe has given up hope of finding a job, even though he has completed law school with a brilliant record. He spends all of his time alone in his room or wandering about the house. He masturbates openly, using intimate apparel belonging to his mother. He has told his mother that he desires sexual intercourse with her.

By now, *Giuseppe's illness dominates the life of the family.*

Ten minutes of the first session have gone by. The father, the mother, and Giuseppe are present. Giuseppe is sitting between his parents and seems very tense. He looks at the floor with an expressionless gaze while his parents talk about him.

THERAPIST (*to the father*). I'd like to find out how Giuseppe is feeling because I would feel very uncomfortable in his place.	*The therapist interprets Giuseppe's nonverbal messages and makes them explicit. He reads his behavior, which in other contexts is considered inappropriate, as a manifestation of a plausible state of mind. He shows that he is in-*

GIUSEPPE. I don't feel at all uncomfortable.

T. Right now you look extremely uncomfortable... even the way you're sitting...

G. Now I'm pissed off.

T. Hmm... let's say you're pissed off... about being here?

G. (*more decidedly*). No, I'm pissed off because of my goddamned tricks.* I don't need sympathy from anyone, I don't need any help with my damn tricks, I can manage perfectly well by myself.

T. Give me an example of what you mean by tricks, because maybe the way we use the word in Rome is different from the way it's used where you live.... Maybe you don't mean what I am thinking of.

G. (*provocatively*). I want a woman so I can shove it up her ass, but I've never done anything.

T. You want to...?

G. Shove it up her ass.... But I've never done anything...

T. Do you mean you've never shoved it up a woman's ass, or

terested in the patient as a person and not only in his symptomatic behavior.

The patient's response to the therapist is clearly provocative. The mother and father appear worried, grieved, and resigned to their role as parents of a mentally ill son.

The therapist does not retreat from Giuseppe's linguistic assault; on the contrary, he calls attention to it and uses it himself. The way that the therapist calmly repeats and analyzes Giuseppe's words gives his behavior a connotation of normality.

The therapist insists on concrete, specific answers, which makes

---

*Giuseppe uses the slang expression *puttanata*, from *puttana* ("prostitute"). A *puttanata* is something unworthy; it also has the connotation of a "gyp" (translator's note).

you've never had sexual relations of any kind?

G. I've had some sexual relations ... but only using certain methods. Anyway, only with hookers.

T. Well, they are more willing, aren't they? What is the problem? I mean about shoving it ...

G. (*surprised*). What did you say?

T. I mean hookers really are more willing, aren't they? They have a more easygoing attitude toward their own bodies. Did you have any problems with them?

G. No.

T. I don't see where the tricks are, except in the literal sense of turning a trick with a hooker. I still don't understand what you mean ... can you explain it better?

G. I'm ashamed, so I get inhibited, I always get inhibited ...

T. You mean you get inhibited about shoving it up a woman's ass or about having sexual relations in general? That's not clear to me.

G. This year, and maybe even last year, too, I made proposals to a few women, but I never got anywhere.

T. Okay, but I still don't know what you mean by your damn tricks.

Giuseppe's statements seem less eccentric. It also deprives the patient of power and reduces the sense of drama in the session.

The therapist's implicit redefinition of Giuseppe's behavior as normal constitutes a counterprovocation of the identified patient and his family. Giuseppe responds with surprise.

MOTHER (*ingratiatingly*). May I...

T. (*to Giuseppe*). You told me that you are pissed off because of your goddamned tricks. I think there are lots of young men your age who would like to take a woman and shove it up her ass.... I don't know what seems so extraordinary to you. Maybe you want some very special kind of an ass... maybe that's what makes you feel bad...

Depriving Giuseppe of the family's support enables him to explore other personal areas.

The initiative is now firmly in the hands of the therapist. He encourages the patient to confront him directly.

G. I think it's something I'll never be able to obtain...

T. From yourself or from women?

G. What did you say?

T. From yourself or from women?

The context is now completely appropriate. The difference between the "patient" and the other participants is losing all significance.

G. From women.

T. Are you sure?

G. I think so.

T. Because from the way you talk, it sounds as though you have some problems of your own.

At this point the father and mother intervene, trying to convince the therapist that Giuseppe's behavior is really very seriously disturbed. The therapist responds:

T. I really don't understand.... You have taken a long trip by train, you even had to sleep in Rome last night in order to come here today.... If the problem is

The therapist explicitly denies that the identified patient is mentally ill.

183

just shoving it up someone's ass, I can't see why the situation is so serious.

FATHER. But he has tried to commit suicide because of that...

T. Yes, I know, but so far I have no idea of how that all happened. It doesn't seem to be a problem that deserves so much attention and so many doctors...

The parents now start relating a series of episodes to support their conviction that Giuseppe is in fact very ill. The therapist interrupts them and again resumes his provocation of Giuseppe.

T. Would you please wait a moment, Mrs. Fraioli, because Giuseppe is still pissed off and I can't work with a family with a son who is... how old (*to Giuseppe*)?

The therapist blocks the parents' attempt to reinstate Giuseppe as "the patient." He circumscribes his objective, keeping Giuseppe under fire.

G. Twenty-eight.

T. Twenty-eight years old. If you were only ten, I could accept your sitting here in silence and looking pissed off while your parents talk about you. But since you're twenty-eight, I can't accept it... so either we have to end this meeting or talk about why you are pissed off.

Since the therapist refuses to let the patient continue playing the role of the sick member who needs protection, he cannot accept the patient's silence. He therefore defines Giuseppe's silence (and all of his other behaviors in the sessions) as voluntary.

G. I'm in this mood because...

T. Perhaps I had better explain this to you better: a person can be depressed, or worried, or sad—but if he's pissed off, he certainly won't cooperate. Do you see what I mean? That's what worries me... if you are pissed off, you won't be able to help us. If your mother or father or I... if any of us were pissed off, he wouldn't be able to help. So if we don't deal with the fact that you are pissed off, I can't go on. I even had to interrupt your mother who was trying to tell me what happened in 1972.... Maybe you are pissed off at me...

G. (*animatedly*). Yes, as a matter of fact, while I was waiting to come over here, I was saying, "Now I have to go to see that pain-in-the-ass."

Giuseppe returns the provocation...

T. I'm glad you call a spade a spade. I like that, you are frank.

... and the therapist redefines it in a positive sense.

G. Of course, since...

T. But I want to know just one thing. Why are you pissed off, here, today.

G. You want to know what's bugging me?

The therapist again invites the identified patient to deal directly with a concrete issue.

T. Yes, precisely.

G. Because by now this situation has become a tremendous nuisance, I'm fed up, I'm pissed off, I'm furious. For example, I'm continually bugging my parents... but naturally I don't do the same thing to my brothers and sister because they would think I was nuts ... so I don't do it to them.

T. Just a minute, I understood everything up to a certain point, but then I couldn't follow you anymore... because in my opinion it's

By surpassing the patient's own use of provocative language, the therapist implicitly defines Giuseppe's behavior as appropriate. We begin

not that they would think you were nuts—but that they would tell you to shove it up your ass.

to notice a difference between the parent's protective attitude, based on the premise that Giuseppe is mentally ill, and the reactive behavior of his siblings, based on the assumption that Giuseppe's behavior is voluntary and responsible.

G. You are right.

T. That's different from thinking that you're nuts.

G. They would think I was nuts, and they would also tell me to shove it.

It is interesting to note that Giuseppe labels his own behavior as pathological.

T. No, I think that they would tell you to shove it because they don't like to consider you nuts. It's a completely different story with your parents. They protect you because they're worried and they're afraid that you are nuts—so they think they can't tell you to shove it.

G. What did you just say? My parents are afraid that...

T. Basically, your parents are worried because they think you aren't capable of behaving like an adult, or of being independent—and they think that if they tell you to shove it up your ass, you will get worse.

The therapist does not attack the parents directly. He points out how their love and concern for Giuseppe lead them to protect and stigmatize him.

The following excerpts from the subsequent session illustrate how the family counterreacts.

M. You probably don't know about it, but after we were here last Tuesday, Giuseppe was worse than ever on Wednesday, Thursday, and Friday. He was in a terrible state, locked up in his room all day...

As predicted, the family claims that the situation became worse as a result of the previous session. Their message is clear: "Therapy is useless, even dangerous ... but ...

Interaction in Rigid Systems

F. In complete isolation.... Now what do you think we should...

... help us anyway."

M. He was just lying there on his bed almost the whole time. We were worried... we talked to Doctor X about putting Giuseppe in the hospital for a while...

G. I brought my law books to the hospital with me so I could study a little, because at the end of October I have to get sworn in as a practicing attorney... I guess I was still thinking about continuing work with my brother, who's a lawyer.

Simultaneously, an autonomous aspect of Giuseppe's behavior comes to the fore: his concern about exams and his future career as a lawyer. Giuseppe implicitly calls attention to the absurdity of his hospitalization, which he planned to utilize as a normal study period.

T. I don't understand who it is that thinks you are better off in the hospital in these circumstances.

G. Are you asking me?

T. Yes, because I have a feeling that you want me to think that your family wants to get rid of you. But it really looks as though it's your system for gaining a sort of Pyrrhic victory over them.

The therapist continues to focus directly on the identified patient.

G. In what way?

T. By creating a big fuss, by going into the hospital to create a fuss. That's clear, isn't it?

The therapist affirms that Giuseppe's hospitalization was voluntary. It was Giuseppe himself who decided to go to the hospital, not because he was sick but to attract attention.

G. By creating a fuss in what sense?

T. In the sense that your parents would have to visit you, worry about all sorts of things, stay with you all the time...

G. But they seem to be just as worried when I'm home, since lots of times...

T. Don't shift the problem to your parents.

The therapist persists in his efforts to deprive the patient of control over family relations and to prevent the other family members from intruding into Giuseppe's personal space.

G. My mother told me several times that the situation is intolerable.

T. Let's not talk about your mother... you are the one who chose to go to the hospital.

The therapist reemphasizes the voluntary aspects of Giuseppe's behavior.

G. It's not true that I chose to go, I really didn't want to go there ... but my brother and my cousin bugged me so much that I just had to go.

T. You know, I can accept the fact that you don't want to cooperate—but last week you were more frank.

G. What do you mean about accepting that I don't want to cooperate?

T. What I mean is that you are playing the part of the guy who needs a crutch, and you force your parents to try to convince you to be a good boy...and then you even try to insinuate that they should feel guilty about the way you behave. Right now you *(to the parents)* seem to be very upset by Giuseppe's efforts to blackmail you—he tries to kill himself if you don't pay

The therapist explicitly affirms that every member of the family has a specific role and function and that these are reciprocally complementary. This is the reason that any change would be dangerous, unless it serves to reinforce the system's homeostasis. The therapist's position amounts to strategically denying therapy, or, "I am doing therapy to avoid doing therapy."

enough attention to him. So we can't begin family therapy unless this situation remains exactly the way it is. You will have to avoid changing anything, because you have all learned how to live with this situation, and you all accept it.

The therapist prevents the family from replying by getting up, saying good-bye, and terminating the session.

Phase 3: The Strategic Disqualification of Improvement

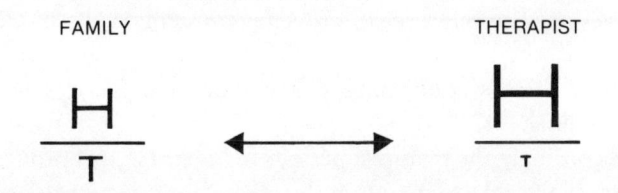

FAMILY	THERAPIST
$\dfrac{H}{T}$ ⟷	$\dfrac{H}{T}$
PROVOCATION	COUNTERPROVOCATION
THINGS ARE GOING BETTER (analogic message) BUT THINGS ARE WORSE (verbal message). YOU ARE NOT HELPING US, BUT HELP US MORE.	THINGS ARE EVEN WORSE THAN YOU THINK. IF YOU WANT ME TO HELP YOU, COOPERATE BY NOT CHANGING ANYTHING.
The identified patient has shown obvious improvement, but the family either denies this or defines it negatively (he has become worse). The family seems to have a more favorable attitude toward therapy, even though they claim that it is counterproductive.	The therapist, observing that the situation has improved, *asserts that things are much worse,* confirming his stated view that nothing can or should change. He solicits greater collaboration in maintaining the status quo *by prescribing the family's own dysfunctional rules.*

In this phase, the characteristics of the encounter between family and therapist change with respect to the preceding phase. The behavior of the family in the sessions is now incongruous in a different way. The members no longer present a united front. The patient has clearly improved, but the other members claim the contrary. While on the one hand the family communicates through its official spokesman that progress has occurred, on the other hand the system cannot afford to *define the situation as improved.*

The family members, particularly the parents, implicitly express a desire to continue therapy. They realize that as an outsider, the therapist is in a position to establish a direct and outspoken relationship with the identified patient. An open confrontation of this kind could not occur within the family itself, because it represents a modality of encounter prohibited by the system's present transactional rules. Although at one level these rules are dysfunctional, at another level they serve to protect the family's cohesion.

On the basis of these premises, we have developed a therapeutic strategy designed to reinforce improvement pragmatically by *disqualifying* it. That is, the therapist defines the improvement as a worsening of the situation, thereby confirming his stated opinion that it is better not to change anything.

Accordingly the therapist persists in his strategy of provocation by instructing the family to maintain the status quo—just at the time when changes are beginning to occur. The therapist justifies his position by pointing out the potential risks inherent in these changes. Once again, the therapist attacks the system through the identified patient, this time provoking him on the question of his improvement.

Paradoxically the therapist's provocation has the effect of reinforcing the system's tendency toward transformation. The therapeutic strategy is actuated in three successive moves:

1. *Refusal to recognize any improvement.* The therapist behaves as though he were totally unaware of the first signs of improvement.
2. *Redefinition of improvement as dangerous.* The therapist warns the family of the risks involved in change, thereby activating the family's own worst fantasies and fears concerning possible modifications of the system. Once these fears are brought to light, they lose their destructive power, and as change begins to appear less menacing, the process of change that is already under way is strengthened.
3. *Prescription of nonchange.* The therapist prescribes behaviors intended to accentuate the system's dysfunctional rules. He

presents the prescription as a necessary precaution to avoid change. Thus he paradoxically supports the improvement taking place and creates a new sense of cohesion among the family members. The family must now struggle to demonstrate that it *is* capable of changing.

Giuseppe participates more actively in the following session.

T. (*a few minutes after the beginning of the session*). Giuseppe, I'd like to ask you right away whether you've had any new problems this week, because I can see from your face you are... less on guard than usual.

The therapist immediately disqualifies the obvious improvement.

G. What do you mean?

T. You are less on guard. What has happened?

G. A little confusion.

T. I'm not interested in the usual things. I want to know if there's been some big problem, something exceptional.

The therapist envisages a situation that is worse than the family's most dire fantasies. Therefore whatever the family members say about the deterioration of the situation will fall short of the therapist's expectations.

G. (*surprised*). No, no really big problems.

T. I must be mistaken then, but...

F. We had an enormous problem in bringing him here, because this morning...

T. But that's just a normal problem... Giuseppe, I definitely have the feeling that you are less on guard.

G. What do you mean? I don't know what you mean.

M. Forgive me for butting in, but maybe the doctor is talking about the fact that you did some extra activities...

T. Mrs. Fraioli, you must have a sixth sense.

M. I think you (*to Giuseppe*) should tell the doctor that you worked at your desk two or three times...

T. Ah, that's the reason you seem less on guard.

The therapist continues to define Giuseppe's improvement negatively.

F. Even though he said that everything is useless, that it doesn't do any good. You said that right afterwards, didn't you? You said you would do something self-destructive.

G. I know perfectly well that if some day I decide to do the same things my brothers do, I'll manage perfectly well, but I would have to give up...

T. Your *function*.

G. I don't know what... I'd have to give up a fantasy world.

T. Your *function*, and I think you're being very naive by behaving differently. Naive because you are under the illusion that someone else can or wants to take over your function... that perhaps someone else could do it better than you. Can you suggest someone?

The therapist makes the situation explicit: he warns Giuseppe not to abandon his function within the family system. Being less on guard means losing his control over the system, abandoning his role as family "watchman." The therapist's message is obviously provocative.

G. What did you say? I didn't hear you.

T. Can you suggest someone else... someone who can take over your position at home, who would be as watchful as you are?

The therapist persists in defining Giuseppe's new attitude as inopportune and dangerous for the family's stability. He terminates the session by assigning a task intended to reinforce the system's dysfunctional rules:

- The parents are instructed to observe closely all abnormal behavior on Giuseppe's part. They are to discuss his behavior each evening, recording all details in a notebook.
- Giuseppe is told to stay at home for the following two weeks. He is not to modify his usual behavior in any way. Any adult behavior on his part, whether voluntary or prompted by his parents, will be considered a breach of the agreement and a failure to uphold his vital function in the family.
- Giuseppe and his parents are asked to guarantee that the instructions will be scrupulously carried out. They are asked to note any transgressions in writing.
- The following session will be held only if the participants submit the written material requested.

The therapist reconfirms his support of the family's homeostatic tendencies by defining any future autonomous moves by Giuseppe as a betrayal of his family function. He actually instructs Giuseppe to persist in his symptomatic behavior and requests the family to observe certain family rules faithfully. The rules that the therapist specifically prescribes are those concerning Giuseppe and his parents' close surveillance of each other's behavior. In carrying out these instructions the family will be forced to take cognizance of its real situation, which will rapidly appear intolerable to each of the members. The ultimate objective of this strategy is to strengthen generational boundaries and to permit greater individual autonomy.

Giuseppe and his parents bring a series of written notes to the following session. These notes are utilized by the family to contradict the therapist's view concerning the importance of Giuseppe's function. Moreover the notes indicate that Giuseppe went out of the house on several occasions to visit a friend and that he was irritated by his parents' continual anxiety.

The therapist expresses his disappointment in the family in general for its failure to cooperate in therapy and in Giuseppe in particular for relaxing his vigilance over family life.

Phase 4: Testing the New Structure

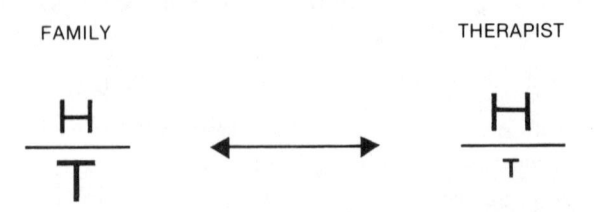

FAMILY   THERAPIST

$$\frac{H}{T} \longleftrightarrow \frac{H}{T}$$

WE DISAGREE WITH YOU BECAUSE THINGS ARE REALLY CHANGING.	I'M NOT CONVINCED. PROVE IT WITH FACTS.
The family contests the therapist's definition of the situation "things are worse and nothing should change") and insists that improvement has occurred in the identified patient's behavior as well as in family interactions in general.	The therapist responds with disbelief of the structural changes that the family claims are taking place. *He warns the members of the risks involved and states that he will accept modifications of the situation only after real changes have been ascertained* at the level of family subsystems.

The underlying *family structure* can now be seen more clearly. The system is more willing to reveal its real relationships and inner tensions. Therefore the therapist can more easily verify hypotheses concerning the family's modality of functioning, the composition of its subsystems, and the differentiation of functions and their respective boundaries.[6] Previously the behavior of the identified patient was determined almost exclusively by his function as the sick member; during this phase, he begins to differentiate himself within the various subsystems.

Improvement is now more evident, both in the patient's symptomatology and in the interactional modalities of the entire system.* The family now feels directly responsible for the changes that have occurred. Therapy has progressed from an earlier phase in which improvement actually occurred but was denied to a phase in which the family vindicates the merit of having modified the situation through its own efforts. However, since these changes were achieved in an effort to prove that the therapist was wrong, the results may prove to be unstable. The family is really in a *new state of abnormality,* even though it has taken a step forward in dealing autonomously with its own difficulties.

Whereas at the beginning of therapy the family expected to delegate all responsibility for treatment to the therapist, the entire family is now participating actively in the therapeutic process. This change has come about because the system is now more willing to risk change, despite the intrinsic threat to its previous equilibrium. The family now "transfers" its homeostatic tendencies to the therapist, so that he becomes responsible for maintaining the system's homeostasis, thereby relieving the family of a considerable burden.

The therapist now expresses greater willingness to accept the movements occurring within the family system. However, he demands that they be *tested.* In other words, he asks the family to demonstrate that the stated changes actually lead to verifiable results. These changes are to be tested first in the sessions and then at home, thus reinforcing the movement toward change and extending the therapeutic process beyond the weekly sessions.

While working out new transactional modalities for the therapist, the family members have an opportunity to experience the advantages of change and they learn to function autonomously. The therapist's specific requests encourage the family to deal with the difficulties inherent in change, thereby deepening their understanding of the interactional dynamics that interfere with the realization of their goals.

As the family structure becomes more evident, the therapist expresses doubts concerning the family's desire for change. He points out the advantages of the status quo and underscores the dangers of the unknown. Instead of threatening family homeostasis, he presents obsta-

---

*The two aspects are inseparable: an improvement in the symptomatology of the identified patient is a response to modified interactional patterns, which are in turn elicited and reinforced by the identified patient's responses.

cles to the family's request for change. It is through the process of dismantling these obstacles that the family gradually achieves greater autonomy—to demonstrate to the therapist that his fears are unfounded.

Once the family has become more flexible, we can apply a typically *structural* approach, promoting new interactions among and within the various subsystems.[5]

The following excerpts from the 13th session, in which only the parents participated, illustrates this phase of therapy.

M. Now I'm feeling tired, beat, I think I'll take a little rest...

F. But I can sum things up. It's true, Giuseppe has changed recently... he hasn't stayed in bed at all. He went to court a few times with his brother, he has done some studying... he is always carrying his books around...

In this phase, the father participates more actively and responsibly.

T. Children's books?

The therapist interrupts, expressing incredulity. His tone is provocative.

F. No, law books. He really has made an effort to straighten out. True, if I ask him about it, he says, "I'm doing this but I'm convinced it's all over for me...." But he used to be consistent in this completely negative attitude... he stayed at home. Now, if his brother calls him down to the courthouse, he goes.

T. I'm not convinced by all of this. I'm surprised that after all of the experiences you've had, you believe in it so blindly.

F. It's not that I believe in it.... I'm wondering, I'm telling you about it...

T. I'm trying to tell you that I don't believe in it. I didn't expect to find any improvements today. At the most, a few well-rehearsed scenes... but nothing that would be so dangerous for all of you.

M. In my opinion, Giuseppe is making progress.

Now both parents agree that an improvement has taken place. It seems as though the therapist's doubts have reinforced the parents' conviction.

F. But don't you understand that just a minute ago the doctor said that he doesn't believe in Giuseppe's efforts to rehabilitate himself? He said it in so many words: "I don't believe in it," and maybe he has good reasons. It's true that Giuseppe says, "I should look for a job"—and then he says, "But I can't."

M. At this point I want to say something. From the fifteenth to the twenty-sixth—I've got it written down right here—those were all good days. Giuseppe spent all of those mornings at his brother's office, and he stayed home very little.

F. We shouldn't be convinced, I agree. The boy might do something crazy tomorrow.... But in fact ... another positive thing has happened. Giuseppe won a case and we only found out about it from the newspaper. We didn't even know he was working on this case, so I think that if we're careful not to get our hopes up too high—even Franco (*the oldest son*), who is always cautious and never goes overboard in his judgments, said to my wife yesterday that...

The parents want to convince the therapist that an improvement has occurred. If the therapist accepts this view, the family's collective efforts toward improvement would probably come to a halt. The therapist does not budge from his position of incredulity. This position is paradoxically reassuring to the family and allows the system to move further in the direction of change.

M. He has noticed that Giuseppe seems more interested in his work.

F. Yes, he says that Giuseppe has some real interest in his work.

T. I still don't trust all of this—it's too risky. Giuseppe can't just give up his function like this. You haven't given me sufficient guarantees.

The therapist implies that his doubts can be allayed only if more substantial changes can be demonstrated.

Even though the therapist has introduced the idea of further change, he spends the rest of the session warning the family not to modify their habitual modalities of interaction. In particular, the therapist insists that Giuseppe should continue to play the role of watchman—a role that is extremely useful to everyone and that he plays with perfect self-abnegation. Implementing the therapist's instructions creates considerable stress and increased family tensions, which are expressed through the identified patient. An explosion occurs in the following session, and Giuseppe refuses to participate in subsequent sessions:

G. This idea of going to a psychiatrist and talking about your own fucking business is completely ambivalent. NO! You can all go and shove it up your ass. I accept my life just as it is, so stop bugging me. Goddamn it all, I don't bug you, so lay off me. Then we'll be even!

T. I think Giuseppe is telling us in his way that he doesn't feel like whining today. I'm very pleased. I wasn't expecting it.

The therapeutic team interprets Giuseppe's absence from the subsequent sessions as a positive development. It confirms that an important structural change has occurred. Previously the family system could not tolerate any distance between Giuseppe and his parents, and particularly between mother and son; therefore the parents' decision to continue therapy without Giuseppe is indicative of an important structural modification. According to the parents' reports, we learn that Giuseppe

Interaction in Rigid Systems

has also become more autonomous. Several sessions are devoted to consolidating the newly established distance between parents and son. The therapist then sends a letter to Giuseppe via the parents.

The therapist's letter to the identified patient is intended:

1. To acknowledge Giuseppe's efforts to consolidate a more autonomous position.
2. To renew the strategy of provocation by again prescribing the patient's symptomatology.
3. To further a sharper delineation of boundaries between the spouse subsystem and the patient.
4. To establish an equivalence between Giuseppe's autonomy and that of the parents.

This is the text of the letter:

Dear Giuseppe,

I realize that you have been making a considerable effort to participate more effectively in family therapy. Your participation from a distance is particularly constructive for you, because there is no risk of your becoming dependent or passive toward therapy. I hope that you will continue to behave as creatively as you have in the past (stay in bed as much as possible, masturbate frequently, bug the rest of the family, threaten to commit self-destructive acts, don't work, etc.) until you are absolutely certain that your parents will be able to carry on alone and that they no longer need your function.

The therapist gives the letter to the parents with the following instructions:

- *The letter should be read aloud daily by either the father or the mother in the presence of the other spouse and Giuseppe.*
- *After each reading, all three should discuss their thoughts about it.*
- *If Giuseppe refuses to participate, the letter should be read by the parents at the set hour in another place or outside of the house.*
- *The following session will be held only if these instructions have been carried out.*

The letter reinforces the general strategy utilized in this phase, redefines Giuseppe's behavior as creative, and focuses attention on the functional characteristics of the family system. Although the letter is formally addressed to Giuseppe, it is really addressed to the entire family system. In fact, the entire family reacts to it. The third instruction (the parents should read the letter outside of the house if Giuseppe is absent) provides another opportunity for the parents to confront each other and strengthen their conjugal relationship while separating themselves from their son. Progress toward this objective—of increasing the parents' independence from Giuseppe—began with the parents' decision to continue therapy without Giuseppe's participation.

In the following comments by the mother, made after implementing the letter-reading task, it seems as though the parents have achieved a deeper and more objective understanding of how the family functions:

> ... it might appear that we parents are the ones who benefit from Giuseppe's functions in order to be able to carry on ourselves. But it also seems to me that we are very much involved in and influenced by our son's behavior. This influence would no longer exist if he behaved logically, like an adult. In any case, I, his mother, realize that we parents have to force ourselves not to be influenced by his function.

The parents seem bravely determined to struggle—with *the help* of the therapist—*against* their own need for Giuseppe's function.

Phase 5: Disengagement from the Therapeutic System

FAMILY | THERAPIST

$$\frac{H}{T}$$ $$\frac{H}{T}$$

THINGS HAVE CHANGED. WE THINK WE CAN CARRY ON BY OURSELVES.	YOU HAVE DEMONSTRATED WITH FACTS THAT YOU ARE ABLE TO CHANGE. YOU NO LONGER NEED ME.
The family no longer utilizes the identified patient, who has lost his central position in the system. All of the members function more autonomously in the various family	The therapist *expresses his satisfaction* with the real change that has taken place.

subsystems as well as outside of the family group. A new family cohesiveness makes it possible to disengage from the therapeutic system.

By progressively decentralizing himself, he facilitates the family's disengagement and encourages the individual members to achieve further personal autonomy.

In this phase of therapy, therapeutic progress can be easily evaluated because there is now very little difference in the way the family functions in the therapist's presence and the way it functions in daily life. The family's ability to interact more freely is a result of both the deeper level of comprehension attained within the therapeutic system and the reduction of the family's defenses. It becomes relatively easy, therefore, to draw a detailed family map. It is surprising to find how frequently the family itself is able to make an astute evaluation, describing its own situation in simple terms that nonetheless reveal a remarkable comprehension of the system's structural realities. One of the most striking characteristics of the system at this time is the decentralization of the identified patient. Giuseppe's position is both less preeminent and more personalized. He has begun to deal autonomously with his own authentic needs and desires, and his behavior no longer draws the constant attention of the other family members. Similarly the other members feel freer to experience and deal with the satisfactions and difficulties arising in their own personal lives.

At this point, the "healthy" family begins to feel a need to test out its newly acquired autonomy without the help of the therapist. In an earlier phase (which we described as a "new phase of abnormality"), the family was able to progress only through opposition to the therapist. Now, in moving toward a more genuine autonomy, the danger remains that the family's fears may cause a return to an earlier phase. To avoid this risk, the therapist reassures the family concerning their new situation and helps them to understand the process of change more clearly. Each member is encouraged to reexamine the various aspects of the changes brought about by the group's collective efforts.

After the therapist and the family have jointly evluated the present situation, the time has come to plan differentiated programs for the future. The therapist encourages each member to plan creatively and realistically. He offers to remain available for further periodic meetings in which progress toward fulfillment of these plans can be jointly examined.

In this terminal phase, the therapist's general strategy and his specific interventions seem so simple and clear that it is easy to underestimate their importance. But superficiality or haste can cause the therapist to make serious errors. The therapist's moves at this time should lead to his own decentralization and to a gradual diminution of his power, which is no longer essential to the success of the therapy.

If the therapist fails to abandon his central position, he will block the movement toward autonomy that is under way. In working with families with a schizophrenic patient, it is more difficult to achieve a situation of equality between therapist and family than in work with other family groups. This process requires considerable time and caution, so that separation does not occur too abruptly.

We will now briefly describe developments in the Fraioli family during the concluding phase of therapy. The material that follows confirms the validity of the program laboriously carried out in the last sessions.

Giuseppe repeatedly sends news about the progress he is making, and he now defines his behavior as "normal." His symptoms have not reappeared, although he says that he has not yet resolved all of his problems. He adds, however, that he will no longer resort to self-destructive behavior. He expresses some worries about the future, but he is leading an active life and no longer withdraws to his former regressive positions.

He has passed the bar examination and is running a law office together with his brother. He is also studying in order to increase his professional acumen. He has taken vacations with friends and found this new experience gratifying. He has become friendly with a boy of his own age with whom he spends part of his free time. He also frequently visits his oldest brother, who lives in a nearby city, and has established a close and meaningful relationship with him. He is enthusiastically planning a trip through Lazio and Umbria for next year's vacation.

The parents, early in therapy, had begun to spend a few extra days in Rome each time they came there for the sessions. Then, for the first time in their lives, they planned and actually took a vacation without any of their children. They were surprised and pleased to find that they did not talk about Giuseppe, nor did they feel guilty about this. They were amazed by the fact that Giuseppe had gone off by himself on a trip to Assisi, a few days before their own vacation began. They said they felt as though he had "beaten them to it."

Some tensions emerged that they attribute to their "differences in personality." However, they feel that their relationship has been revitalized by discussing their conflicts. The father says that he has "rediscovered" Giovanna, his adolescent daughter, and that his relationship with her, which had been interrupted without his realizing it, has been renewed.

The gradual disengagement of the family from the therapeutic system renders the members more independent. Each one must now assume responsibility for the family's modified situation, in which each participates with fuller understanding. The individual members now have broader areas of personal autonomy and are less bound by family functions. Each one is now taking stock of his or her new position and the opportunities that it offers.

SUMMARY

The authors classify families as flexible or rigid on the basis of their capacity to modify the equilibrium between homeostatic tendencies and their capacity for change during the family's life cycle.

The authors analyze the ways in which rigid systems attempt to enmesh the therapist in their own dysfunctional roles, and they present an original model of strategic intervention. Since the rigidity of the system is expressed through provocative messages addressed to the therapist, the therapist responds with a counterprovocation intended to force the system to move in the direction of change.

Four basic phases of therapy are described and illustrated by transcripts of sessions with a family with a schizophrenic patient.

REFERENCES

1. Andolfi, M. Paradox in psychotherapy. *American Journal of Psychoanalysis,* 1974, 34, 221–228.
2. Andolfi, M. La ridefinizione in terapia familiare. *Terapia Familiare,* 1977, 1, 7–27.
3. Andolfi, M. *Family therapy: An interactional approach.* New York: Plenum Press, 1979.
4. Andolfi, M., & Menghi, P. La prescrizione in terapia familiare: Parte seconda. *Archivio di Psicologia, Neurologia e Psichiatria,* 1977, 1, 57–76.
5. Menghi, P. L'approccio strutturale nella terapia con la famiglia. *Terapia Familiare,* 1977, 1, 53–74.

6. Minuchin, S. *Families and family therapy.* Cambridge, Mass.: Harvard University Press, 1974.
7. Selvini Palazzoli, M., Boscolo, L., Cecchin, G., & Prata, G. *Paradox and counter-paradox.* New York: Jason Aronson, 1978.
8. Whitaker, C. Psychotherapy of the absurd: With a special emphasis on the psychotherapy of aggression. *Family Process,* 1975, *14,* 1-16.

13

Communicational Aspects of Therapeutic Systemic Transaction with the Psychotic Family

Philippe Caillé Charlotte Buhl
Pål Abrahamsen Bente Sørbye

Systems-oriented family therapy involves a special kind of transaction between therapists and family over a limited period of time. In this form of therapy, a successful outcome (i.e., the restructuring of rigid, homeostatic rules) is largely determined by the very form of what is conveyed to the family. In the psychotic family, the form of communication is of so great a significance that one may say that the way a communication is expressed is almost synonymous with its meaning. Because the form a message takes is so important to these families, the therapists must be especially sensitive in talking to this kind of family. Consideration of this issue requires the therapists to use time, space, and their relationship with each other as it is manifested to the family in order to formulate effective and adequate communication. In other words, the therapists should be rigorous in planning their use of digital and analogue communication.

Digital and Analogue Communication

In practical situations, it may be difficult to make a sharp distinction between the digital and analogue aspects of communications because they are expressed simultaneously. One may try to distinguish them by defining the written transcript of an interview as the digital part of the interaction. In order to be meaningful, such a transcript must contain sequences of words that have both symbolic content and logical order. This digital language allows a rapid transmission of abstract concepts to the reader. However, it cannot sufficiently express the emotional quality of human communication; the finer gradations of intensity and the more subtle nuances are lost.

The analogue part of the communication is everything else that takes place during the interaction: the way words are pronounced, modulation of the voice, facial expressions, body movements, activity in the room, etc. The analogue language contains a wealth of detail for the description of relationships between people. It is not dichotomized as is digital communication.

It is important to note that the analogue part of the communication always tells something about how the digital part is to be interpreted. The expression "I hate you" accompanied by a big smile and seductive body movements will bring the receiver to understand the word *hate* more as meaning "sexual attraction" or "love." On the other hand, it is impossible to influence digitally how the analogue part of the communication should be perceived. One cannot deny with words that one smiles or looks angry.

The analogue part of the communication is on a higher logical level than the digital part; it expresses a communication about communication, that is, a metacommunication.[10] Digital messages, like this paper, will not reproduce adequately the real interaction that takes place in therapy or elsewhere.

The Family and Its Myth

We shall here describe a clinical situation to illustrate the complexity of the phenomena.

> A family with five members comes to an outpatient clinic. The mother has called and told the therapist that the oldest daughter, Marie, 20, has a problem in controlling her weight. She has been depressed from time to time, lacks initiative, and appears withdrawn. Mother and Father are in their 50s. The two younger sisters are Eva, 19, and Anne, 14.
> Mother and Marie sit down beside each other, their post-

The Psychotic Family

ures almost identical. Father sits on the opposite side of Marie, somewhat further away from Marie than Mother. Eva and Anne sit closely together opposite the other three, and the therapist takes an empty chair beside them.

The therapist addresses Marie and politely asks what is the matter with her. Each time he asks, Marie, in a weak and depressed voice, begins to explain her depression or her previous attempts to lose weight. Mother, however, soon interrupts and takes over the description of Marie's symptoms in a detailed and rather determined manner. Father volunteers some rather unimportant details, but the two younger sisters do not seem to be interested. They discretely move their feet, apparently playing some kind of game.

The therapist becomes somewhat uncertain in this situation. Is the problem in this family that Mother needs a sick daughter, or is it that Marie needs parents, particularly a mother, who believe in her pathological condition?

It is very unlikely that a question (i.e., the digital mode of communication) will clarify this. Instead, the therapist decides to make use of analogue communication. He asks Marie to sit between her sisters, while he takes the now empty chair between the parents. If it is true that Mother needs a sick daughter and Marie has to be loyal to her mother's need, the new situation could create relief in Marie when the physical space between Marie and Mother is increased, not as a result of her own will but as prescribed by the therapist.

The opposite happens. Marie displays irritation in her new position between her sisters. They abruptly stop playing and seem slightly worried. The parents seem relieved, especially the mother, who allows Marie to speak without interruption. Now the therapist begins to perceive the family myth. Marie defines herself as sick and demands that the others be loyal to her. Her parents must be supportive and understanding. The sisters must not consider her one of them; Marie is a separate subgroup, the "sick sister."

The therapist continues to explore the situation analogically. He defines all family members at a symmetrical level by asking each one if he or she has had any eating difficulties, weight problems, depressive periods. Marie now shows increased irritability and becomes openly aggressive. In this way, she makes it clear that it is of no use to compare her difficulties to problems that other family members may have experienced. Her problems are so special that the others can not possibly understand them. They must limit themselves to showing empathy and respect for her suffering.

The present family myth (i.e., their shared interpretation of their difficulties) now is easy to see: Marie suffers deep internal conflicts that only she herself fully understands. All other members of the family are concerned about her condition and will do everything they can to help her, especially Mother. However, their empathy is of little real help to Marie. This represents a difficult situation for all of them, and thus the family has agreed to come for a family therapy session.

The Psychotic Family

In psychotherapeutic work with psychotic families, we are confronted with situations much more complex than was the case in the previous example.

The family myth in psychotic families might more correctly be compared with Chinese boxes. The investigator opens one box, only to be faced with a new, smaller box, which in its turn contains another box. It appears as if there is no way he or she can solve the problem.

This appearance results because the psychotic families' defenses, and also their sufferings, are built upon a very complex definition of the relationship of the family members to each other. Role definitions may seemingly originate in the remote past; one may even discover patterns that are stable across two or more generations. The functional value is lost; only the homeostasis-preserving function still persists. It becomes a mask confirming other masks in a meaningless, tragic, and seemingly inevitable performance.

The point of departure for a possible change is the paradoxical situation that is created when the family seek therapy. They present the therapists with the wish that the disturbing symptom in the sick member should disappear. At the same time, they say that this most probably will not be possible, because they have already tried every means of changing

The Psychotic Family

the unwanted behavior. They seek change, but none of the family members is willing to take advice or follow instructions.

Members of such a family are extremely anxiety-ridden in presenting their wish for change, and they obviously believe that the family and its members will be destroyed should they abandon their belief in the family myth.

It would be of little use here to apply a linear, explanatory way of understanding the family's situation. Every attempt to explain or clarify, to make distinctions between cause and effect, will be opposed or disqualified. The family will either stop coming, or they may outmaneuver the therapists by increasing their symptoms.

The only possibility is to challenge every paradoxical definition given by the family with an adequate therapeutic counterparadox. The basic counterparadox is to state, as an expert, that the family is at the moment forbidden to change. The therapist will then acknowledge the existing behavior in the family as necessary at the present time, even if it is not fully understandable. By doing this, the therapist forces the family into a new situation. They may continue to follow their previous rules, but they are now prescribed by the therapist. Hence they acknowledge the authority of the therapist, which is a change. Or they may oppose the therapist's prescriptions and have to set up new rules among them, which also is a change, but of a different kind.[9]

Psychotic families are experts in redefining relationships in a paradoxical way. Every prescription by a therapist will be disqualified if possible, leading to an apparent redistribution of roles, and the situation may soon look as hopeless as before. This form of stability may express itself in a change of symptoms within the defined patient, the onset of symptoms in a different family member, or the failure of the family to come for therapy. Neither one single therapist nor two opposite-sexed cotherapists may fully avoid being taken in into the power field of the psychotic family. Live supervision is therefore, in our experience, essential. The observer(s) stays behind a one-way mirror and may from there study the family's rules as expressed in the therapy situation. Observers are less prone to become involved, and they may contribute with logically based evaluations of the situation and suggest potent interventions.

The therapists will have to consider carefully the number of paradoxical messages to be used and their content. Interventions should support homeostasis when the family seems about to change. On the other hand, they should be challenging when the family is in a homeostatic phase or when the family seems to be on the verge of taking control of the therapy. The therapist must also evaluate what should be conveyed digitally and analogically. It is also important to take care that the interventions fit the social context, in order to avoid unnecessary conflicts.

Social Context of the Therapeutic Intervention

There tend to be certain stereotypes that define what attitudes and expectations patients and therapists have about therapy. In our Western culture, the therapists are supposed to be experts, representatives of a rationally based science. Their tasks are to diagnose abnormal behavior and to ameliorate or remove psychiatric symptoms. The family members are expected to be worried about the abnormal behavior of the sick member and to give him or her much attention.

Some therapists regard this cultural context as limiting and attempt to free themselves and their clients from such expectations. This, however, is a pointless stuggle. We cannot escape the set of rules and myths that govern the larger system, the society, to which both families and therapists belong.

From the first session, the therapists are met with a sum of digital and analogue signals that, in our cultural context, point to a possible chain of causality, that is, the explanatory myth.[3,4] If the situation is experienced as so difficult that it becomes threatening, the therapists may easily be drawn into one of two types of destructive stereotypical reactions.

The first type of reaction is to start a logical argument (on the digital level) about the adequacy of the myth. The Siberian shaman who is requested by the family to liberate them from evil spirits will not bring about a cure by denying the base of such a superstition. Neither is the Western therapist of much help if he or she starts to discuss who is really sick and what psychiatric illness is all about. On the other hand, it would be destructive if the Siberian shaman or the Western psychiatrist naively believed that the cause of the problem was found exclusively in the power of supernatural forces or in the attack of a hypothetical psychiatric illness.

The first step is, therefore, not to be caught in one of these stereotypes. The aim is to attempt to understand the digital, analogical,

The Psychotic Family

and cultural components of the family myth as it is presented by the family and to give this understanding back to the family. This approach may consist of a redistribution of roles within the old myth, a strengthening of this myth, or a new myth introduced by the therapist. A situation implying a possible choice is in itself a change. It is of little interest if the family accepts or rejects the hypothesis. There will therefore not be any power struggle between the family and the therapist about who is right. The family's definition of their problems is respected and becomes the point of departure for the therapists in making their next move in the therapy.[6]

Choice of Therapeutic Intervention

In the difficult therapeutic work with psychotic families, the therapist's ability to respond adequately to the different moves made by the family is of crucial importance to the therapeutic process.[7] In the following pages, we will describe selected incidents from different therapies. These descriptions, however simplified, will illustrate the use of different modes of communication in the interaction between family and therapist. The chosen examples are not necessarily crucial to the outcome of therapy.

Case 1

An analogical intervention may challenge the logical explanation given by the family for their problems:

> A couple in their 30s with two small children apply for family therapy. They have seen several therapists for a number of years but have never really felt that this therapy has been of help. The husband is chronically depressed and has periods with acute aggression when he breaks the furniture. Suicidal attempts and aggressive conduct have led to his admission to a psychiatric clinic. The wife is more controlled and is cold and shrewish toward her husband. She declares that it is only a question of time before she collapses. The children seem inhibited, possibly retarded, in this family where the conjugal drama dominates. Conflict is apparently the only means of relating in this family. The therapists are

asked to change a situation that is defined as unchangeable. To probe into the possible reasons for this conflict will analogically imply that the therapists take over the responsibility for solving the problem. What other reason could there be for asking questions? On the other hand, it would create much anxiety in this family should the therapist admit any incompetence. Such an admission might force the family into a new, panic-stricken search for therapy, perhaps with new dramatic episodes.

In this case we chose to let the two opposite-sexed therapists be seduced into allying themselves without compromise with the spouse of the same sex. They sit next to "their" partner in sessions, take identical body postures, and speak more or less the same words. After a few sessions the situation is dominated by a forceful argument between the therapists about the marital conflict. The spouses are called upon to elaborate only when the therapists need details about their conflict.

The spouses are hence placed in a paradoxical situation. They are now the experts and may only comment upon the statements made by the therapists on their marriage. Their only chance to get back to their roles as patients is to redefine their relational problems.

Case II

Splitting the sessions into different phases may also be a way of reframing the family myth:

A married couple and their three children come for family therapy. The problem is the father's uncontrolled use of alcohol and his destructive aggression. The children's reaction appears to be a combination of hyperactivity and withdrawal. During therapy sessions, the father is obviously guilt-ridden and at times berates his wife. The mother usually is kind and forgiving, but at times she rejects and humiliates her husband. The spouses define their problems in a rather detached way and have no real expectations from this therapy.

After five sessions, we declare the marriage to contain so much suffering that it is unlikely ever to change. We ask the children to leave the therapy room so that the parents may have a

The Psychotic Family

chance to discuss with the therapists alone how they can protect their children from the bad influence of the marriage. After half an hour with the parents alone, we suggest that the parents go to the waiting room and we invite back the children. We now wish to teach them how to protect themselves from the bad influence of the parents' marriage.

In this way, we have underlined the family's definition: the spouses are helpless and the marriage makes them irresponsible parents. We will offer parents and children separate guidance to protect the minors from the bad marriage. This redefinition will allow the family to reframe the problems, and maybe it will bring about roles more appropriate for parents and children.

Case III

To support the family members' positions may also be a way to redefine the family myth. A well-known technique in working with psychotic families is to prescribe the psychotic behavior during the first session with the patient and ask him or her to try not to cover psychotic outbreaks but willingly to follow every such impulse. The "spontaneous" or "irresistible" psychotic behavior will then often soon disappear temporarily, making it possible to work with patients defined as difficult or dangerous, for example, in an institution.

To obtain more lasting changes, however, it is important to instruct all family members, not only the symptom carrier, not to change their behavior.

> A family consisting of two parents in their 50s and three children in their teens begins treatment. Their reason for seeking therapy is that father has been anxious and depressed for some years. His memory is poor and he functions badly at work. The worst problem, however, is his alcohol consumption. He is not able to determine whether he drinks to calm his nerves or whether he is an alcoholic. This uncertainty makes him despair, and he now drinks all kinds of alcohol, from light beer to hard liquor. The mother criticizes the father not so much because of his alcohol intake but because of his weakness and his unrealistic plans for the future. The children seem rather uninformed about the problems in the family. They are criticized by the parents for their lack of interest.

> The therapists conclude that it is absolutely necessary to determine the nature of father's use of alcohol. As is well known, we tell them, an alcoholic is a person whose use of alcohol does not limit itself spontaneously. To understand the father's drinking pattern, we ask him to drink exclusively the strong beer for which he has a preference during the next few weeks. He is to drink as much as he finds natural. The mother is to help the father by being critical of any suggestion that reveals his tendency to promise more than he can give. Even if the children may feel tempted, we say, they are not to stay at home more than usual, and they are not to influence the situation more than is natural. In this way, everybody's conduct is prescribed by the therapists.

Such redefinitions with main emphasis on analogue communication have been used by many family therapists. An example is the "therapeutic meal" used by Salvador Minuchin in the treatment of anorexia nervosa. The family is invited to share a meal during the session. They are asked by the therapists to behave as naturally as possible. The feared meal situation is thus reframed, and the use of food symbols is made impossible. The therapist has created a new, relational context, offering a possibility for redefinition.[8]

Case IV

Use of the spatial dimension—for example, a change of the seating arrangement in the therapy room—is also a way to redefine or comment on the family myth.[1]

> Let us consider a family of six members where the father and mother are in their 50s, the two daughters are 30 and 25, and the two sons are 20 and 17 years old. At the start of therapy, both boys are inpatients in a psychiatric hospital, diagnosed as psychotic. During the first session, the mother seems to need to control the men in the family. On her left sits her husband, whom she time and again interrupts by hitting him and shouting. This man, who has achieved a high-ranking position outside the home, does not get a chance to finish one single sentence in his own family.
> On the mother's right are the two boys, whom she treats as small children with kisses and cuddles. The daughters sit opposite

The Psychotic Family

the mother, apparently representing the sane part of the family. However, it soon becomes clear that they must send messages about mood changes to their mother in a ritualized way in order to maintain their "freedom."

In the fourth therapy session, the female therapist seats herself on the mother's left and places the daughters on her own left. The male therapist chooses a chair on the mother's right, taking on his right the boys and then the father. Both therapists declare their concern for the mother, because she has too much responsibility in the family. They hope that all the family members will meet in the parents' home to listen to the mother at fixed intervals. They must not interrupt or discuss, only listen.

At this point one of the sons was discharged, as his behavior had normalized; the other was considered "better" by the hospital staff. The mother was anxious, restless, and often mildly intoxicated during the therapy sessions.

An effective redefinition of the family situation was obtained by placing the mother in a protected position between the therapists and declaring her the central and most threatened person in the family. At the same time, an important part of the family myth was exposed by placing the men (the "weak persons") on one side with the father at the periphery and the women (the "strong persons") on the other side. In this way we were able to comment upon the situation without expressing any form of criticism or wish for change.

Case V

The following example demonstrates the difficult transition period that frequently occurs when treatment is to be terminated. This often leads to a power struggle between the therapists and the family, and the family may express anxiety and denial of any improvement in order to continue therapy:

Two parents in their 50s have a daughter of 26 and a son of 22 years. The son is the designated patient. He is a student, and during the past year, he has felt that he has been criticized and followed. Therefore he has isolated himself from his fellow students. Initially he displays a bizarre and rigid posture; his face is distorted by involuntary grimaces. Toward his parents, he is cold and accusing, yet at the same time, he seems to feel responsible for their relationship.

After eight sessions, the son has markedly improved, and the relationships in the family seem to have changed. However, if the therapists suggest termination, we feel that we might risk a panic reaction and a worsening of symptoms.

The ninth session starts with a statement from the son that he has forgotten to write in his diary about the state of his health as prescribed earlier by the therapists. The analogue part of this statement seems to be that he does not consider this activity necessary any more. The only complaint he now has is that his student obligations have not been very demanding lately, with the result that he has not been able to test himself fully. At the end of this session, the female therapist carefully and calmly reads a conclusion stating in essence that the therapists have evaluated the situation as improved, both for the young man and for his family, even though they are aware that the young man's study situation is not as demanding as expected. We suppose, she says, that it will not be too optimistic to have the family come back in six months.

The male therapist gives no support while she is reading. He seems to be worried and moves restlessly in his chair. In this way, he conveys analogically that the therapists may not agree and diminishes the implications of the oral message given by the female therapist.

The message is very well received. The parents are nodding approvingly, and the boy smiles triumphantly. The family feel safe and are willing to take upon themselves the responsibility for the future. Each of the therapists denies the importance of the changes obtained, thereby underlining the family homeostasis.

Conclusion

Different forms of psychotherapy have very different explanatory models. These will often be fundamentally contradictory and thus impossible to unify. However, it is interesting to note that certain basic principles seem to be generally valid in facilitating change during therapy.

One such principle is that the therapist must carefully evaluate the timing and the content of the therapeutic interventions. A correct intervention may not work or may even be destructive if it is introduced too early— or too late—in therapy. The concept of premature interpretation is well known from psychoanalysis.

Also there seems to be an agreement among most schools of psychotherapy that important changes in behavior take place abruptly, not smoothly and progressively, as one might logically conclude. Again, this finding is supported by psychoanalysis, where the important phenomenon of insight seems to come all of a sudden and often dramatically during the course of therapy.

Some contemporary schools of family therapy seem to disregard this common knowledge and base their efforts on a pedagogical model. These therapists teach patients to express the same message both digitally and analogically, to be congruent. Our daily life experiences, however, ought to make it clear that this is a very moralistic and utopian aim for psychotherapy.[2] Investigations of families randomly picked from the general population have shown that every family member makes use of analogue communication to dilute, modify, or even deny the digital part of communication. The view that double-bind messages or incongruences can in themselves create mental illness in a family has long since been abandoned.

Systems-oriented family therapy pays much attention to the timing, form, and content of therapeutic interventions. A well-chosen challenge to the family's myth may indeed cause surprising and profound changes in the family's internal balance.[5] Alarming, long-standing symptoms may suddenly disappear, and at the same time, one may observe attitude changes in family members other than the patient.

Correct therapeutic intervention of necessity requires good theoretical knowledge of systems thinking, interest in the family as an emotional unit, and an imaginative use of the available modes of human communication. The therapist must be able to appreciate the complexity of human interaction and make use of this complexity in his or her therapeutic interventions. Even if it might be tempting, it does not pay off in the long run to try to simplify human phenomena that one intends to work with seriously.

REFERENCES

1. Andolfi, M. *La terapia con la famiglia.* Rome: Astrolabio, 1977.
2. Caillé, P. La question des modèles théoriques en psychothérapie de famille. *Annales de Psychothérapie,* 1974, *8,* 4-11.

3. Caillé, P. Qu'est-ce que le syndrome psychiatrique? *Annales de Psychothérapie,* 1976, *12,* 22–27.
4. Caillé, P. Familiepsykiatri. *Tidsskrift for den Norske Laegeforening,* 1977, *97,* 1621–1624.
5. Caillé, P., Abrahamsen, P., Girolami, C., & Sørbye, B. A systems theory approach to a case of anorexia nervosa. *Family Process,* 1977, *16,* 455–456.
6. Ferreira, A. J. The question of family homeostasis. *Archives of General Psychiatry,* 1963, *9,* 457–463.
7. Minuchin, S. *Families and family therapy.* Cambridge, Mass.: Harvard University Press, 1974.
8. Rosman, P. L., Minuchin, S., & Liebman, R. Family lunch session: An introduction to family therapy in anorexia nervosa. *American Journal of Orthopsychiatry,* 1975, *5,* 846–853.
9. Selvini Palazzoli, M., Boscolo, L., Cecchin, G., & Prata, G. *Paradosso et controparadosso.* Milan: Fetrinelli, 1975.
10. Watzlawick, P., Beavin, G. H., & Jackson, D. D. *Pragmatics of human communication.* New York: W. W. Norton & Company, Inc., 1967.

TRAINING

14

Research on Training in Marriage and Family Therapy
Status, Issues, and Directions

DAVID P. KNISKERN
ALAN S. GURMAN

In a recent publication, we reviewed the existing outcome research in the field of marriage and family therapy.[12] Through our study of the literature on the effectiveness of family therapy, we became convinced that previous reviewers (e.g., Beck,[3] Wells, Dilkes, & Trivelli[41]) had underestimated the research base for conclusions about the effectiveness of family therapy in general, as well as the specific factors affecting the outcome of family therapy. In contrast, after reviewing the literature on family therapy *training*, we have to confess our field's collective empirical ignorance about this topic. The paucity of research investigating training in family therapy parallels the state of research on training in individual psychotherapy,[8] despite the substantially longer history of well-developed training models and programs in the individual-therapy field. The deficient research base in the training of individual psychotherapists occurs across theoretical orientations as divergent as behavior therapy and psychoanalysis.

Since research on family therapy training is lacking in most regards, this paper focuses on three areas. First, the existing models and programs of training are discussed, including didactic, supervisory, and experiential techniques. Second, the major issues critical to an evaluation of family therapy training are presented and discussed. Finally, a methodology for the evaluation of training programs is outlined. Where research evidence exists, it is reviewed and used to support particular training models, programs, or techniques.

David P. Kniskern & Alan S. Gurman
Implications of Family Therapy Research for Family Therapy Training

We are unaware of any empirical study of either the process or the outcome of training programs in the family field. *There now exists no research evidence that training experiences in marital–family therapy in fact increase the effectiveness of clinicians.* An increasing body of knowledge about specific therapist factors that influence the outcome of family therapy does exist, however. To the degree that these factors are teachable, learnable, and focused on in training programs, their identification provides indirect support for the potential effectiveness of family therapy training programs.

In the most extensive review to date of the marital and family therapy research literature, Gurman and Kniskern[12] cited family therapists' experience level, therapy-structuring skills, and relationship skills as factors that influence the outcome of marital–family therapy. Of these three factors, the latter two are potentially teachable. High levels of experience, found by several researchers to increase the chances of positive outcome,[7,10,26,29] and by others to decrease dropout rates,[32] cannot be taught or learned. Nor does the literature allow a discrimination between experience as a marital–family therapist and experience as an individual and/or group therapist. One way to gain clinical experience is obviously through a family training program, but some additional gain from training programs, other than increased experience, must be demonstrated for justification of their existence. Furthermore, if family therapy experience per se does not produce more effective family therapists than equivalent amounts of experience in other therapeutic paradigms (e.g., behavior therapy, individual psychodynamic psychotherapy, group therapy), then one would have to confront directly the possibility that there is little about the skills usually thought necessary for practicing effective family therapy (e.g., Thom & Wright[37]) that go beyond those that are salient for psychotherapy in general (cf. Gurman & Razin[14]). While we certainly are not alone in disbelieving that this state of affairs in fact obtains, the null hypothesis is still to be disproved. Moreover we do not know whether there are *additive* positive effects of increasing levels of clinical experience in *both* family and nonfamily treatment methods. Nor do we know, despite common prejudices, whether, as is often argued, increasing experience in nonfamily methods may actually *interfere* with increasing one's competence in family therapy (cf. Haley[15]).

The second set of therapist factors influencing outcome, structuring skills, has been investigated by several researchers.[2,33,34] Included in structuring skills are directiveness, clarity, self-confidence, gathering information, and stimulating interaction. From the existing research, it is clear that the family therapist must generally be active and provide early structure, but without assaulting family defenses too soon.[11]

The ability of a family therapist to establish a positive relationship with his or her patients, as has been found in individual therapy, has received consistent support as the most important outcome-related therapist factor.[11,12] Therapist empathy, warmth, and genuineness, the so-called client-centered triad, appear to be very important in keeping families in treatment beyond the first interview.[30,31,39]

Relationship skills (affect–behavior integration, humor, warmth) have also been shown to have powerful effects on the outcome of family therapy.[4,5,21,38] The most impressive demonstration in this regard has been offered by Alexander et al.[2] Alexander et al. found that while structuring skill discriminated between two levels of poor outcome, only relationship skill was able to discriminate between good and very good outcomes. These factors appear to be related to positive outcome regardless of the theoretical orientation of the therapist.

The apparent importance of therapist relationship skills to family therapy outcome leads logically and directly to a consideration of criteria for the selection of family therapy trainees. While no research on selection has been published, it seems likely that such criteria, when explicitly developed, will prominently feature the personal qualities of the applicants rather than traditional academic credentials alone. Applicants will, in most cases, have been screened several times in their professional training with regard to their intellectual ability, and further screening of this order is likely to be only marginally profitable.

Some family therapy training centers (e.g., Philadelphia Child Guidance Clinic) require personal interviews and a videotape sample of a family therapy interview in their process of selecting trainees with previous professional backgrounds in other disciplines, for example, psychology and psychiatry. The long-range usefulness of such a costly procedure requires cost–benefit justification, yet on clinical and logical grounds it would seem to be an ideal method of trainee selection.

David P. Kniskern & Alan S. Gurman
Current Models of Family Therapy Training

At the present time, family therapy training exists in a wide variety of training centers and encompasses a wide variety of professional disciplines. Family therapy is taught in medical schools, universities, and family institutes to postgraduates, graduate students, undergraduates, and even nonprofessionals. Some programs seek only to train students to be family therapists, while others seek only to acquaint the student with family therapy as one potential modality of treatment worthy of clinical consideration. Some recently published surveys of well-known training centers have appeared (e.g., Beal,[44] Stanton,[36] Williamson[43]) that document the heterogeneity of such training goals.

Current models of training differ in what we consider to be three major dimensions. First, does the training lead to a degree or a certificate in family therapy? For example, academic psychology and social work training programs, regardless of the amount of family therapy training they offer, do not lead to such certificates, while graduate programs in marriage and family counseling do. Second, there is the issue of whether family therapy is the only form of therapy taught at a given training center. For example, even highly focused and specialized marriage and family counseling graduate school programs may require some experience with individual and group therapy, while family institutes generally do not. Finally, training programs vary on the matter of whether previous experience in psychotherapy, in terms of both amount and type, is required for admission. Some agencies expect demonstrated proficiency in individual therapy, while others feel that previous experience is not essential or, as noted earlier, may even interfere with learning to do family therapy.

Factors Influencing Training Models

Historically (cf. Olson[23]), the meaning of the term *family therapy* has been embedded in either of two major, and at times competing, conceptual frameworks. One framework has been concerned with the unit of treatment (i.e., the individual or the family) as the focus of intervention. The other conceptual framework has been concerned with laws of psychopathology (i.e., intrapsychic "versus" systemic). *Family therapy,* in the former framework, refers to the practice of treating the family as a unit. In the latter, *family therapy* has been used to describe a conceptual viewpoint adopted by a therapist, a viewpoint in which the family system is considered the patient, regardless of whom the therapist sees in treatment sessions.

The meaning that one attaches to the term family therapy *will directly affect the way in which one trains family therapists and evaluates that training.* If family therapy is viewed as a *technique,* a training program will focus primarily on the acquisition of technical skill, and the acquisition of specific technical skills will be viewed, accordingly, as the most appropriate criterion of the success of a training program. If family therapy is viewed as a new *conceptual approach* to the understanding of behavior and behavior pathology, then the acquisition of specific intervention techniques becomes a secondary goal. A training program using this latter perspective would focus its evaluation on the changing conceptual framework from which its trainees operate. The pragmatic consequences of the conceptual view taken of what constitutes family therapy are likely to become especially prominent in the substantive methods of training offered by a particular program.

Methods of Training

All family therapy training programs with which we are acquainted utilize three primary methods for training: didactic, supervisory, and experiential. The extent to which these methods are emphasized, however, varies widely. Differences often seem to be based on teachers' intuition rather than on research or even well-articulated hypotheses about essential and nonessential family therapy training components. Given the youth of the family therapy field, it is not really surprising that this state of affairs exists. This intuitive basis for orienting and structuring a family therapy training program is especially predominant in training centers that have a limited number of staff who are expert in this area. Aside from family therapy institutes and a small number of graduate programs in marriage–family therapy, both of which, of course, are very specialized, most family therapy training occurs in more diversified clinical teaching settings, that is, those of psychiatry, psychology, social work, and psychiatric nursing. In these settings, family therapy teachers often lack support from their peers and may find their work disregarded or even disparaged. When this occurs, it is predictable that a family therapy teacher will take a "hard line" and perhaps feel constrained to proselytize a single therapeutic method and to overemphasize a particular training method, at the expense of a more balanced program that includes significant amounts of training in all three spheres.

A more benign interpretation of the forces influencing this sort of intuitive program planning is, simply, that the marriage–family therapy field is still so young that it is actively struggling to develop effective curricula and that the multiple models of training emphasis thus reflect, in the field at large, a healthy attitude of experimentation.

Didactic Methods. The literature about family therapy is a disorganized hodgepodge of articles and books on a variety of topics. Few books or articles offer a comprehensive and integrated point of view about family therapy practice, either in general or according to a particular school of thought. Trainers of family therapists have few satisfactory choices for introductory texts or readings for beginning family therapists. Most family therapy training centers suggest a variety of readings to students, reflecting the diversity and "school" orientation of family therapy.[19] Schools of family therapy typically have focused on the work of a single well-known therapist, for example, Carl Whitaker, Salvador Minuchin, Murray Bowen. Each school has developed its own language and techniques and has often turned a deaf ear to the proponents of other schools, making comparisons by students difficult and frustrating when several viewpoints are presented.

Programs that present a single, integrated approach to family therapy avoid the confusion that might result from a sampling of the field's literature, but they run the risk of producing less creative or flexible practitioners. This situation is well described by Sluzki[35]: "The process of becoming a family therapist includes two tracks: one is identifying with and mimicking as tightly as possible a given teacher, and the other is reading a lot of stuff from different sources with the hope of transforming that melange into one's own private jig-saw puzzle."

Whether a family therapy training program that exposes its trainees to a wide range of views in the field is more likely to yield muddy-headed eclectics or thoughtful, flexible clinicians is unknown. Certainly there is great value in a budding clinician's developing a consistent sense of self-as-therapist, especially in his or her dealing with the understandable anxieties about his or her clinical competence. The precise nature of what is lost for the trainee who receives rather narrowly focused training is unknown. While we personally favor training models that expose neophyte family therapists to a reasonable sample of the multiple viewpoints that exist in the field, we would not want to impose our pedagogical biases on others. Furthermore careful study needs to be done of the *sequencing* of multiple exposure. For example, what are the training and learning costs and benefits of beginning didactic family therapy training from a broad base and then offering advanced training in more focal models, as opposed to reversing this order of exposure?

Supervisory Methods. Most trainers of family therapists would agree[19] that, as is the case in individual therapy,[8] the primary teaching of family therapy occurs in supervision. Techniques of supervision vary widely, from the use of traditional process recording of sessions with an individual supervisor, to group supervision using videotape, to live supervision and cotherapy. Some schools of supervision (e.g., behavioral) focus almost exclusively on the problems of the family being treated, while others focus almost entirely on the therapist, quite independently of specific cases (e.g., Bowenite), or on the therapist's relationship with the family (e.g., existential[42]).

The techniques utilized by the supervisor, and his style of supervision, are heavily influenced by his or her theoretical and therapeutic orientation. A directive, problem-oriented therapist (e.g., Haley[15]) tends to supervise in a direct, problem-oriented way, while process-oriented therapists tend to be more concerned with the personal growth of their supervisees (e.g., Whitaker, Napier, & Keith[42]). Such stylistic differences in supervision will very likely be translated into differences in therapeutic style by supervisees, although no study to date has investigated this very significant impact of training. Obviously these varying supervisory stances about the nature of family therapy, and hence of family therapy training, are saliently affected by whether a supervisor leans toward viewing family therapy as a treatment modality focused on the unit of treatment or as a conceptual perspective focused on principles of human behavior, development, and behavior pathology. Thus, while the conceptual–technical framework continuum referred to earlier is likely to influence all three spheres of family therapy training models (didactic, supervisory, and experiential), where a teacher stands on this continuum is most likely to exert a perceptible influence in the supervisory dimension of training.

The consequences of supervision style for supervisee therapeutic styles are underscored by work such as that of Pagell, Carkhuff, and Berenson,[25] who have reported that individual therapists who receive high levels of therapeutic conditions (empathy, genuineness, and congruence) from their supervisors are more likely to offer higher levels of these conditions to their patients. Such research has not been published with marital or family therapists as subjects, yet it is reasonable to assume that the results would be similar. The salience of factors similar to client-centered "therapeutic conditions" has already been demonstrated in marital–family therapy.[2]

Whether one invokes a psychodynamically based identification interpretation or a social-learning-theory-based modeling explanation to account for the specific mechanisms by which such effects on the supervisee come about, the pragmatic upshot is still the same: trainees learn by what they live in the immediacy of their interaciton with their supervisors.

Experiential Methods. Experiential methods for family therapy training fall into three main categories: personal therapy, whether individual, group, marital, or family; sensitivity training and role playing; and working with one's own family. The first two of these experiential methods are not unusual in the training of individual and group therapists, while the third is probably unique to family therapy training.

Personal therapy is widely recommended for psychotherapists in most training centers, yet few family therapy training programs require psychotherapy for trainees. Those that do have such requirements, not surprisingly, generally espouse a more "psychoanalytic" framework.[19] Family psychotherapy is recommended to family therapy trainees for several reasons. First, it can provide insight into one's own countertransference and transference feelings toward the families one treats. Second, it facilitates the therapist's own growth as a person, which will allow him or her increased flexibility as a therapist. Third, it provides direct experience in the role of patient, thus enabling the therapist to understand better the experience of the family in therapy. Finally, since psychotherapy is a highly stressful profession, one that creates stress that will have effects on the trainee's own family, it provides the opportunity for prophylactic treatment of a family at risk.

Little is known about the effectiveness of personal therapy for family therapists. One recent study,[18] however, found that therapists who participated with their own marital partners in a structured short-term training program, similar in many ways to conjoint marital therapy, showed a significant increase in their clinical skill as rated by experienced clinicians. Garfield's recent review[8] of the effects of experiential training for individual therapists cites several studies indicative of some positive effects of such training. He concluded, however, that "the findings secured are frequently inconclusive and offer little in the way of guidelines for practical training" (p. 72).

Indeed the issue at hand is quite a bit more complex than a simple question of "Does personal therapy make a difference?" For example, there are some data[9] that suggest that the *timing* of such personal therapy may be critical. Thus personal therapy that precedes the core training period may be especially helpful, while personal therapy that is begun concurrent with such a training period may actually either inhibit or decrease a neophyte therapist's clinical effectiveness, perhaps because of the anxiety such a personal therapy may arouse. Obviously such a differential effect of personal therapy on the student clinician's own clinical practice will be mediated by, among other things, the severity of the trainee's own emotional problems.

Finally, another empirically unaddressed issue is whether different types of personal therapy are likely, on the average, to have different effects, both positive and negative, on the neophyte family therapist's own clinical effectiveness. In concrete terms, for example, is an uncovering, intrapsychic, psychoanalytic personal therapy more or less likely to produce direct effects (for better or for worse) on the trainee's clinical practice than a personal therapy that emphasizes interpersonal experience (i.e., marital or family therapy)?

The third form of experiential training, working with one's own family, is probably unique to family therapy. Its use varies from the construction and discussion of one's own family tree, to role-playing of one's own family problems, to visits home, to further self-differentiation. We know of no completed studies that have attempted to assess directly the impact of such procedures nor of any studies that indirectly support such a practice, although at least one such investigation is now being planned.[24]

The Role of Research Training

Perhaps the most neglected area in the training of family therapists accounts for the relative lack of research on family therapy itself, as well as on family therapy training. Family therapists are rarely trained in outcome evaluation skills concurrent with their clinical training in family therapy. Of the professional groups practicing family therapy, only psychologists are routinely extensively trained in research methodology, design, statistics, and the like. Even in psychology programs, however, the special problems that arise in the evaluation of family therapy are seldom discussed (cf. Gurman & Kniskern[12]). For family therapy research to progress rapidly, including the evaluation of training, training centers must teach treatment evaluation skills along with clinical skills and must promote an attitude of scientific curiosity and discovery in their students. Such an attitude may be a healthy antidote to the adoption of the "we-have-the-secret" attitude currently prevalent in some schools of family therapy.

There are some very influential family therapists and teachers of family therapy who believe that it is impossible for family therapists to be highly skilled in both the clinical and the empirical domains. Even more pointedly, such people often argue that the possession of a skeptical, scientific *attitude* toward family therapy may actually interfere with one's effectiveness as a therapist. Other leaders in the field, of course, take the equally extreme position that the only way to practice family therapy responsibly—indeed, ethically—is always to function as a scientist–practitioner. We find both these positions quite destructive, or at least inhibiting, to a field in which so little is really known, yet in which clinicians and teachers often act and speak as though there is little that remains to be learned. Such myopic self-confidence may have a great external political payoff in preventing the field from being drowned in a sea of competing psychotherapeutic models, but it does little to strengthen the internal structure and substance of a field still in its adolescence.

As a minimum exposure to research in the family therapy field, beyond basic courses in experimental design and such, we believe that careful study of the existing empirical literature on the process and outcome of marriage and family therapy (e.g., Jacobson,[16] Gurman & Kniskern,[11,12] Gurman, Kniskern, & Pinsof,[13] Wells & Dezen[40]) should be required of all family therapy trainees at some point in their training, lest dogma be taken as a substitute for data.

Finally, at a metalevel, educators in the family therapy field must address the fact that, just as different types of patients respond differently to different treatment methods, family therapy trainees are likely to vary in terms of their responsiveness to and profiting from different training methods. An important long-range training goal for the family field is to identify the types of experiences that maximize learning and clinical effectiveness for individual trainees. Obviously research on this question is greatly needed.

Important and Researchable Questions Regarding Family Therapy Training

If this paper is serving its intent, the reader should at this point be able to generate an elaborate and impressive list of questions that research could answer about training. Family therapy outcome research has been bogged down for years in trying to answer the too-broad question "Does family therapy work?" It is our hope that by our listing a number of *specific* training-relevant questions, such a state of affairs can be avoided with regard to the analogously inappropriate question "Does family therapy training work?" It is also essential that the field attempt to avoid the predictable competitive struggle of a "we-train-better-than-you" game, as has been so predominant in research on the outcomes of virtually all psychotherapies.

One needs to keep in mind, however, that not all of the following questions should be considered in an investigation of the training conducted at a particular training center. A finding, for example, that personal therapy with one's spouse with a growth-oriented therapist does not improve a trainee's ability to do behavioral contracting does not generalize necessarily to other types of therapy training, in which such personal therapy experiences may enormously heighten a neophyte family therapist's clinical effectiveness. The broad research question implicit here, then, is: *What types of training experiences are especially potent in producing effective therapists within a particular model of therapy?*

With regard to *selection,* some of the crucial questions are the following:

- What type(s) of previous training best prepares a trainee for family therapy training?
- Are there any types of previous training that inhibit family therapy training?
- What personality factors predict success in training, and do these vary as a function of emphasizing different theoretical orientations to family therapy?

- Does the developmental stage of the trainee (e.g., never married versus married) influence success?
- Can success be predicted without a personal interview? Based on what criteria?
- Does a sample of therapy behavior improve selection?

Some controversial questions about *didactic methods* would be:

- Is it better to present one view or many?
- Does reading about families help the trainee learn therapy?
- Should reading be done before, after, or during the bulk of therapy training practice?
- Does the live observation of "experts" help or hinder the development of skills?

With regard to *supervision:*

- When are audiotapes or videotapes most helpful? When are they harmful?
- What are the demonstrable advantages and disadvantages of cotherapy supervision?
- What are the measurable strengths and weaknesses of problem-oriented supervision and of therapist-oriented supervision?
- Should all cases be supervised?
- What differences do different forms of supervision make for different trainees?

Some questions related to *experiential methods* would be:

- What specific changes are produced by different types of personal therapy?
- What are the positive and negative effects of personal therapy when it is required?
- At what point in one's training in family therapy are personal therapy experiences most beneficial, and when may they be harmful?
- Does working with one's own family (e.g., via family genograms) facilitate cognitive (conceptual) change more than it facilitates personal emotional change?
- When working with one's own family becomes the primary method of training, what is the effect on outcome for the families in treatment with such trainees?

- Are role-playing experiential methods more effective in producing technical skill than in reducing neophyte family therapists' anxieties about their competence?

Obviously, different training centers and programs need to generate questions that are especially relevant, or even unique, to their own training goals.

Assessment of the Outcome of Training Procedures

Since there now exists a body of research that indicates that family therapy produces both positive and negative effects on families and individuals,[11] it is important that assessment allow for the possibility of detecting a worsening of some trainees' skills as the result of training. In addition, the evaluation of training should be made from a number of perspectives (e.g., trainee, supervisor, independent judge) and on several dimensions.

Change in trainees should be assessed in *at least* the following ways. First, does the trainee increase his or her *conceptual knowledge* of families? Even more specifically, does the trainee increase his or her knowledge of family dynamics and interaction patterns and of the theoretical understanding of different treatment models? These questions can probably best be answered by a written examination given prior to and following training. While not all programs give equal stress to this dimension as a goal for training, all would expect that a trainee be better able to understand and explain the dynamics of families and their dysfunctions. Naturally such measures would need to be school-specific and would probably have to be "graded" by experts of that school. Obviously most family therapy training programs or centers unfortunately do not have family experts representing a wide variety of conceptual viewpoints.

A second area for the assessment of change would be in the trainees' *in-therapy behavior*. Ultimately all training in family therapy expects change to be translated into the therapist's actual interventions during treatment sessions, although the mechanisms and direction of change would be viewed differently. Such a change would best be assessed by a combination of trainee self-report, supervisor report, and objective observer. Each perspective could be used with videotape before and after training to assess change in this domain. It should not be expected that the observations from these vantage points will agree.

A third area would be that of the trainee's *personal life*. While not all types of family therapy training predict such change, in the absence of evidence to the contrary some assessment of this type should be made, since not all changes that follow from a given model of training are likely to be predicted by that model. Change could be assessed by the trainee himself or herself through self-report, by paper-and-pencil or projective personality tests, and by some significant others in the trainee's life (e.g., wife, parents, friends).

The fourth area for assessment—in many ways, the most important, sensitive, and difficult—is that of the outcomes of the families treated by the trainee. *No training program can responsibly be said to be effective unless its graduates can be demonstrated to produce more positive effects and fewer negative effects with the families they treat after receiving training than before receiving training.* The evaluation of outcome in families is a complex endeavor in and of itself and is one that we have treated in detail elsewhere.[12,13] Despite the difficulties inherent in such an assessment, it is essential to the evaluation of training programs and techniques of training.

Setting-Specific Training Effects

Klein and Gurman[17] recently raised an important issue rarely addressed in discussions of the generalizability of results obtained in psychotherapy outcome studies. That is, are the positive treatment outcomes documented in a setting in which a particular method of treatment was developed—what Klein and Gurman called the "parent setting"—generalizable to other (second-generation, as it were) treatment settings? For example, Klein and Gurman raised the specific question of whether the cognitive therapy of depression,[27] developed at the University of Pennsylvania, would be equally effective when applied in other treatment settings, *even if* the therapists had been expertly and thoroughly trained in the method at that other setting. If a treatment method is very effective (for a specific clinical disorder) *only* in the setting in which it was originated, or if it is substantially less effective, though still effective overall, in other settings, the power of the method per se would need to be questioned.

Research on Training

Analogous concerns should be raised about the efficacy of training methods applied outside the settings in which they were first developed. Thus, for example, even repeated demonstrations that the training methods used to teach structural family therapy[22] at the Philadelphia Child Guidance Clinic are highly effective would not logically preclude the possibility that the use of the same methods of teaching structural family therapy at Family Institute X might be considerably less effective, even given unquestionable expertise in the clinical and training methods of the teaching staff.

The point here, then, is that family therapy training methods must not be assumed to be powerful across training settings. The "child" training setting may mimic the "parent" training setting in marvelous detail and may be "just like" the parent. But the child can never *be* the parent.

The possibility of setting effects in family therapy training is an enormously significant issue, given the charisma that has characterized so many leaders in the family movement and the cultism that has so often characterized their followers.

In conclusion, the field of family therapy is a rapidly growing one by any standard used to assess such activity. Special training programs are being developed in many locations, and more existing psychotherapy centers and clinics are including family therapy in their training programs. Now is the time to integrate evaluation with the training process, so that the next generation of family therapists can benefit fully from our mistakes rather than blindly repeating them.

REFERENCES

1. Abel, T., Bruzzese, D., & Wilson, J. Short-term family therapy for short-term hospitalized patients: A vehicle for training as well as treatment. In L. Wolberg & M. Aronson (Eds.), *Group therapy 1974: An overview*. New York: Stratton Intercontinental Medical Book Corporation, 1974.
2. Alexander, J., Barton, C., Shiavo, R., & Parsons, B. Systems–behavioral intervention with families of delinquents: Therapist characteristics, family behavior, and outcome. *Journal of Consulting and Clinical Psychology*, 1976, 44, 656–664.
3. Beck, D. Research findings on the outcomes of marital counseling. *Social Casework*, 1975, 56, 153–181.
4. Beck, D., & Jones, M. *Progress on family problems: A nationwide study of clients' and counselors' views on family agency services*. New York: Family Service Association of America, 1973.

5. Burton, G., & Kaplan, H. Group counseling in conflicted marriages where alcoholism is present: Clients evaluation of effectiveness. *Journal of Marriage and the Family*, 1968, 30, 74-79.
6. Cleghorn, J., & Levin, S. Training family therapists by setting learning objectives. *American Journal of Orthopsychiatry*, 1973, 43, 439-446.
7. Freeman, V., Klein, A., & Rubenstein, F. *Final report: Family study project*. Pittsburgh: Allegheny General Hospital, 1964.
8. Garfield, S. Research on the training of professional psychotherapists. In A. Gurman & A. Razin (Eds.), *Effective psychotherapy: A handbook of research*. New York: Pergamon Press, Inc., 1977.
9. Garfield, S. L., & Bergin, A. E. Personal therapy, outcome and some therapist variables. *Psychotherapy*, 1971, 8, 251-253.
10. Griffin, R. Change in perception of marital relationship as related to marriage counseling. *Dissertation Abstracts International*, 1967, 27, 3956A.
11. Gurman, A. S., & Kniskern, D. P. Deterioration in marital and family therapy: Empirical, clinical and conceptual issues. *Family Process*, 1978, 17, 3-20. (a)
12. Gurman, A., & Kniskern, D. Research on marital and family therapy: Progress, perspective, and prospect. In S. Garfield & A. Bergin (Eds.), *Handbook of psychotherapy and behavior change: An empirical analysis* (2nd ed.). New York: John Wiley & Sons, Inc., 1978. (b)
13. Gurman, A. S., Kniskern, D. P., & Pinsof, W. Family therapy research: Toward an integration with training and practice. In A. Gurman & D. Kniskern (Eds.), *Handbook of family therapy*. New York: Brunner/Mazel, Inc., 1981, in press.
14. Gurman, A. S., & Razin, A. M. *Effective psychotherapy: A handbook of research*. New York: Pergamon Press, Inc., 1977.
15. Haley, J. *Problem-solving therapy*. San Francisco: Jossey-Bass, Inc., 1976.
16. Jacobson, N. S. A review of the research on the effectiveness of marital therapy. In T. Paolino & B. McCrady (Eds.), *Marriage and marital therapy: Psychoanalytic, behavioral and systems theory perspectives*. New York: Brunner/Mazel, Inc., 1978.
17. Klein, M. H., & Gurman, A. S. *A proposal for collaborative research on the psychotherapy of depression*. Washington, D.C.: National Institute of Mental Health, 1978.
18. Lange, A., & Zeegers, W. Structured training for behavioral family therapy: Methods and evaluation. *Behavioural Analysis and Modification*, 1978, 2, 211-225.
19. Liddle, H., & Halpin, R. Family therapy training and supervision literature: A comparative review. *Journal of Marriage and Family Counseling*, 1978, 4, 77-98.
20. Matarazzo, R. Research on the teaching and learning of psychotherapy. In A. Bergin & S. Garfield (Eds.), *Handbook of psychotherapy and behavior change*. New York: John Wiley & Sons, Inc., 1971.
21. Mezydlo, L., Wauck, L., & Foley, J. The clergy as marriage counselors: A service revisited. *Journal of Religion and Health*, 1973, 22, 278-288.

22. Minuchin, S. *Families and family therapy.* Cambridge, Mass.: Harvard University Press, 1974.
23. Olson, D. Marital and family therapy: Integrative review and critique. *Journal of Marriage and the Family,* 1970, *32,* 501–538.
24. Orfanidis, M. M. Personal communication, May 1978.
25. Pagell, W., Carkhuff, R., & Berenson, B. The predicted differential effects of the level of counselor functioning upon the level of functioning of outpatients. *Journal of Clinical Psychology,* 1967, *23,* 510–512.
26. Roberts, P. The effects on marital satisfaction of brief training in behavioral exchange negotiation mediated by differentially experienced trainers. *Dissertation Abstracts International,* 1975, *36,* 457B.
27. Rush, A. J., Beck, A. T., Kovacs, M., & Hollon, S. Comparative efficacy of cognitive therapy and pharmacotherapy in the treatment of depressed outpatients. *Cognitive Therapy and Research,* 1977, *1,* 17–38.
28. Santa-Barbara, J., Woodward, C., Levin, S., Streiner, D., Goodman, J., & Epstein, N. *The relationship between therapists' characteristics and outcome variables in family therapy.* Paper presented to the Canadian Psychiatric Association, Banff, Canada, Sept. 1975.
29. Schreiber, L. Evaluation of family group treatment in a family agency. *Family Process,* 1966, *5,* 21–29.
30. Shapiro, R. Therapist attitudes and premature termination in family and individual therapy. *Journal of Nervous and Mental Disease,* 1974, *159,* 101–107.
31. Shapiro, R., & Budman, S. Defection, termination and continuation in family and individual therapy. *Family Process,* 1973, *12,* 55–67.
32. Shellow, R., Brown, B., & Osberg, J. Family group therapy in retrospect: Four years and sixty families. *Family Process,* 1963, *2,* 52–67.
33. Sigal, J., Guttman, H., Chagoya, L., & Lasry, J. Predictability of family therapists' behavior. *Canadian Psychiatric Association Journal,* 1973, *18,* 199–202.
34. Sigal, J., Rakoff, V., & Epstein, N. Indications of therapeutic outcome in conjoint family therapy. *Family Process,* 1967, *6,* 215–226.
35. Sluzki, C. *Treatment, training and research in family therapy.* Paper presented at the Nathan W. Ackerman Memorial Conference, Cumana, Venezuela, Feb. 1974.
36. Stanton, M. D. Family therapy training: Academic and internship opportunities for psychologists. *Family Process,* 1975, *14,* 433–439.
37. Thom, K., & Wright, L. M. *Family therapy skills.* Unpublished manuscript, University of Calgary, 1978.
38. Thomlinson, R. A behavioral model for social work intervention with the marital dyad. *Dissertation Abstracts International,* 1974, *35,* 1227A.
39. Waxenberg, B. Therapists' empathy, regard and genuineness as factors in staying in or dropping out of short-term, time-limited family therapy. *Dissertation Abstracts International,* 1973, *34,* 1288B.
40. Wells, R., & Dezen, A. The results of family therapy revisited: The nonbehavioral methods. *Family Process,* 1978, *17,* 251–274.

41. Wells, R., Dilkes, T., & Trivelli, N. The results of family therapy: A critical review of the literature. *Family Process,* 1972, 7, 189–207.
42. Whitaker, C. A., Napier, A. Y., & Keith, D. V. Process-oriented family therapy. In A. S. Gurman & D. P. Kniskern (Eds.), *Handbook of family therapy.* New York: Brunner/Mazel, Inc., 1981, in press.
43. Williamson, D. Training opportunities in marriage and family counseling. *Family Coordinator,* 1973, 22, 99–102.
44. Beal, E. Current trends in the training of family therapists. *American Journal of Psychiatry,* 1976, 33, 137–141.

15

A Model for Training in Family Therapy*

MAURIZIO ANDOLFI
PAOLO MENGHI

Choosing an Experience

If we accept the broadly held supposition[7,8,9,10,11,14,19] that the family represents the fundamental nexus between the individual and the community and that family therapy is a form of social psychiatry, then we must assume that those who work in community service (mental health centers, family counseling centers, schools, hospitals, etc.) are the people who would truly profit the most from a thorough course of study in family therapy.

These groups, more than others, are subject to the daily frustrations of trying to interpret individual problems in terms of social problems, facing the difficulties involved in exploring new territory. For this reason, many community service groups are now interested in learning methods of intervention that prevent the cloistering of mentally disturbed persons in hospitals or in the offices of psychiatrists. The wished-for situation is that of observing these persons within the context that creates their disturbance. Family therapy, involving all the directly interested parties in the therapeutic intervention, is the most coherent discipline for moving toward this goal.

Four years ago, we conjectured that although there were difficulties inherent in teaching family therapy to community service groups, there existed also great advantages, for the teachers as well as for the

*This article is the first general formulation of the training program carried out by the Italian Society for Family Therapy, held at the Family Therapy Institute of Rome.

students. It seemed to us, in fact, that these community service groups possessed far greater therapeutic potential than more heterogeneous student groups, constituted as they are of people intensively sharing much common terrain besides the goal of learning family therapy.

Because these groups would already be working together on actual cases, we would have an opportunity to discover relationships between family problems and other social realities and would be able to test the quality of learning during training as well.

We decided, therefore, to teach family therapy to existing institutional teams, especially units working in community mental health centers, psychiatric hospitals, and schools.* We also added a control group composed of persons not working in a common area who, however, had the requisite professional background and motivation.

The decision was made to have the teams come to the Family Therapy Institute in Rome for biweekly, weekly, or monthly sessions, which varied in relation to the phase of training and the geographical distance (some of our groups came from remote parts of Italy).

The decision to have the groups come to the Institute was based on practical matters: convenience for the teachers and the availability of special equipment such as one-way mirrors and audiovisual aids. We then discovered incidentally that in coming to us, the group somehow left behind the old logic of the "institution," the preference of "crash" therapy to a broader and deeper comprehension of the problem.

In Rome, a sort of laboratory situation was created to which the teams contributed fragments of their past experience, such as interviews with families, taped sessions, or discussions of clinical cases. These were observed, discussed, analyzed, and synthesized in the light of new knowledge. Through experimentation with this new type of intervention within the learning situation, the students were able to test their ability in the day-to-day working reality.

Motivation of Training and the Redefinition of Expectations

The request for training almost always results from dissatisfaction shared by the team over a period of time: "We don't know what to do any more;

---

*Six to ten persons constituted a group, among whom were psychiatrists, social workers, sociologists, nurses, and school consultants. The composition varied in relation to the services rendered by each team. The course required four years of training comprising a total of 1,200–1,500 hours.

A Training Model for Family Therapy

public assistance doesn't work; our mental health center just prescribes drugs; the problem isn't technical but political; the definition of *assistance* must be changed; the chief of our unit doesn't believe in psychotherapy." Phrases such as these have been constant themes in our interviews with requesting teams. All of them contain some truth. All of them express the sense of impotence felt by those wishing to give some sense to their work in the community. But how to do it? Dissatisfaction with their work seems to be the most important unifying element of the team, but beyond this, the dissatisfaction appeared to us also to cover tensions and difficulties in relationships within the team itself. In this sense, we can draw certain parallels with the family system: the incapacity felt by the team acts as the symptom does in the family; it is real and it, too, makes for difficulty in interaction.

When we inquire as to what has motivated the teams to seek training in family therapy, the answers are similar: "To try to help one person isolated from his social context makes no sense; we want to avoid hospital commitment or pharmaceutical dependence; if the family cooperates, it's easier to help the patient; family therapy seems to consider the real needs of the community."

The request for training in itself implies interest in becoming a more effective therapeutic unit. Family therapy is perceived as a way of increasing the team's "technical baggage" and of seeing mental illness in a broader frame than the merely individual.

But no one ever asks *to learn to see himself or herself as an integral part of the therapeutic process.* Even if those who question their own role rarely regard themselves or the interaction within the team or of the team within the institution as relevant components in the analysis of mental disturbance. When this does occur, these components are usually perceived only intellectually, with no accompanying modification of the habitual, familiar, and reassuring interaction.

What would happen if one were to expand the problem beyond the patient and the family, to include the therapeutic team? The focus on the disturbance would have to move from the mind of the patient to include not only the family and community but also *the therapeutic system,* that is, the interaction between family and therapist. We feel that to acquire competence in this sort of approach, one must personally experience the interaction within a learning context that lends itself to the analysis of systematic meaning. In this way, one learns to alternate between a position of personal involvement and a detached, systemic analysis.[15] We elected to pursue this line of training with our groups.

Maurizio Andolfi & Paolo Menghi

The Group as Laboratory: The Search for a New Structure

When the team arrives, each member feels anonymous and protected by the same request for training. Although each member may feel dissatisfied and frustrated, he or she is disposed to cover these feelings in an attempt to maintain a "united front" that masks tension and offers protection from the fear of individuation. If we hope to initiate a process of differentiation, we have to clash with this sense of security that the apparent group unity supports in each member. This clash gradually breaks through the defense-based unity, which gives way to a new structure. In order to facilitate this passage from an apparent unity to a real unity, the trainer, while respecting each individual, must decisively and directly assume a strongly provoking position.* Rather than shielding each member from embarrassment at self-individuation within the group, the trainer must force them to a real openness. Stress and confusion are unpleasant but essential components of the process.

Without attempting to clarify the time progression of this process, we will illustrate the principal points, including the most significant techniques.

The *hot seat* is an incisive technique with which we begin. The trainer places a chair in the center of the room and asks each member in turn to sit there and tell something about himself or herself while the others, in a circle, listen without interrupting. Each one is given this personal space, well differentiated from the protected position within the circle. The trainer, as well, takes the hot seat.

If someone wishes to pass his or her turn, claiming to be timid, the trainer invites that member to define himself or herself as timid from the hot seat. The physical act of going to that seat, to speak from there about this difficulty (saying that he or she cannot do it), allows the member to overcome the difficulty while avoiding the embarrassment of not participating.

The content of what is said is not as important as the fact that everyone, including the trainer, participates. The direct visual confrontation between the individual and the group, as well as the physical distance, reduces the possibilities of control to a noticeable degree. Through the restructuring of space, we act on emotional closeness or distance and on the processes of exclusion or inclusion. The students are generally

---

*Through a balance between provocation and support, the rapport between trainer and student develops and is shaped in time.

A Training Model for Family Therapy

amazed by the uncommon emotional expression released by the simple rearrangement of individuals in space, learning, from their own experience, ways of working when they put themselves to the test with families in therapy.

The encounter between teacher and group has barely been initiated but the methodological pattern is already clear.

The definition of leadership, the division into subsystems, the internal coalitions, and the attempts at alliance with the trainer are the first aspects of the group dynamic that we try to clarify and make visible, although their existence is often not admitted verbally. After this, we can begin to activate the free flow of exchange within the group. We can *focus on a problem in group interaction* (making it larger than life) through its symbolic representation.

The trainer sometimes sees a fixed pattern in the rules of rapport between two or more students, and he or she asks them to act it out in the presence of the others. Often a situation is revealed that points out the rigid and contradictory aspects of this rapport. Following is an example of an exchange between Carla, a social worker, and Francesco, one of the three psychiatrists of the same team.

TRAINER (*placing two chairs touching back to back in the center of the room*). Now, Carla and Francesco, sit here so that you can't see each other's faces. You, Francesco, tell Carla what you don't like about the way she acts.

FRANCESCO. What do you mean? In what situation?

T. You make the choice. However I'd like you to do it in a courteous way; try not to show annoyance ... and try to keep a calm demeanor. (*Turning to Carla.*) Your job is very easy: you must only say "yes." With or without words, you must show agreement, letting Francesco know how much you appreciate his criticism of you. I'd like both of you to try very hard.... You can begin.

Carla's and Francesco's inability to express their reciprocal dissatisfactions openly is represented metaphorically by the chairs placed back to back. A demonstration of Francesco's disappointment in Carla is openly solicited.

The incongruity of Francesco's real irritation with his feigned courtesy toward Carla is explicitly prescribed.

Carla is asked, in an even more provocative way, to expand her usual response to Francesco's ambivalent messages by appearing agreeable when she is, in fact, anything but.

(Therapist and group sit in a circle around them.)

F. *(after a silence of a few minutes during which the two of them seem most uncomfortable)*.... I don't know where to start.... It's difficult to speak to someone you can't see.... Well ... the fact is ... the most annoying thing about you is that you tend to be passive in all the situations in which I, maybe because of my personality, would like to see more determination ... so to speak ... a different sense of security ... of autonomy.

What occurs habitually now seems embarrassing and difficult to recreate.

CARLA *(initially smiling, now serious, indicates she well recognizes this situation)*. Yes, yes, I agree.... *(Her tone is mocking.)*

T. I asked you to keep smiling.

The trainer solicits an altered interaction by negating it. Carla begins to ask for help, which is totally new.

C. How can I keep smiling when he's always criticizing without ever trying to understand my problems.

F. What are your problems?

T. Excuse me, Francesco, I didn't ask you to question Carla. I just asked you to tell her the negative qualities you see in her.

The trainer doesn't allow Carla and Francesco to get into an argument. He focuses attention back on their habitual mode of interaction. The tension grows.

F. Okay ... okay ... but what kind of dialogue is this anyway?

Francesco emphasizes the impossibility of an exchange ...

C. It's what it always is and always has been ...

... and Carla retorts openly.

A Training Model for Family Therapy

F. Look, I'm not talking about faults... I probably have many more.

C. Oh, now he's beginning the paternal bit. Look, I'm tired of being treated like a kid who needs advice.... I don't give a damn.... Why don't you look at your own weaknesses?

Carla expresses her need for autonomy and becomes aggressive because she cannot satisfy that need.

T. That's enough. Let's stop here. I thought it would be easier for you to respect the rules.

The trainer continues the provocation, thereby maintaining the tension.

(The trainer asks Carla and Francesco to sit outside the circle to listen to the comments on the scene just enacted.)

The rest of the group analyzes the observed interaction. What is stated in the discussion increases the discomfort of the protagonists but at the same time stimulates the search for new solutions.

In this case, the trainer underscores the impossibility of altering the malfunctioning rules of their interaction. By emphasizing the maintenance of the status quo, he provokes increased tension, which acts as a catalyst to unblock the rigidity in their interrelationship.

Our attention now focuses on how individual members use themselves within the group rapport.

The trainer presents concrete experiences based on the use of the body and of movement.[3,17,18] The most complex and involving experiences presented are "sculpting" one's own family and the group in training. In both cases, the same method is used: the students are asked to re-create symbolically the state of mind and the emotions they feel within their families and within the group by arranging a three-dimensional representation of these perceived relationships. By prohibiting verbal communication, we elicit the expression of these feelings visually. As a result, emotional states and ways of expressing that were formerly dormant seem to be freed. The final outcome is the symbolic representation of a system: in one case that of the family, in the other that of the group in training. Alliances, conflicts, and triangulation are all arranged in the visual sphere. The use of sensory and symbolic representation gives broader opportunities for the communication of emotions. Often it is exhausting and even embarrassing to derive "sculpture in space" from the core of one's creativity, but sooner or later, everyone manages to present his or her own perception of the significant relationships linking him or her to the others and linking all the rest of the team to one another.

This method, more than any other, seems to favor reciprocal awareness, to increase intimacy, and to reinforce cohesion within the group. Each one begins to think of the group and the family as systemic units. Each moves from the role of observer to that of actor of his or her own "living."

To visualize and recompose the structure of one's own relational systems is the first step toward analyzing one's own process of change. It is also the first step toward understanding the history and the evolution of the system of learning across time.

A link from this phase, based on individuation and group cohesion, to the following one of actually facing the family is the simulation of therapeutic intervention.

Real as well as hypothetical cases encompassing the most varied problems are suggested to the group, who then become parents, children, brothers, and therapists, as required.

The students-as-actors assume specific roles and relationships, therein reproducing true therapeutic encounters. Each one puts himself or herself to the test as a therapist; the rest, as observers, analyze the situations produced in terms of nonverbal communication, incongruence between the objectives of the therapist and the approaches used, the rules of the therapeutic system, dissonance between verbal and analogical expression, the dynamics of the subsystems, and the examination of power hierarchies. The exercises have limited, precise objectives and tend to be brief: to show an accusatory situation for a mother or a protective one for an identified patient,[2] to restructure flux in a situation of confrontation between a father and a daughter or within a couple,[13] or to attempt to express the emotions of the diverse members of the family. Anger, affection, solitude, pain, hope, contentment, mistrust, humor, all become feelings to "touch" and to be "touched."

We frequently videotape these scenes to allow us to reobserve certain sequences[1] and to search collectively for an alternate mode of intervention. To observe oneself in action is a patently incisive and instructive experience. To what degree can each student recognize himself or herself, his or her own actions, as compared with an idealized self-image? The response at this stage of the game is very little. The students seeing themselves on tape are comparable to musicians hearing their own false notes, and the distance between what they would like to be and what they in fact are seems almost unbridgeable at this point.

Through direct experience and analysis within the learning system, the technical "baggage" of each one is extended and deepened. The first phase turns the group's attention inward on their own group interaction; the second phase turns their attention on that of their respective family systems. The next phase brings the team to the analysis of their clinical experience through the observation of their work in their respective institutions.

Many different family situations are examined in the light of both the theory and the practice of our therapeutic method. Now the students may permit themselves the luxury of observation before the necessity of intervention. It is hoped that they have by now gained some facility in seeing reality through a relational vision and looking at their own work in a systemic frame of reference.

FORMATION OF THE THERAPIST AND THERAPY: PARALLEL PROCESSES

The moment has arrived for each one, after having tested himself or herself within the group interaction, to attempt a first experience as therapist with a family, supported by the direct supervision of the trainer.[12,16]

Here we are often asked why the encounter with the family generates so much tension and anxiety in the student therapist. We don't see this as the anxiety of an initiation into therapy, since most students have already had therapeutic experience with families within their institutions. We think, instead, that this reaction is more plausibly the result of an analysis of the union between the learning system (trainer–student) and the therapeutic system (supervisor–therapist–family). The student entering the session sees himself or herself caught in a cross fire with no way out. The student, in fact, in his or her work with the family, is open to the analysis of the supervisor and the observing group; as therapist, he or she is the communicating link between the two systems, which are spatially separated by the one-way mirror. He or she will be alternately part of one system and then of the other, putting into action the models of confrontation and individuation previously experienced in the group. His or her expertise must evolve in the "field."

The trainer–supervisor bears full responsibility for the family and the students in training. He or she must give both family and therapist a structure within which they can safely face each other and interact. In searching for a balance between the impulse to replace the student therapist and the impulse to leave all the responsibility of the therapeutic process to the student, the trainer is also forced to examine his or her own flexibility.

We have learned that the success of therapy is directly proportional to the understanding that exists between supervisor and therapist. If they are capable of openly examining the relational problems that arise in their dynamic, the family will feel itself moved to do the same.

Between sessions, students, therapists, and supervisor examine what process of change is taking place or what is preventing it. Through the analysis of videotapes, sculpture, and enactment of the observed interactive sequences, the group members learn and together continue the parallel process of formation and therapy.

The one-way mirror is the permeable screen between the therapist–family system, which is directly involved, and the supervisor–group system, which is less emotionally involved and can therefore take a more objective view of what is happening.[3]

During the sessions, the supervisor may communicate with the therapist by intercom (Scheme 1), making suggestions that should be made effective in immediate action.* The therapist may also leave the room of his or her own wish or by the request of the supervisor to exchange information, to interrupt a nonproductive situation, or to clarify a strategic intervention (Scheme 2). When the therapist enters the supervisor–observer system, he or she becomes temporarily detached from involvement in the therapy session. Under certain conditions, the

---

*A supervisor of this type is justified by the certainty that every family may enmesh the therapist in its habitual interaction, preventing the possibility of change. In other words, the therapist might end up behaving with the family so as to reinforce the same transactional style that brought them into therapy in the first place.

A Training Model for Family Therapy

supervisor may be the one who temporarily leaves the observation room to enter the therapist–family system (Scheme 3), thus changing the dynamics of the context by his or her presence. At other times, the family will move from one place to another: one or more family members may be asked to observe behind the one-way mirror, thereby joining the supervisor–observer system (Scheme 4). This spatial separation permits the exploration of specific interaction at the level of the subsystems.[4]

Four Examples That Illustrate the Aforementioned Schemes

Scheme 1

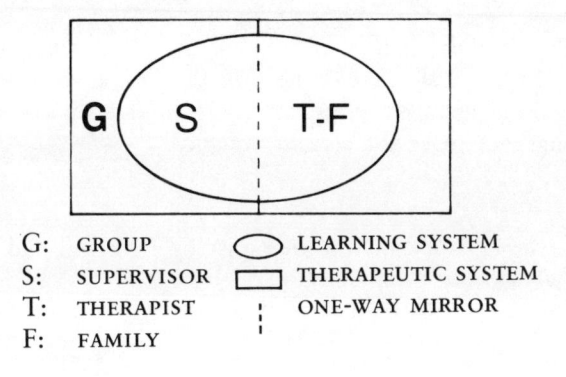

G: GROUP — LEARNING SYSTEM
S: SUPERVISOR — THERAPEUTIC SYSTEM
T: THERAPIST — ONE-WAY MIRROR
F: FAMILY

The therapist is involved with Maria, a 16-year-old anorectic patient. The girl is seated between her parents. The session is supervised from the observation room by the trainer, in the presence of the group.

MARIA. I can't accept the role of a woman, because I reject the adult figure—that is, a female. It's useless to hope that I can want something that I rejected long ago.

"It's useless to hope"... Maria tells all of those wishing for her recovery that it's all wasted effort. The rejection of sexuality and the refusal of food simultaneously represent symptom and power sphere. Her language is cerebral and detached.

SUPERVISOR (*calling the therapist by intercom*). Be provocative on the sexual level. Move the idea of sex from her head to her body. Make it tangible and use strong language.

The suggestion of provoking the girl in her power sphere—her choice of asexuality—demands that the therapist change the situation brusquely through the open use of strong sexual language.

THERAPIST. Okay. (*Coming back to sit down and turning to Maria with visible embarrassment.*) Now I'd like you to tell me... that is, I'd like you to list for me how girls your age undergo sexual change.

Despite the supervisor's suggestion, the intervention of the therapist is as cerebral as Maria's.

M. (*decisively*). I don't understand. If you could explain it better...

T. (*sitting rigidly with arms crossed*). Yes... well... tell me about the more apparent physical changes that take place at a certain early age...

The therapist's embarrassment and the nonproductive situation elicit a foreseeable interruption of this sequence.

The supervisor calls the therapist by intercom and asks him to leave the room.

Scheme 2

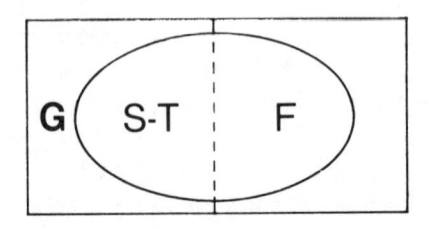

G(S-T | F)

The following discussion occurs between supervisor and therapist before the group in the observation room.

S. I didn't ask you to give a lesson on the reproduction of butterflies to a five-year-old.

The supervisor doesn't shield the therapist from embarrassment; on the contrary, he openly provokes

T. (*embarrassed*). I don't think I can get Maria to answer in such a sensitive area for her.

S. (*interrupting*). I'd like you to change the context. It's too rigid and cerebral. And get Maria out of that lineup between her father and mother. Talk more about thighs and breasts—and get Maria to talk about them, too.

T. (*with a tight smile*). Easier said than done... besides it's not my style.

S. I wonder if you always hold conferences in bed.

T. (*increasingly annoyed*). I don't see the connection, but here I go. (*Leaves the observation room.*)

it. A sort of investigating sequence develops between the two that activates the idea of what should be taking place between the therapist and Maria.

By protecting Maria from embarrassment, the therapist protects himself, thereby sustaining the girl's power.

The girl and her parents are a "united front" that limits the attempts of the therapist. The supervisor therefore suggests a restructuring of the spatial relationships. He uses the same provocative language the therapist should use now with Maria.

Style is here confused with inhibition and embarrassment. The therapist is up against his inability to be open in that situation. Style is simply beside the point.

The supervisor directly provokes the therapist, leaving the family apart. He seems to be crudely breaking into the therapist's personal area. In reality, he is helping him to overcome his embarrassment, which will be replaced by annoyance with his own inhibitions. Acting on the rapport between therapist and supervisor may be more complex than explaining a strategy; it is also more broadly effective for the therapist (formation) and for the family (therapy).

The provoking of the therapist acts as a catalyst, making him challenge the girl. Tone of voice, gesture, and words become decisive and irritating. Language that goes beyond that expected in a therapeutic context[6] has a liberating effect on both therapist and patient.

Scheme 3

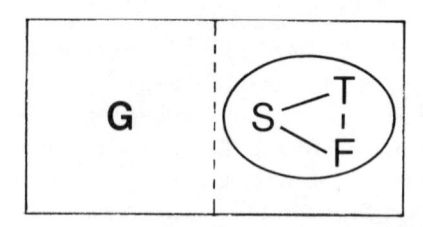

$$G \quad | \quad S {<}^{T}_{F}$$

The Calò couple are arguing during a session. After a quarter of an hour of shouts and insults, the therapist hasn't yet realized that her apparent "neutrality" acts as a reinforcement of this fighting. In paying diligent attention to not allying herself with husband or wife, she has overlooked the skillful complicity of the couple in avoiding the need to face each other. Every real confrontation is brilliantly turned aside by polemics on what hour to rise in the morning, the character of a certain friend, or whether it is better to take a sporting vacation and go camping or have a shorter vacation and go to a hotel and live royally; all of this is punctuated by the persuasive and insidious "What do you think about it, Doctor?"

The supervisor, without being announced, enters the therapy room.

S. (*He greets the couple hurriedly and sits in front of the therapist. His gaze is directly on her, and he excludes the couple.*). Apart from this useless yelling of Mr. and Mrs. Calò, it bothers me to accept their reasoning (*he motions to the couple while still looking at the therapist*) that they come here because they don't get along.... However, my complaint isn't with

The entrance of the supervisor reunites the therapeutic system in a single space. The subsystem supervisor–therapist is seen in this sequence.

The problem is not the quarreling but the way the couple use it to cover their reciprocal dependence and protection.

The first message is for the couple, but it is directed at the them. It's with you for so blandly accepting their reasoning.

therapist, and it becomes the opening wedge toward talking with the husband and wife.

The supervisor criticizes the reinforcement given to the couple's definition of the problem by the therapist's attempts to remain a neutral party.

HUSBAND. But we ...

S. I'm not talking to you; I want to talk to Doctor Conforti.

The exclusion of the couple is an attempt to get the therapist started on another approach.

T. I agree with you but it's very hard ...

S. You can't agree with me or you wouldn't let them (*indicating the couple*) fill this room with anger and reproaches, which they throw around like boomerangs.

The strategy becomes reinforced by the open disagreement between supervisor and therapist, which is the more effective as it is spontaneous.

T. It seems to me there must be a possibility ... of speaking differently.

The therapist offers an alternative course of action before the family can.

S. I see that you don't really agree with me at all. Up till now, I haven't heard any possibility, maybe because there is such chaos in this room.

T. (*turning to the supervisor*). How can I help that?

S. Instead of killing time talking about hours and vacations, change your direction and see if you can find some useful reason for them to come back here.

The supervisor moves from provocation to offering an alternative. The therapist now must channel her accumulated aggression toward the supervisor in such a way as to allow her to explore the alternative without useless argument.

T. But they (*pointing to the couple*) see their problems as tied to these other matters, and that makes it difficult.

S. Yes, well, for them it is understandable.... How long have you been married?

WIFE. Seven years.

S. Seven years. They've been playing this game for seven years, and they're entitled to it. What I can't approve is that you accept it! They have a right to see things as it suits them. You, no! (*He gets up and leaves the room.*)

The apparent acceptance of the couple's "rights" is strongly challenging, all the more so because these "rights" are denied the therapist.

The supervisor's abrupt entrance into the therapy room and his open disagreement with the therapist, expressed freely in front of the couple, force a brusque change in the line of the discussion and make the couple and the therapist look directly at their "complicity." Rather than remaining neutral and thus reinforcing the couple's protective routine (arguing), the therapist must be the agent who breaks the circuit. The couple are constrained to give up their useless game and begin to cooperate with the therapist, after both have been so directly challenged by the supervisor.

After the session, supervisor and therapist analyze what happened before the group. The other students help in tracing all the contributing factors in the therapeutic system. Each one sculpts his or her perception of the interaction between supervisor and therapist and the effect produced by this interaction on the rapport of the couple.

Scheme 4

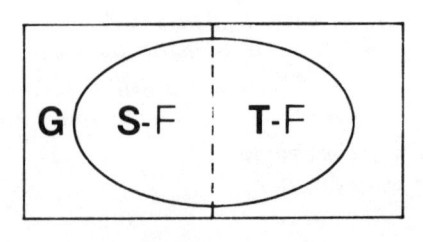

A Training Model for Family Therapy

Anna Lisa, a girl of 10, has been caught stealing at home and in a department store. The parents give differing weight to the problem, the father viewing it very seriously and the mother tending to minimize it. The mother sees herself as extremely insecure at mothering and unable to assert herself with her husband, from whom she feels continual criticism and interference. The father does, in fact, regard her as completely incompetent in her role as mother.

The supervisor and the therapist agree to separate the family, with the mother, Anna Lisa, and a younger brother, Ruggero, playing together in the therapy room while the father observes their interaction from behind the one-way mirror.

Delighted by the situation, the children immediately invent a game. The mother and the therapist are two diners in a restaurant being waited on by the children, who also dance and sing for the customers. The children and their beaming mother appear to be having a fine time together. The father, forced to see the gaiety and naturalness of the mother's participation, mumbles phrases of surprise in the observation room.

The therapist and the supervisor make the spatial separation clear, permitting the mother to "let herself go" in the game even under the critical gaze of her husband; the supervisor's presence lends importance to the husband's observation. The supervisor also provocatively congratulates the husband on his choice of such a capable wife.

In the second part of the session, with the family together again, the situation seems changed. The mother appears less subordinate and therefore more ready to meet her husband on a reality level. He, too, must now relate openly rather than by criticism and interference.

In this example, the therapeutic system is divided into two subsystems. The therapist demonstrates her own adaptability, "letting go" in the subsystem with the mother, while they are observed by the subsystem supervisor–group–father. Being able to relax and enjoy the therapy is a pleasant novelty for the student, who is often so caught up in the stereotype of professional sobriety that he or she habitually inhibits any show of his or her own emotions.

Verification of Four Years of Work

Many data issuing from the comparison of the learning in the teams and the learning in the control groups seem to confirm many of our initial hypotheses. We found that in the former approach, learning was both more rapid and more complete, not because individual potential was not comparable but because of the nature of team structure. In these institutional teams, in fact, the individuation and comparison experienced within the group and with families uncovered fruitful material that could be tested on the actual work scene. As a result, the teams were able to develop a "team culture" through an interdependent period of reflection and formation (in the training) and a period of operation (at the institution).

The control group, which had no shared work place, lacked the opportunity to apply their group learning experience. They tried to fill this need by discussing relevant information and questions relating to their respective work in an evident attempt to implement the use of the knowledge they were gaining. This control group were required by their training to deal with a multifaceted reality, but a situation was created in which individual expectations became disproportionately high. There were only limited possibilities for them to find an external support system that would permit their testing of the newly acquired knowledge. They were, therefore, understandably, looking for more practical and resolute answers in their training, paying the price, however, of not broadening their vision as fully as one might have hoped.

The lack of a shared background often led them to seek special privileges or, at least, special recognition. In observing the group process of defining internal leadership, we learned that an individual might show himself or herself as clever and gifted about his or her own work, but not so much to share knowledge with the others as to assure the possibility of becoming the leader within his or her group. We were struck by the fact that these maneuvers, along with the formation of both alliances and exclusions, were often subterranean and were vigorously denied at the conscious level.

We do not say for certain that these things didn't occur as well within the working teams, but the dynamics evolved in different ways and at different periods. In these groups, denial over a long span of time would be impossible to sustain, given the day-to-day reality of their working relationships. Their difficulty was more the modifying of their relational interweavings, which were often frozen into roles and functions within the institution.

In the course of teaching, we shared many tensions, at times dramatic, and we often felt quite impotent, thinking that so much—too much—energy, ours and the group members', was being wasted in trying to unwind a mass too tangled to be unraveled by our mutual effort.

Luckily some of the results beginning to be verified in the teams' respective institutions justified our commitment. Concrete support from the administration of the institutions was forthcoming in response to the increasingly apparent competence and cohesion manifested by the teams. All the institutions paid for the training as for working hours, contributing also to travel and lodging costs; some financed the entire program. The teams were also provided with space and equipment adapted to facilitating their newly learned mode of family therapy as well as their collective working out and working at their own experience.

As we were well aware of the constitutional reluctance of psychiatric systems to open themselves to new, concrete therapeutic approaches, these supportive steps, approved and undertaken with such alacrity, were as gratifying to us as they were surprising.

Our initial euphoria was redefined soon enough, however, by the realization that the logic of the institutions could not be changed by our teams, which didn't carry enough weight to radically alter their home institutions to the extent that they themselves had changed during the training program. We did achieve a certain extension of our ideas, however, in that members of the trained teams started sharing with their colleagues many of the things they had learned and tested in their training. We assume that any hope for broader institutional change will require much more time and also the training of other members of these therapeutic communities.

Redefining the expectations of the group as a working unit doesn't in any way subtract from the advantages culled from the training experience. In fact, we assert that the attempt to lay the foundation for working as an operating unit within the psychiatric structure enriched each member.

The formulation of this article has aided us in thinking through the first results of a teaching model that had passed through the great uncertainties tied to our own evolution and maturing as therapists and as trainers. Through unavoidable trial and error, we have identified certain central key points in our way of teaching therapy.

We have concluded that family therapy can be construed as similar to pharmacotherapy in its pragmatic effects; that is, if you give the family a new medicine and their sole responsibility is to swallow it, the use of the strategic substance can have dramatic results. These results, however, will be limited if the family and the therapist are not the architects of their own process of change.

As the family can become protagonists in searching for solutions to their own problems, so can the student seek to avoid "swallowing" techniques and the trainer avoid writing the prescriptions. Both student and trainer can draw on their respective creativity, allowing for the nurture of their capacity to grow together.

REFERENCES

1. Alger, J. Audio-visual techniques in family therapy. In D. Bloch (Ed.), *Techniques of family psychotherapy.* New York: Grune & Stratton, Inc., 1973.
2. Andolfi, M. La ridefinizione in terapia familiare. *Terapia Familiare,* 1977, *1,* 7-27. (a)
3. Andolfi, M. *La terapia con la famiglia.* Rome: Astrolabio, 1977. (b)
4. Andolfi, M. A structural approach to a family with an encopretic child. *Journal of Marriage and Family Counseling,* 1978, *4,* 25-29.
5. Andolfi, M., & Menghi, P. La terapia con la famiglia. *Neuropsichiatria Infantile,* 1976, *180,* 487-498.
6. Andolfi, M., Menghi, P., Nicolò, A. M., & Saccu, C. L'interazione nei sistemi rigidi: Un modello di intervento nella famiglia con paziente schizofrenico. *Terapia Familiare,* 1978, *3,* 35-65.
7. Andolfi, M., Stein, D., & Skinner, J. A system approach to the child, school, family and community in an urban area. *American Journal of Community Psychology,* 1977, *5,* 33-43.
8. Aponte, H. L. The family–school interview: An ecostructural approach. *Family Process,* 1976, *15,* 303-312.
9. Auerswald, E. H. Interdisciplinary vs. ecological approach. *Family Process,* 1968, *7.*
10. Cancrini, L. *Bambini "diversi" a scuola.* Torino: Boringhieri, 1974.
11. Flomenhaft, K., & Carter, R. Family therapy training: A statewide program for mental health centers. *Hospital and Community Psychiatry,* 1974, *25.*
12. Haley, J. *Problem-solving therapy.* San Francisco: Jossey-Bass, Inc., 1977.
13. Menghi, P. L'approccio strutturale nella terapia con la famiglia. *Terapia Familiare,* 1977, *1,* 53-74.
14. Minuchin, S. The use of an ecological framework in the treatment of a child. In J. Anthony & C. Koupernik (Eds.), *The child in his family.* New York: John Wiley & Sons, Inc., 1970.
15. Minuchin, S. *Famiglia e terapia della famiglia.* Rome: Astrolabio, 1977.
16. Montalvo, B. Aspects of live supervision. *Family Process,* 1973, *12.*
17. Nicolò, A. M. Techniche di azione in terapia familiare: La scultura. *Neuropsichiatria Infantile,* 1977, *190,* 421-441.

18. Papp, P., Silverstein, O., & Carter, E. Family sculpting in preventive work with well families. *Family Process*, 1973, *12*.
19. Zwerling, I. Terapia familiare e psichiatria di comunità. *Terapia Familiare*, 1978, *3*, 13–20.

16

Family Therapy Training at Hahnemann Medical College and Hospital

ROBERT GARFIELD

The parable of the sower and the seed in the Bible teaches that in order for the sower's seeds to grow and bear fruit, they must fall on "good soil." The parable certainly applies to family therapy training and the institutional soil in which it develops. It is often naively assumed that family theory and technique can be taught in any academic or clinical setting, just as though this teaching meant simply introducing additional ideas and skills that are compatible with the frame of reference of the individuals in these settings. Haley,[5] Framo,[4] Selig,[7] and Liddle[6] have described the numerous difficulties that are involved in bringing family therapy approaches into institutional settings that are organized along traditional, individually oriented lines and the turbulence that regularly arises when they are introduced. To simplify a not-so-simple truth in the language of Gregory Bateson,[1] family therapy is not merely another *member of the class* of therapies that precede it in its development, it is rather a *distinct class of therapy,* representing a unique view of human behavior that is in many ways incompatible with the models that preceded it. Therefore, family therapy training requires special and receptive "institutional soils" in which it can successfully flourish.

This chapter describes the development and the current status of family therapy training in the Department of Mental Health Sciences at Hahnemann Medical College and Hospital in Philadelphia. The author's purpose here is to portray the necessary "soil ingredients" that exist in the department's training setting that support the growth of family therapy training. The following sections describe the recent history and structure of the Department of Mental Health Sciences at Hahnemann, as well as the nature, extent, and philosophy of family therapy training within the department's academic programs and clinical training settings. The last section focuses largely on the department's most concentrated effort in family training, the Master's of Family Therapy Program, a relatively recent two-year graduate program that provides specialized, intensive training in family therapy and leads to a master's degree.

THE HAHNEMANN DEPARTMENT OF MENTAL HEALTH SCIENCES: HISTORY AND STRUCTURE

In 1973, Dr. Israel Zwerling became the chairman of the Department of Mental Health Sciences at Hahnemann Medical College and Hospital. Dr. Zwerling began to institute a social-psychiatry training model within the department, one that stressed interpersonal and sociocultural aspects of patient care and clinical training of the students in the community. The model had been developed previously at Bronx State Hospital at Albert Einstein Medical College, where C. Beels and A. Ferber had run the Family Studies Section under Dr. Zwerling's administrative direction.

Since its inception, the social-psychiatry training model at Hahnemann has influenced the many academic programs within the Department of Mental Health Sciences. These include basic and child psychiatry residency programs; doctoral programs (Ph.D. and Psy.D.) in psychology; a psychiatric nursing program; specialized graduate programs in creative arts (art, movement, and music); mental health evaluation; group process and therapy; and family therapy. The department also sponsors undergraduate mental-health technology and mental-health associate-degree programs.

Over 400 regular and clinical faculty work in the department. The core Hahnemann faculty is interdisciplinary and almost all of the members teach in other programs as well as in their own. The student body, similarly, is large, numbering 226. Students in the department have many interdisciplinary classes with students from other programs. This latter feature of student training fulfills a valued departmental objective, which is to teach students to work in team-member capacity with professionals from other disciplines as well as from their own.

The students' clinical training occurs primarily in the department's clinical facilities. The largest of these is the Hahnemann Community Mental Health/Mental Retardation Center, whose satellite outpatient clinics and inpatient and emergency services serve a multiethnic, low-income population in central Philadelphia. Students also work in the department's private child and adult clinics. They learn individual responsibility in these settings and also how to ask for help and to work in team-member capacities under the supervision of clinic staff. The teaching faculty from the college are strongly committed to teaching in the community; each community facility with students has one or more senior faculty educators assigned to teach both staff and students throughout the year.

Family Therapy Training at Hahnemann

Administrative support for this social-psychiatry teaching model (an academic setting in which students are taught by faculty from several different specialties) and the clinical teaching setting (which stresses a team approach) creates a climate at Hahnemann that is especially conducive to family therapy training. Most of the programs in the department—including those in psychiatry, psychology, creative arts, and mental health technology—include courses in family therapy in their curricula, and all of the departmental programs include at least some lectures on family therapy and theory. The chairman of the department himself teaches family therapy in several of these programs and is an active member of the family therapy section. In accord with the department's commitment to training in the community mental health center, the senior faculty who are family-therapy-oriented give weekly family case conferences in the center clinics where family therapy is done. These kinds of conferences are also given in the department's private psychiatric clinics to students and staff alike.

The department has a family therapy section that meets on a monthly basis and functions to provide and monitor family therapy training throughout the department, in the academic programs as well as in the clinical facilities. The family therapy faculty are both locally and nationally known family therapists, many of whom have contributed to the literature in the field. The core faculty consists of Mrs. Jean Barr, Dr. Ivan Boszormenyi-Nagy, Dr. Ilda Ficher, Dr. Robert Garfield, Dr. Florence Kaslow, Mrs. Myra Levick, Dr. Pirooz Sholevar, Dr. John Sonne, Dr. Edward Volkman, and Dr. Israel Zwerling. Many of these faculty members serve as the administrative heads of other training programs and clinical facilities in the department.

Dr. Ivan Boszormenyi-Nagy is the head of the family therapy section in the department. Dr. Nagy's theoretical contributions most heavily influence the philosophy of family therapy training that prevails in the department. His relational, or contextual, mode of family therapy[2,3]

> integrates all components of relevant, valid knowledge (in the family field) on individual and transactional systemic levels. In addition, it introduces the utilization of dynamic ethical interrelatedness of the welfare of all family members, including that issuing from intergenerational and transgenerational ledgers of reciprocity and expectations of legacies.

The advantages of this model are twofold. First, it provides a kind of theoretical suprastructure within which the vital schools of family theory and the numerous technical contributions that have been made in the field can be included and can find a relevant perspective. Second, it offers an explicit value system through which therapists in training can learn to work in behalf of the welfare of all members of the family system. The integrative spirit of this model allows students the opportunity to learn and assimilate the major significant ideas and techniques that exist in the family field as well as to develop unique personal styles of their own as family therapists.

THE MASTER'S OF FAMILY THERAPY PROGRAM

The major concentrated focus of family therapy training in the department is the Master's of Family Therapy Program (MFT Program), which is directed by Dr. Robert Garfield. This program was designed to provide students with a specialized expertise in family therapy and theory and the capacity to work in team-member and consultant roles with mental health professionals from other disciplines.

The MFT Program is a two-year, full-time graduate program that follows a clinician–scholar model of training, one that emphasizes practical clinical learning as well as academic coursework. The MFT Program is in the Graduate School of Hahnemann Medical College, which is fully accredited; graduates of the program receive accredited master's degrees in family therapy (MFT degrees).

The overall program design is made up of three components: the core curriculum, the practicum, and the thesis. These components are sequenced in a two-year training experience that is divided into three

12-week trimesters per year. During the first year, students spend two full days in classes and then two additional days, which may include some evening hours, in their clinical settings. Times for outside supervisory meetings and administrative meetings are also scheduled into their week. During the second year, the students' clinical and thesis research responsibilities increase, while their classroom time tapers off throughout the year.

Core Curriculum

The core curriculum consists of graduate-level courses in family theory and therapy that provide students with comprehensive in-depth knowledge of the family field. The content of these courses is planned as a partial fulfillment of the specific instructional objectives of the training program.

The courses are given in classroom settings in which the instructors utilize various teaching techniques, ranging from didactic lectures and student presentations to more experiential methods involving role playing, family sculpting, and videotape feedback. Field trips and guest speakers are also utilized in this teaching. Examinations and papers are assigned to students, and they are evaluated on a quarterly basis by their instructors. All students take a comprehensive examination at the end of the first year. The students receive graduate credits for their coursework, as well as for the work they do in their practica and thesis research. An important function of the classroom experience is to help students to conceptualize and plan around their clinical experiences with families, which are occurring simultaneously.

The flowchart below gives a picture of the sequence and overall content of the course material.

MFT CORE CURRICULUM

FIRST YEAR

First Quarter	*Second Quarter*	*Third Quarter*
1. Individual Dynamic Theories of Personality and the Family	1. Community Agencies and Family Treatment	1. Treatment of the Dyadic Relationship

FIRST YEAR (continued)

First Quarter	*Second Quarter*	*Third Quarter*
2. Transactional and Communication Models of Family Therapy	2. The Child as the Identified Patient a. Child Development in a Family Context	2. continued --------→ b. Child Psychopathology in a Family Context
3. Depth Models of Relational Theory and Therapy	3. continued --------→	3. continued --------→
4. The Therapist's Experience in Family Relationships	4. Psychosomatic Illness and the Structural Approach	4. Legal and Judicial Implications of Family Therapy
5. Historical and Sociocultural Influences on the Family		5. Preventive and Educational Implications of Family Treatment
6. Introduction to Theory and Process of Family Therapy a. Individual Process in a Relational Context	5. continued --------→ b and c Theory and Process of Family Therapy	6. continued --------→
		7. Thesis Writing Course ½ quarter

SECOND YEAR

First Quarter	*Second Quarter*	*Third Quarter*
1. Advanced Relational Theory and Its Application	1. continued --------→	1. continued --------→

2. The Creative Arts and Family Treatment	2. continued ---------------------→	2. The Family in Literature
3. Treatment of Sexual Dysfunction	3. Group Theory and Its Relation to Family Process *a.* Didactic and Experiential	3. continued ---------------------→ *b.* Experiental
4. Crisis Intervention and the Family		
5. Continuous Family Case Conference	4. continued ---------------------→	4. continued ---------------------→
6. Medical Information for Nonmedical Therapists		

Practicum

The practicum provides students with an intensive supervised clinical experience working with dysfunctional families in a variety of clinical settings. It offers a context in which students can integrate the various theoretical and practical concepts from the classroom and can develop clinical competence as family therapists while working along with students and professionals from other mental health disciplines.

Students begin their clinical work at the onset of the training program, working in clinical settings, or "site placements," for a minimum of two days a week throughout the entire year. These settings are located both within and outside of the Hahnemann system. They include private psychiatric clinics, outpatient community-mental-health-center clinics, family service agencies, child welfare agencies, inpatient and residential treatment settings, hospital liaison services, and the Philadelphia public school system. In each of these settings, students have experienced on-site supervisors who help them to acquire family therapy cases and to work with these cases in treatment. During their second year, students spend two evenings each month working in the Hahnemann emergency room as student family therapist members of a psychiatric crisis-intervention team. In this setting, students are able to observe and begin to develop skills to help family members who present at times of severe emotional distress.

The objectives of the practicum are that the students gain clinical competence as family therapists and the capacity to work as resource personnel along with therapists from other mental health disciplines. Students develop, in this experience, the skills that are necessary to evaluate dysfunctional families adequately and to plan and implement treatment strategies that can be helpful to the family. Each student is expected to treat a minimum of 5 cases during the first year and 6–10 family cases during the second year. In addition, the students are expected to be able to work with a range of family types; to develop prevention strategies in their treatment plans, especially in dealing with families with emotionally "vulnerable" children; and to be able to assess when termination is indicated and to carry cases through to completion. Supervisors work along with students to help them toward these goals and to provide feedback about their progress during the year.

The supervisory experience is seen as the most critical variable in the students' acquisition of clinical competence. Students receive both on-site and outside supervision from experienced family therapy supervisors with whom the students have the opportunity to demonstrate and discuss their clinical work and to receive feedback about their clinical progress. On-site supervisors provide a special additional function in helping students to deal with the administrative aspects of their work, particularly agency dynamics and the agency's reactions to family therapy approaches. This "political" education, we have found, is invaluable to beginning family therapists.

Students have individual and group supervisors with whom they meet on a weekly basis. The focus and form of supervision varies depending on the students' level of competence and the supervisors' personal supervisory styles. Beginning students sit in with supervisors or observe them working with family cases. They also observe videotapes of experienced therapists working with families. Later, supervision involves the students' verbal reports, audiotapes, or live supervision and videotapes of the students' work, depending on what is seen as most useful by the supervisor. Many supervisors help students explore issues with their families of origin that interfere with their clinical work. Overall, supervisors help to alleviate the students' initial anxieties about therapeutic work and teach the students to conceptualize dysfunctional patterns in families and to design and implement treatment strategies in their work.

Supervisors evaluate the students' clinical work on an ongoing basis throughout the year. Evaluation benefits the students' work most directly when it is conducted as a part of the continuous feedback process between the students and the supervisors and when trusting relationships have been established between them. Formal evaluation of the students' work occurs at the end of each quarter, when students and supervisors are asked to meet to discuss the students' work, their strengths, their needs for improvement, and their overall progress. The results of these discussions are recorded on evaluation forms, signed by supervisors and students, and are sent to the program director and the program evaluator. The program director maintains contacts with the students and supervisors during the year to monitor the overall evaluation process. Students are also asked to evaluate their courses, their supervisors and instructors, and their practica experiences in a similar fashion. All clinical supervisors meet on a quarterly basis with the core teaching faculty. The purpose of these meetings is for supervisors to give feedback to the faculty about the students' progress and the relevance and applicability of material in the courses to the students' clinical learning experience. This is a valuable component in the feedback process for ongoing modifications of the program's design. A second important purpose is for the supervisors to exchange information and views on supervisory styles. We have begun to introduce formal presentations of different supervisory techniques so that faculty can share and learn from each other. These meetings provide a most valuable context in which the program's commitment to an integrative teaching model is strengthened through the exchange of viewpoints between faculty members.

Thesis

Students, with the aid of a faculty committee, select an area or topic of significance in the field of family therapy to explore as an investigatory research project. This research occurs primarily in the second year, and results in a scholarly written work that meets the graduate school standards for a master's thesis. The purpose of these projects is to stimulate creative thinking in students and to encourage those who might be inclined to make future contributions to the literature and practical developments in the field of family therapy to begin to develop their interests. Various faculty members who are doing research in marital and family therapy have begun to invite students to join them in these undertakings.

The Students

Twelve students are recruited for each MFT Program class. This class size is considered large enough to provide a good range of ages, sexes, and disciplinary backgrounds and yet small enough to support an active group process. The students tend to be older and more goal-directed than students in "first" master's programs. They are recruited from a variety of backgrounds and settings. The program has a strong commitment to the recruitment of minority students. The general criteria for student selection are (1) the applicants' demonstration through prior academic work that they can adequately meet the responsibilities of graduate-level course work; (2) their demonstration through prior clinical or related work that they have the capacities to become competent psychotherapists; and (3) their demonstration through personal interviews with faculty members that they have the interest and emotional maturity to become competent family therapists.

The specific guidelines for applicants are that they possess a master's degree in a mental-health-related field (psychiatry, psychology, social work, counseling, or psychiatric nursing, for example) and prior clinical experience in the mental health field. The master's degree requirement is occasionally waived for a candidate who has unusual clinical experience and demonstrates unique potential to become a competent family therapist. We are currently evaluating the factors, including the criteria for candidate selection, that predict the successful performance of students both during and after graduation from the program.

Students play an important role in the decision-making processes of the MFT Program, particularly in the area of program modification. Aside from their feedback through course evaluations and critiques of their clinical experience, the students have representatives who participate directly in faculty meetings and on curriculum, job placement, and guest speaker committees. Their enthusiasm about and interest in the program has resulted in a continuous, stimulating exchange with faculty instructors and supervisors.

Family Therapy Training at Hahnemann

PROGRAM EVALUATION

The MFT Program has a major commitment to its own ongoing evaluation. Through this evaluation process, the program hopes to strengthen its own design and to make this design replicable for other family therapy training programs. The evaluation procedures that have been planned and instituted seek to answer the following questions: (1) How successful are the students in acquiring the knowledge, attitudes, and skills set forth in the program's instructional objectives? (2) How effective is the program in communicating these objectives to students? (3) How do students fare after graduating from the program with regard to obtaining jobs as family therapists, performance in and satisfaction with their work, and sense of preparedness for working in the chosen setting? (4) What factors in the students' experience are most closely related to their successful practice of family therapy after graduation? The variables that will be considered here include the students' academic and clinical performance during the program, their own perceptions of the most salient aspects of the training experience, and factors related to the process of selecting students.

Data used in these evaluations will be drawn from course instructors' and supervisors' ratings of the students' progress during their training and from written and videotaped assessments of students' knowledge, skills, and attitudinal changes measured early and late in their training experience, as well as the students' self-evaluation reports. Additional data will be provided by the students' quarterly ratings of their courses, instructors, and clinical supervisors and of their practicum experiences. These data are used in part to aid in the yearly modifications in the program's design. Finally, postgraduate reports from the master's students and their employers, as well as recognition through publications, presentations, and membership in national societies, will provide data for assessing the students' success after graduation. We plan eventually to publish the results of these evaluation procedures in family therapy and other journals, so that this information may be available to persons in other settings and particularly to those who are interested in replicating this kind of program.

REFERENCES

1. Bateson, G. *Steps to an ecology of mind.* New York: Ballantine Books, Inc., 1972.

2. Boszormenyi-Nagy, I. Philosophy of family therapy training—The relational model. In *Master's of Family Therapy Training Grant Application,* # 1-TO 1 MH 15432-01, 1977, Appendix A.
3. Boszormenyi-Nagy, I., & Spark, G. M. *Invisible loyalties,* Hagerstown, Md.: Harper & Row, Publishers, 1973.
4. Framo, J. Personal reflections of a family therapist. *Journal of Marriage and Family Counseling,* 1975, 1, 15–28.
5. Haley, J. Why a mental health clinic should avoid family therapy. *Journal of Marriage and Family Counseling,* 1975, 1, 3–12.
6. Liddle, H., & Halpen, R. Family therapy training and supervision literature: A comparative review. *Journal of Marriage and Family Counseling,* 1978, 4, 77–98.
7. Selig, A. L. The myth of the multi-problem family. *American Journal of Orthopsychiatry,* 1976, 46(3), 526–532.

17

The Future of Family Therapy

Donald A. Bloch

The focus of this report is on the future of family therapy, with special emphasis on family therapy in the community. At the outset, I would like to assure you that the future is as opaque to me as it is to others; my crystal ball is as cloudy as that of any other magician. But the topic does provide an opportunity to do a little focused dreaming.

In a short report, it is not possible to begin to deal fully with all issues, and certain simplifying assumptions must be made. Thus I will not attempt to prove the truth of such propositions as that there will be a future (my cautious guess is that there will be) or that the human race will be a part of it (again, I vote on the side of optimism). Since the death of the family has been widely predicted—even, on occasion, prayed for—we might briefly examine, though, the question as to the likelihood that that social form will cease to exist. The question is important since "community" is often placed in opposition to "family."

In most general terms, by *family* I mean that specialized human social institution that reproduces itself in a unique and endlessly fascinating fashion. It has developed machinery over many millennia at the biological, psychological, and social levels for generating its own component parts: people. The family is a true self-reproducing automaton. All other social institutions, including the community, recruit members from outside their boundaries and indeed from families, either directly or indirectly.

Therefore it seems to me to be nonsense to talk of the death of the family. There is not *the* family; there always will be *a* family. The membership, internal organization, foreign relations, psychopolitics, and economics of this intimate human group will always be changing, at times rapidly and at other times with a glacierlike slowness. At this moment in history, the pace is exceedingly rapid. A recent survey of households in the United States—a household being defined as those persons physically living together under the same roof—showed only half the households to be made up of an adult couple, married to each other for the first time, with or without children, the traditional nuclear family. Of the balance, 11% were remarriages with children, 12% were single-parent families, 19% were single adults, and 6% in some communal, unmarried-parent, or common-law arrangement, with two generations under the same roof. (An additional 4% were three-generation families living in some effective kin network, the most traditional form.)

The statistics appear to point convincingly toward a steady increase in the number of acceptable family format options. These include: remaining single, establishing a household as a couple, being either married or unmarried (for example, in Sweden today less than half of the couples establishing households choose to marry when they do so), postponing to a later date the birth of the first child (and therefore reducing the total number of children), or remaining childless. As is well known, male and female gender roles are rapidly changing, as for example in the two-career family, with a resultant shift in domestic power allocations. (It is not always to be assumed that the woman does the dishes.) We are moving to permit homosexuality as a legitimate sexual preference without penalty, leading to Lesbian and gay "families" seeking treatment. Sexual fidelity, monogamy, and a lifetime exclusive dyadic contract between marital partners are no longer taken for granted, with consequent revisions of the career line of being a married person.

In societies that do not legislate conformity in these matters, it is likely that we will see ever more variation, although the rate of change may slow. Science fiction may provide us with other scenarios, but it is a safe wager that for a long time, most humans will be born into and acculturated by one intimate network, the family of origin, and will live bound to other humans in some form of a family of procreation. (The actual biological relations of these persons may vary. Indeed, some time ago I was led to predict that the family of the distant future would very probably be a Lesbian commune. Even so, the general model holds.)

Nor will pain and dysfunction disappear from the human scene. The special contribution of family therapy lies in demonstrating how some varieties of human misery grow out of the character of the two families we are all part of (our contexts): the original and current families.

The Future of Family Therapy

We are dealing here not simply with a new set of techniques but with a radically altered view of causality, of the relationship between human events.

This leads us to a view of the human condition for which the god Janus might best be invoked as the appropriate deity. He is the god with two faces for whom the month January is named. Looking both forward and backward, inward and outward, at systems and at context, Janus is the god of interfaces.

Thus we speak about the emergence of a new paradigm, which should be called, I believe, the *general systems paradigm*.

Among its elements that seem to me to be important are:

- The abandonment of notions of linear causality for conceptions of feedback and circularity. (We may call this the *end of blame*.)
- The permanent and irrevocable placing of the participant-observer (in our case the therapist) as part of the phenomena to be studied and modified. (We may call this the *end of objectivity*.)
- Steady attention to the hierarchy of meaning systems, relevant to the phenomena being studied. Associated with this is an awareness of the *limitations* of the sharing of systems that can occur and a deepened understanding of the consequences of the failure to share these. (We may call this the *end of absolutes*.)

This emphasis on context and circularity is a bit like peeling an onion from the inside out. It is hard to know when to stop—perhaps when too many tears make it impossible to go on. In any case, family *is* context and *has* context. This brings us to community. For example, government and social policy planners must take into account the variety of family forms I spoke of earlier. If one chooses to live as a couple and not be married, how is society to define this status? What patterns of income maintenance favor what kind of family organization?

How do we provide legal services to divorcing families? What right of self-determination does the adolescent member of a family have about her own decision to have an abortion? Or not have it?

As to education—should we have a school for families, as opposed to a school for individuals?

In the work place: How do one's career choice and work conditions relate to the ongoing developmental phases of the family? Consider for a moment an aspect of the career line of family therapist. Her or his working hours must be at times (usually the evening) when other families are available. What happens to her or his own family?

Special note should be taken of the need for consideration of the relation between physical illness in the family and the doctors, nurses, and others who make up the health care system. This is a largely unexplored conceptual area of major importance: "family somatics" in John Weakland's[1] phrase.

In all of these domains, the general systems concepts that I have spoken of before provide us with a useful orientation as to *what* to study, the proper boundaries of the phenomenon we hope to change.

Turning in a slightly different direction now, I wish to draw your attention to the increasing politicization of the "family," both as a field of endeavor and as an issue in general politics. What is at stake is the control of a symbol system—what we always fight about: the definition of meaning. As an illustration, let me quote from *The New York Times* of Monday, June 19, 1978. I have taken this excerpt from an article by Roger Wilkins:

> The White House Conference on Families—once seemingly the simplest of President Carter's campaign promises to keep, but recently mired by controversy, rumor and suspicion—has been postponed from December 1979 to 1981.

> The specific precipitating cause for the suspension was the inability to select an executive secretary for the conference. Patsy Flemming, a black divorced mother of three teenage sons, had been appointed and then subsequently withdrew:

>> ... her appointment was sharply criticized by the Rev. Andrew Greeley, a Roman Catholic priest who writes a syndicated newspaper column, on the ground that it was inappropriate for a divorced person to head such a conference.

>> ...

>> Blacks both within and outside the Administration immediately seized upon the Fleming incident as an indication of strong Catholic pressure to focus the conference on intact, middle-income, white families, thereby causing a decrease in the attention to be given to poor and female-headed families, which account for a large proportion of the people served by H.E.W.

>> ...

Among those issues needing to be faced are abortion, the desire of homosexual groups to participate, the extent to which it is wise for government to involve itself in family issues, the degree to which program money intended for families should be tied up by Federal program requirements, and the extent to which the conference should place emphasis on the interests of ethnic groups in the middle class as opposed to minority and poor families.

As family therapists, we may regard all of these issues as beyond our level of competence, and to a degree that is certainly so. Yet it is foolish to believe they will not affect us or that in the long run our position on these issues can be developed entirely within the limits of the consulting room.

The systems approach and the tie to the family as the system *primus inter pares,* first among equals, is a tool powerful yet humane. We should not stand back from participating in these struggles.

Turning to family therapy itself, in looking to the future, I see a particular concentration, both clinically and theoretically, on the problem of appropriate systems levels. The familiar form of the systems-level problem concerns the relation among psychological levels of explanation, familial and small-group levels, and cultural and large societal levels. The student of human behavior seeks explanations at the organic and cellular systems levels as well (for example, what are the unchangeable characteristics of the human brain as they determine modes of experiencing, what is family to the left brain and to the right, what are the genetics of patterns of family interaction?). Our interest in culture and community should not put us into opposition to explanation at other levels. Depression may be related on a chemical basis to hormonal imbalance, on a psychological basis to the inward turning of hostile affect, on a familial basis to an equilibrium-maintaining operation, on a societal basis to a shift in gender identity. This list is merely illustrative. I am sure you all can think of other explanatory models at different levels in addition to those I have chosen.

For polemic and heuristic purposes and to avoid an unruly eclecticism, family therapists have wisely insisted on eliminating levels of explanation at the biological and psychological levels. But it is necessary now to undertake that work.

We must also renew our attention to the past, to time. Our assumption that we did not need to pay attention to time was based on the notion that the analogue for memory at the family level of conceptualization lies in the organization of the family, its structure and rules. The family does not need to remember, it *is*. The timeless stance—that is, the position that we deal with only the here and now—is also a convenient fiction and has been valuable clinically and for teaching purposes. My impression is that the theorizing of the next decade will reopen that issue and that the many kinds of time, and timelessness, that families experience will be cataloged and explored. Out of this exploration, I expect we will have a better opportunity to consider how experience is coded, and stored, and made into the model of the past that guides and shapes new experience.

Family therapists have had to scale down their ambitions because of the ever-increasing awareness of the inherent stability of the family system, which should not particularly surprise us. Any biopsychosocial system is multiply redundant in regard to its control and its homeostatic maintenance functions. We are, after all, dealing with a complex product of the entire evolutionary process.

Consider for just a moment the 5-billion-year journey from the remote beginnings of time to this moment. With small exceptions, the same chemical elements are present here as were present at the beginning of this planet, neither fewer nor more, with the exception perhaps of the meteors and the stardust that have joined the earth, and the space junk that we have recently placed in orbit or out among the stars. The evolution of the most simple form of life has been required to go against the eternal drag of entropy, to say nothing of that recent wrinkle in time we think of as mammalian evolution and the tiny corner of human history and prehistory. This organization and relationship of elements, and their formation into systems capable of maintaining and reproducing themselves, must fill us with the most unspeakable, profound awe. In regard to the family, we are alerted once again to the complexly metastable nature of the system we propose to influence.

Such diverse clinical innovators as Haley and Selvini, Watzlawick and Minuchin, have struggled with developing new and more effective techniques for gaining power over these phenomena, recognizing the magnitude of the forces with which they contended.

It is beyond the scope of a brief presentation to attempt a forecast of the new directions other than to say that they will steadily work to enlarge the power of the therapist as a change agent in the family system.

Certainly, much of what we can expect is a better selection of the right time to do therapy, when the family is at its most labile, and a better selection of goals, so as to result in more effective joining. We will try to improve our ability to induce crisis in families, a sort of controlled thermonuclear reaction, if you will, and work toward a better conceptualization of the therapist's use of self.

The self of the family therapist has not been studied very much and is rarely included as a significant conceptual issue. Some groups—the Milan group, for example, and my colleagues at Ackerman—have considered the personal characteristics of the therapist of major importance, with the presentation and use of the therapeutic self being critical.

It was early observed in regard to communication that one cannot *not* communicate. Equally—indeed, it is really another way of saying the same thing—one cannot *not* relate. Even if one chooses *not* to consider the personality and family of the therapist, one has a massive organizing influence on the therapeutic system by taking that stance. Indeed, it is fully analogous to the power and the informational content of silence.

This orientation should lead in time to a more sensitive orchestration of therapeutic elements. To illustrate, let me very quickly touch on a few ways in which this might work. We might, for example, actively work at matching certain characteristics of the family of origin of the therapist with characteristics of the family being treated. General systems theory would lead us to regard the therapeutic unit as being at an interface between these two families, much in the same way as a new marriage is the location of an interface between the two families of origin of the new marital partners. We ask what kind of joining is appropriate to the therapeutic model being invoked.

Some therapeutic models require a cool, apparently uninvolved, distant use of the therapeutic self. There are, after all, good cool marriages. In these instances, we might emphasize choosing therapists whose personal style is cool, remote, and authoritarian and whose position in their families of origin facilitates this and is different from that of the index patient in the family being treated.

For those therapeutic approaches that emphasize affectivity, including emotional involvement of the therapist with the family, we might look for completely different kinds of matching so as to increase the mutual-identification and projective processes. We might look for high complementarity of families of origin, for example, so as to create the analogue of a good "hot" marriage.

Thus, instead of asking ourselves what is the best therapeutic strategy or tactic, we ask ourselves what is the best match between family of therapist and treated family, given the tactics that are to be employed in the particular instance. The critical reason for focusing on this issue is that acquisition of power along the lines I have spoken of earlier must take place through this route.

However defined, this field has been growing at an exponential rate. New journals and books appear almost daily. It is said that 40,000 people have been trained to some extent in its techniques.

Thus, beset by the dangers of success, family therapy, to paraphrase Charles Dickens, lives in the best of times and the worst of times. Clearly, there is an important and meaningful place for those who propose to study the inner dynamics of the family and to intervene in its processes. I believe it is appropriate to close on a note of very cautious optimism. It does seem as if the struggle to be of help to our patient families may make a broader contribution to the well-being of humans generally.

REFERENCE

1. Weakland, J. "Family somatics": A neglected edge. *Family Process,* 1977, 16(3), 263-272.